Christening

CHRISTENING:

The Making of Christians

Mark Searle

The Liturgical Press

Collegeville   Minnesota

Library of Congress Cataloging in Publication Data

Searle, Mark, 1941–
 Christening: the making of Christians.

 Includes index.
 1. Baptism—Catholic Church. 2. Confirmation—Catholic Church. 3. Lord's Supper—Catholic
Church.
 I. Title.
BX2205.S4   234'.16   80-19454
ISBN 0-8146-1183-4

Nihil obstat: Joseph C. Kremer, S.T.L., *Censor deputatus.*
Imprimatur: ✠ George H. Speltz, D.D., Bishop of St. Cloud. June, 1980.

FOREWORD

When we received the new Rite of Baptism for Children in 1969 we got a great deal more than a new rite. Not only was it the first time that there was a specific rite for the baptism of children that "took into account the fact that those to be baptized are infants" (SC, 67), but there was also considerable emphasis placed on the communal nature of the sacrament and its celebration, as well as a firm commitment to the proper indoctrination and preparation of parents, godparents and others. For many years, prior to the reforms of Vatican II, there had been developing among some in pastoral ministry the conviction that the faith community could be better served if there were more in the way of presacramental catechesis for parents and others, and if the communal celebration of the rites for the entire assembly was stressed. Now that the premise has been established there must be no hesitation in implementing it.

In all trades and professions one of the most important requirements is to have good tools. Pastoral ministry is no exception. We too must have good tools and we must respect them and use them well. But this is not enough. We must also distinguish between the facile "how to" tools that move from the old to the new without much depth of perception or insight, with little consideration for history and tradition, Scripture and theology, from those that take into consideration all the basic elements and show reverence and respect for true liturgical tradition and practice.

This book is more than a good tool. It is obviously the work of one who respects scholarship and its rightful place in the growth and development of the faith communities that form the Church. There is a most gratifying admixture of scholarship and clear vision and understanding of the pastoral needs and desires of the assembly at prayer and worship.

There is enough history of the development as well as the disintegration of the rites of baptism, confirmation and Eucharist to provide more than an adequate basis to comprehend the place and function of Christian initiation among the faithful and to facilitate a fruitful celebration for all. Perhaps it is not too much to hope that this stimulating presentation may lead many to a further investigation and study of Christian initiation that may eventually bear fruit as a commitment to baptism as an open-ended process of conversion all the way to the Eschaton.

The body of this work consists of an exciting account of the step-by-step journey through the entire rite of Christian initiation. With an excellent combination of history, liturgical tradition, Scripture, theology and pastoral insights, it presents a most workable prebaptismal catechesis for all who will participate in the celebration. There is more material here than could be used in any one celebration; one can envision a long-term catechesis of the entire faith community over a period of many years' celebration of Christian initiation.

The chapters devoted to confirmation and Eucharist are not exhaustive but they present a clear picture of the integrity of Christian initiation as a three-act process that is best celebrated as an integral whole and in the order developed in the primitive Church. The author protests that this is not a book on how the sacraments are to be celebrated and he is correct; it is a great deal more. Nevertheless, as one with forty years of pastoral experience, I must protest that at the present time it is the best source book available for catechesis before and after the celebration of Christian initiation.

Fr. James D. Shaughnessy
Pastor, St. Cecilia Church
Peoria, Illinois

(Fr. Shaughnessy was the first director of the Notre Dame Center for Pastoral Liturgy, Notre Dame, Indiana.)

INTRODUCTION

This book, it must be confessed, lays no claim to originality. Its aim is simple and unpretentious: to give the general reader some understanding of the history and theology of the rites of Christian initiation, the sacraments of baptism, confirmation and Eucharist. The purpose is not academic but pastoral, and the method employed is that of commentary on the present rites of initiation. It is not a book about how these sacraments might be celebrated, nor a critique of the revised initiation liturgies. The revised rites are themselves the product of centuries of evolution, or more precisely they are the precious heritage bequeathed by countless generations of praying and celebrating Christians. Our hope, then, will be that we can learn to listen to these "testimonies of faith" in such a way that our eyes are opened to the rich mystery which they reveal, to "the riches of the glory of this mystery, which is Christ in you, the hope of glory" (Col 1:27).

Too often in the past, theology and catechesis have suffered by being pursued at a level quite remote from experience, whether that be ordinary human experience of life or the more specifically sacramental experience of liturgical celebration. The value of this approach thus lies in its attempt to draw faith and experience together and to recognize the liturgy as being the celebration of them both. The liturgical celebrations of the Church point to the meaning of our experience of life in the world and help us to understand it; they express our faith and they shape it. Instead of just asking practical questions about when and how sacraments should be conferred, we need also to learn from the liturgy itself by being attentive to the profound meaning of the rites we have inherited. This was done by those who revised the rites; it has not yet become common among those who celebrate them.

Baptism, confirmation and Eucharist are called the sacraments of Christian initiation. They are the stages marking a person's gradual incorporation into the body of Christ which is the Church. As such, and because they are precisely rites of *initiation* and *formation*, they have much to tell us not only about the process of becoming a Christian but also about the full Christian life itself. Consequently, although this book takes as its starting point the rite for the baptism of children, it will refer frequently to the rites of adult initiation since in many respects these reveal more clearly the full implications of becoming a Christian. In any case, it is hoped that what is written here will be of interest not only to those who, as parents, teachers, or pastors, have special responsibility for the delicate task of making Christians, but to everyone who, having been baptized into Christ, is concerned, in the words of the ancient Roman baptismal liturgy, "to know who he is and who he shall be."

Mark Searle

SOURCES QUOTED

Abbot, W. (ed.), *Documents of Vatican II*, NY, 1966.
Augustine, *The First Catechetical Instruction (de catechizandis rudibus)*, tr. and ed. by J. P. Christopher, ACW 2, Westminster, Md., 1946.
Bettenson, H. (ed.), *Documents of the Christian Church*, OUP, London, 1967.
Cyril of Jerusalem, *Lectures on the Christian Sacraments*, ed. F. L. Cross, SPCK, London, 1951.
Denziger-Schoenmetzer, *Enchiridion Symbolorum*, Herder, 1963.
Donovan, J. (tr.), *Catechism of the Council of Trent*, Dublin, 1867.
Eusebius, *History of the Church*, tr. G. A. Williamson, Penguin, 1965.
Fisher, J. C. D., *Christian Initiation: Baptism in the Medieval West*, SPCK, London, 1965.
Mitchell, L. L., *Baptismal Anointing*, SPCK, London, 1966.
Palmer, P. F. (ed.), *Sacraments and Worship* (Sources of Christian Theology, vol. I), London, 1957.
Tertullian, *On Baptism*, ed. E. Evans, SPCK, London, 1964.
Whitaker, E. C. (ed.), *Documents of the Baptismal Liturgy*, SPCK, London, 1970.
Wilkinson, J. (ed.), *Egeria's Travels*, SPCK, London, 1971.
Wilson, H. A. (ed.), *The Gelasian Sacramentary*, Oxford, 1894.
Yarnold, E., *The Awe-Inspiring Rites of Initiation*, Slough, 1971.

ABBREVIATIONS USED

AG   *Ad Gentes*. Decree on the Church's Missionary Activity.
GICI   General Introduction: Christian Initiation (1969).
LG   *Lumen Gentium*. Dogmatic Constitution on the Church.
RC   Rite of Confirmation (1975).
RBC   Rite of Baptism for Children (1969).
RCIA   Rite of Christian Initiation of Adults (Study Edition, 1974).
RR   Rite of Reception of Baptized Christians into Full Communion with the Catholic Church (1974).
SC   *Sacrosanctum Concilium*. Constitution on the Sacred Liturgy.
DS   Denziger-Schoenmetzer, *Enchiridion Symbolorum*.

CONTENTS

PART ONE

THE HISTORY OF
CHRISTIAN INITIATION

THE HISTORY OF CHRISTIAN INITIATION

"Christians," wrote Tertullian in a lapidary phrase, "are made, not born" (*Apol.* xviii). Christian initiation, or "christening," is the process which a person goes through while being transformed into a new creation, modelled in the likeness of Christ himself. The sacraments of initiation mark the stages of that transformation and help to bring it about. They are the celebrations of the believing community, the Church, through whose mediation Christ acts to summon the individual to conversion of life and to transform that person by the gift of his Spirit. Yet initiation, as the name implies, is just a beginning; for it launches a person on a journey, a journey back to God from whom one came. It is a journey each of us must make, yet one which is only made by following in the footsteps of Christ in the company of his disciples. If Christian initiation is only a beginning, the rites of initiation nevertheless anticipate both the direction of that journey and its conclusion, so that from them we may learn both what the cost of discipleship may be and what hopes we may have for our final homecoming.

The history of Christian initiation is a help towards understanding the meaning of the sacraments of initiation which we celebrate in the Church of our own time, but it is also, implicitly at least, the story of how Christian people, our forebears in the faith, have from generation to generation shouldered the cross and set out full of faith to follow the Lord in his passing from this world to the Father. The evidence we have of the rites they celebrated gives us an indication of how they viewed the Christian life, with what conviction they embraced it and at what cost they were prepared to follow it. For this reason we shall be looking to such evidence to understand the different features of the rites of baptism and confirmation; but it would be helpful to begin with a sketch of the history of Christian initiation as a whole. This will enable us to see the organic development of the whole practice of making Christians, as well as to situate in their historical context some of the great teachers of the past whose insights we shall be sharing.

1

1. THE BEGINNINGS OF CHRISTIAN BAPTISM

The gospels are all concerned to announce, each in its own way, the good news that a new era has opened up in the relations between God and human-kind, thanks to the wonders he has worked through Jesus. Matthew, Mark and Luke each begins his proclamation of the gospel with baptism (Mark 1:1ff; Matt 3:1ff; Luke 3:1ff) and ends it with the promulgation of a new baptism (Mark 16:16ff; Matt 28:19; Luke in Acts 1:5). John does the same, but, like his whole theology, his approach is more intricate and less obvious. The first baptism is that preached and practiced by John the Baptist. The second is that inaugurated by Christ. The difference between the two is explained by all that happened in between times: the whole life, preaching, signs, suffering, death and resurrection of Jesus himself. It would seem from the Acts of the Apostles that the disciples of John continued his work after his death, and that for a while at least, the baptism of John and the baptism of Jesus were administered to the respective converts of each group of disciples. But they really belonged to different ages. The baptism of John was a rite of preparation for the age to come; the baptism inaugurated by Jesus was a rite of entry into the new age.

This difference is summed up in the words attributed by Mark to John the Baptist himself: "I have baptized you with water, but he will baptize you with the Holy Spirit" (Mark 1:8). It is the presence among us of the creative and redemptive Spirit of God which characterizes the new era, and it was fitting enough that the presence of that Spirit was first manifested in the presence of John the Baptist when Jesus came to submit to his baptism in the Jordan. John testified: "I saw the Spirit descend as a dove from heaven and it remained on him. I myself did not know him; but he who sent me to baptize with water said to me: 'He on whom you see the Spirit descend and remain, this is he who baptizes with the Holy Spirit'" (John 1:32-33).

This incident has traditionally been understood as the beginning of Christian baptism, although it was not until after the resurrection of the Lord that the disciples began to baptize, in accordance with the Lord's command (Matt 28:19). It was not until Jesus himself had passed through life and death and so into the glory of the Father that the way to the Father was open for the rest of the human race. Only then, as Jesus had promised, was the Spirit given to others to "complete his work on earth and bring us the fulness of grace" (see John 14:12, 26; 7:39). But after his glorification, the apostles, themselves baptized with the Holy Spirit (Acts 1:5), began to preach the Good News of what God had done, with conviction and with power. The people who heard them "were cut to the heart, and said to Peter and the rest of the apostles, 'Brethren, what shall we do?' And Peter said to them, 'Repent, and be baptized every one of you in the name of Jesus Christ for the forgiveness of your sins; and you shall receive the gift of the Holy Spirit'" (Acts 2:37-38).

On that occasion, Luke claims, three thousand were added to their number. Even if this incident is untypical, it seems as though Christian baptism was administered with little preparation and less formality. The various individuals and households mentioned in Acts—such as the Ethiopian eunuch (Acts 8:26-39), or the family of Cornelius (10:47-48), or Paul's jailer (16:30-33)—seem to have been baptized with a minimum of instruction. There is a sense of urgency about it all, an almost irresistible drive of the Spirit which seizes people as they hear the gospel preached, so that they are overcome with conviction concerning the truth of what they hear and submit to the Lordship of Jesus and are baptized without further ado. This is what is meant by "baptism in the name of Jesus" (Acts 2:38; 8:16; 10:48; 19:6). This is no longer the baptism of John, or a Jewish ritual washing, but a public profession of faith in and commitment to God who had worked new wonders through Jesus' life, death and resurrection. To be baptized was to become part of this new economy of salvation, numbered among the company of believers, trusting not in the Jewish law and ritual, but in faith in Christ. The result, as Peter had promised, was the forgiveness of their sins and the gift of the Holy Spirit.

Baptism, then, simple though it was in its execution, nevertheless marked a total conversion of a person's life. Its implications were enormous, and with the passage of the years they began to become clearer. The teaching of the New Testament on baptism is already the fruit of a generation or more of celebrating baptism, and is evidence of growing insight into both the sacrament of initiation itself and the Christian life to which it gave entry. To be accurate, one would have to speak of various theologies of baptism in the New Testament, rather than of a New Testament theology of baptism, for it is clear that different writers and the different communities to which they belonged shared a variety of different insights into the meaning of their initiation rites. This is only to be expected, since it is of the nature of symbolic rituals such as the Christian sacraments that they should be rich in meaning and inexhaustible sources of new understanding.

Thus the Johannine writings tend to revolve around the theme of baptismal rebirth (John 3:1-21; 1 John 3:9; 5:1, 4, 18) which makes us children of God (1 John 3:1ff.) through faith in the Son of God (1 John 5:1; John 3:18) and through baptism in water and the Spirit. This rite links us to the saving death of Christ and enables us to share his life (1 John 5:6; John 19:34) in the fellowship of his disciples in the Church (1 John 1:3; 3:14). Like John, Paul attributes our new life equally to faith (Rom 5:1) and to baptism (Rom 6:1ff.), but both are effective because they are the work of the Spirit (1 Cor 12:3, 13). Baptism is initiation into a life of faith lived in the Spirit (Gal 5:16ff.), whereby we are conformed to the image of the crucified Christ (Gal 5:26; Rom 6:2-4). Unlike the deutero-Pauline writings which suggest that we are already raised with Christ (e.g., Eph 2:4-6, "God . . . made us alive together with Christ . . . and raised us up with him, and made us sit with him in the heavenly places in

Christ Jesus"), Paul himself stresses that baptism has initiated us into a life of dying with Christ *in the hope that* we shall share likewise in the pattern of his resurrection (see Rom 6:4-5, 8; 1 Cor 15:22). In this way, we are introduced into a new way of life lived in the Spirit (Gal 5:16ff.), a life which is "in Christ" (Gal 3:27; Rom 6:3) and in his body, the Church (1 Cor 12:12ff.).

The New Testament writers are not concerned to describe the rites of baptism, since those to whom their writings were addressed had been baptized and were familiar with the ritual. Consequently, it is virtually impossible for us to reconstruct the apostolic rites of initiation. The very term *baptizein* implies that they included immersion in water "and a form of words" (Eph 5:26), which may have meant a profession of faith such as "Jesus is Lord" (1 Cor 12:3) or a declaration of the fact that the baptism was carried out in the name of the Trinity (Matt 28:19) or in the name of Jesus (Acts 2:38). Perhaps Paul's talk of "casting off" one's old life and "putting on" the new life of Christ (see Rom 13:12-14; Eph 4:22; etc.) means that the inevitable undressing and dressing were already seen as significant. The profession of faith in Christ was certainly explicit, and there is so much talk of Christian life as a warfare against Satan that some form of baptismal renunciation of Satan may well have been customary.

Almost contemporary with the later New Testament writings, however, is the ancient Judaeo-Christian compilation called the *Didache*, or Teaching of the Twelve Apostles. The material it contains is older than the collection itself and may well reflect first century practice. It opens with six short chapters on the way of life and the way of death, a form of moral instruction for candidates for baptism. Chapter VII then goes on to deal explicitly with the rite of baptism:

> Concerning baptism, baptize in this way. Having first rehearsed all these things, baptize in the name of the Father and of the Son and of the Holy Ghost, in living water. But if you have not living water, baptize into other water; and, if thou canst not in cold, in warm. If you have neither, pour water thrice on the head in the name, etc. . . . Before the baptism let the baptizer and the baptized fast, and others if they can. And order the baptized to fast one or two days before . . . (c. 7; Bettenson, p. 64).

In Chapter IX, the *Didache* orders that no one except the baptized should take part in the celebration of the Eucharist, but it is noticeable that there is no reference here to any rite, apart from water-baptism, for the conferring of the Spirit, although a couple of passages in the Acts of the Apostles suggest that a separate laying on of hands after baptism was already being associated with the gift of the Spirit (Acts 8:14-20; 19:6). On the other hand, there is in the *Didache* evidence of a developing pattern of preparation for baptism, both in the form of instruction and of fasting.

Pre-baptismal instruction, doctrinal and moral, as well as preparation by prayer and fasting, are also recorded in a description of baptism given by St.

Justin. He was a Palestinian living in Rome, and he addressed his first *Apology*, or defense of Christianity, to the Emperor Antoninus Pius in the year 160.

> I shall now lay before you the manner in which we dedicated ourselves to God when we were made new through Christ . . . As many as are persuaded and believe that these things we teach and describe are true, and undertake to live accordingly, are taught to pray and ask God, while fasting, for the forgiveness of their sins; and we pray and fast with them. Then they are led by us to a place where there is water, and they are reborn after the manner of rebirth by which we also were reborn: for they are then washed in the water in the Name of the Father and Lord God of all things, and of our Savior Jesus Christ, and of the Holy Spirit . . .
>
> After we have thus washed him who is persuaded and declares his assent, we lead him to those who are called brethren, where they are assembled, and make common prayer fervently for ourselves, for him that has been enlightened, and for all men everywhere, that, embracing the truth, we may be found in our lives good and obedient citizens, and also attain to everlasting salvation (c. 61–62; Whitaker, p. 2).

It is hard to know whether Justin is describing everything that happened, or whether, in addressing a pagan emperor, he was simplifying matters and perhaps holding back on some of the deeper mysteries such as, for example, the gift of the Spirit, which he does not mention. On the other hand, baptism is clearly seen here as giving entry into the Christian community. In fact, Justin goes on to describe how, the prayers once over, the newly baptized and the whole community share the kiss of peace and then go on to celebrate the Eucharist. But the community obviously takes a hand in the preparation of candidates for baptism, too, both in offering the necessary instruction leading to the conviction of faith and in the preparatory period of prayer and fasting. The whole community seems to be involved.

Less than fifty years later, in North Africa, the priest Tertullian was writing his treatise *On Baptism*. From this and scattered references in his other writings, we get glimpses of a much more developed ritual. The minister of baptism is the bishop, or priests and deacons delegated by him (c. 17). The water used for baptism is blessed (c. 4). The candidates prepare for the sacrament by prayer, fasting and night vigils, as well as some form of confession of sins (c. 20). Initiation is preferably, but not exclusively, given at Easter or during the Easter season (c. 19). A public renunciation of Satan is made before baptism, and again in the course of baptism itself. The candidates stand in the water, renounce Satan and profess their faith in Christ, and are submerged three times in the names of the Trinity. Coming up out of the water, they are anointed, and "next follows the imposition of the hand in benediction, inviting and welcoming the Holy Spirit" (c. 8). It was certainly customary at this time to baptize the children of Christian parents, for Tertullian argues against the practice: "Let them be made Christians when they have become competent to know Christ" (c. 18); but in this, as in his opinion that baptism should not be administered to young single people, Tertullian was not widely followed.

Tertullian, then, witnesses to a development of the rites of initiation in the direction of greater complexity. What seems to be happening is that the Church's growing awareness of the rich symbolic content of the original, simpler ritual is leading to the development of secondary ritual which gives expression to that content. This is just one instance of a consistent pattern of liturgical development: namely, that insights into the meaning of the rites tend themselves to become ritualized, thus leading to greater elaboration of liturgical forms. But the unity of Christian initiation is still retained at this stage. It is still a single process of incorporation into the Spirit-filled community of the Church, which is the Body of Christ. In his work *On the Resurrection of the Flesh,* Tertullian succinctly names the steps of initiation and the sacramental significance of each, while showing how they all lead to their common goal: communion with God in Christ, celebrated in the Eucharist.

The flesh is washed that the soul may be made spotless: the flesh is anointed that the soul may be consecrated: the flesh is signed [with the cross] that the soul too may be protected: the flesh is overshadowed by the imposition of the hand that the soul also may be illumined by the Spirit: the flesh feeds on the Body and Blood of Christ so that the soul as well may be replete with God (c. 8; Whitaker, p. 10).

All this takes place in the course of a single liturgy and the whole complex of rites is included under the single name of "baptism."

2. BAPTISM IN THE THIRD CENTURY

We have seen the gradual development of the rites of initiation from the apparent simplicity and informality of the New Testament period to a more complex pattern of Christian initiation in the second century. In the third century the practice of the Church with regard to baptism and her own understanding of it were influenced very much by the double factors of persecution from without and tensions arising within. Neither of these was a new experience. Indeed, Tertullian himself, thanks probably to his excessive rigorism, ended his days outside the Church as a member of the Montanist sect.

Montanism was one of several puritanical responses to the problem which was growing increasingly urgent and increasingly difficult for the Church as persecution began to ease off, namely, how should the Christian community relate to secular life? Montanists, for example, went so far as to condemn even marriage in their repudiation of the secular world. But other problems arose over those who had denied Christ in order to save their skins when a sudden bout of persecution broke out. Were they really Christians at all? If so, what was to be done with them now? And what was to be made of the baptism administered by Christians who had broken with the Great Church to form their own heretical groups? If baptism was the sacrament of faith, could theirs be a real baptism? If the Holy Spirit resided in the Church, could the Spirit be operative in the liturgical celebrations of those who had broken with the Church? If a person had been baptized as a member of some such heretical or schismatic sect, did that person need to be re-baptized? At one level the problem posed itself in terms of the nature of the Church: is it a community of the pure and the sinless or a field where wheat and tares grow together? What is the status of whole groups who break away from the universal Church? Can such groups confer through their sacraments a Spirit they do not possess? At another level, the problem was one of discipline: how does one care for the weak without discouraging the rest? How does one maintain earlier standards of enthusiasm and dedication when more and more people are coming forward for baptism?

These questions are worth mentioning because they are as relevant today as they ever were, though the conditions under which they are now posed are entirely different from those of the Roman world of the third century. Still, the answers given then have served the Church through the centuries, and are still fundamental to certain disciplinary and theological positions in the Church today. It is hardly the place to go into the controversies as they developed between St. Cyprian of Carthage and Pope Stephen in Rome, but we can simply note the outcome. Briefly, Cyprian and his fellow bishops in North Africa refused to acknowledge the validity of Christian initiation conferred by heretics on the grounds that there is only one Church and that sacraments conferred outside it are meaningless. This view was eventually overruled by the Church universal when it adopted Pope Stephen's position. His was the more traditional one, being content simply to reconcile to the Church those who came over from schism or heresy and not requiring them to be baptized as long as the form of baptism itself was one which expressed the true faith. If the convert had originally been baptized in a Trinitarian faith of the Church, his baptism was accepted and he was reconciled by the laying on of hands "that he may receive the Holy Spirit" (Council of Arles, 314, c. 8; Palmer, p. 114). The Council of Nicea distinguished between different sects, accepting the baptism of some and refusing that of others. Today the same principle prevails and in a much more divided Christian world the Church still acknowledges the baptism of the mainline Christian Churches who hold the Trinitarian faith and baptize in a way which is consistent with the traditional faith and practice of the Church. In fact, this common recognition of baptism is now seen to be the great bond that all

Christians have in common and the starting point for all ecumenical endeavor, whether it be joint action among Christians of different denominations or explicit movement towards Christian reunion.

These third century difficulties also led to the permanent acquisition of certain insights into the sacraments which were to assume new importance at a later period. So, for example, the refusal to rebaptize led to a consideration of why baptism could not be repeated. The fact that you had once been made a Christian meant that you could never totally cease to be one and thus could never be made a Christian again. This led later to the development of the theology of the baptismal "character," the indelible seal of the Spirit of God by which a person is branded forever in the service of Christ. The analogy between the once-for-all character of baptism and the indelible tattoo of the soldier or slave was elaborated by St. Augustine in the early fifth century in his writings against the Donatist sect, and it enabled him to clarify for the Church how a person could be validly baptized and yet the gift of baptism remain unfruitful in his life. In the high Middle Ages it was taken up again by St. Thomas Aquinas and given more positive content by being identified with the Christian's participation, through baptism, in the priestly functions of Christ.

The controversies of which we have been speaking broke out in the middle of the third century, but there is a precious document from earlier in the same century which gives us a very full picture of the process of Christian initiation as it was enacted, probably in Rome, around the year 215. It is a Church order, or book of ritual and discipline, called the *Apostolic Tradition* of Hippolytus. Its central section, "On the Laity," details the steps to be followed in the making of a Christian.

The first striking feature of these rites of initiation is that they are now spread out over a period of time which may be as long as three years. This time is spent in a two-stage preparation for baptism, beginning with the would-be converts being presented to those responsible for such matters in the community by members of the community who will vouch for them, or "sponsor" them. Investigation is made into their motives, life-style, and secular status to ensure the sincerity of their application and to assess what demands conversion to the Christian life is going to make on each of them. They then submit to instruction and formation in the Christian life for up to three years, though the time may be reduced if their progress is good. This period of "catechumenate" involves learning about the Christian faith, but it also demands growth in personal piety and morality and a growing concern for the underprivileged. After each instruction, the teacher, whether it be a priest or a layperson, will pray over those under instruction, laying hands on them to exorcise the spirit of unbelief (chs. 18:1-2; 19:1).

Sometime before Easter, the catechumens are examined again to see "whether they have lived piously while catechumens, whether they 'honored the widows,' whether they visited the sick, whether they have fulfilled every good work" (20:1). If they are seen to be ready, they are then told they will be admitted to baptism at Easter, which is the sign for them to embark on a period of intensive preparation: "If those who bring them bear witness that they have done thus, let them hear the gospel" (20:2). This is almost a lengthy prebaptismal retreat, marked with daily instructions in the Christian faith and daily exorcisms. We may guess, both from Hippolytus' indications of how the community was involved in the preparation for baptism and from later evidence, that this was something the whole local Church knew about and associated itself with. As such, it would come to serve as an occasion for the whole community to renew its own conversion in the annual observance of Lent.

On the Thursday before Easter, the candidates for baptism are instructed to bathe in preparation for the vigil. On Friday and Saturday, the days of Christ's death and burial, they fast and pray. Saturday sees a final assembly of all the baptismal candidates for a session of prayer and exorcism presided over by the bishop himself. That night they gather with the rest of the community for the great annual paschal vigil, which is passed in the reading of the Scriptures and instruction. At cock-crow, the baptismal celebration itself begins with the blessing spoken over the waters of baptism. Then the bishop blesses one jar of oil and exorcises another for use in the rites to follow.

The candidates then remove their clothing and, prompted by the priest, make their renunciation of Satan: "I renounce thee, Satan, and all thy service and all thy works." The priest then anoints them with the exorcised oil, saying: "Let all evil spirits depart far from thee." The candidates are then led by a deacon to the water, where a priest, himself standing in the water, awaits them. Children are baptized first, then the men and then the women. (A member of the family is instructed to speak on behalf of children too young to answer for themselves.) The priest in the water lays his hand on the candidates and asks them if they believe in God the Father almighty. They reply, "I do," and are then submerged in the water. They then profess their faith in the Son and in the Holy Spirit, each time being submerged again. Emerging then from the water, they are anointed with the oil of thanksgiving before drying themselves and putting on their clothes.

When all the candidates have been baptized and anointed and have dressed themselves, they are taken back into the assembly of the faithful and led before the bishop. Stretching his hand over them, he prays for those who have just had their sins remitted by the waters of regeneration, that they may now be filled with the Holy Spirit to serve God in his Church. Then he takes some consecrated oil in his hand and pours it on the heads of the newly baptized Christians, laying his hand on them and marking their foreheads with the sign of the cross, saying: "I anoint thee with holy oil in God the Father almighty and Christ Jesus and the Holy Ghost" (22:1-2). The bishop then greets them with the kiss of peace.

Then, for the first time, the newly baptized are permitted to join the faithful in their prayers and, afterwards, to exchange the kiss of peace with them. The liturgy of the Eucharist then begins and the newly baptized celebrate their incorporation into the body of Christ by sharing in Holy Communion. At long last, after perhaps as much as three years of association with the Church, they are allowed to celebrate and pray with the believing community. It is the climax of the whole process of conversion; and as a sign that they have arrived in the Promised Land, they are given, besides the Eucharistic bread and cup, a cup of milk mixed with honey, as well as a drink of water to signify the purification of the inner self.

We have spent some time describing Hippolytus' baptismal arrangements because they really represent a very clear example of what the rites of initiation were like in the early centuries. Hippolytus himself claimed to be doing no more than preserving the traditional order of things, and certainly there is evidence for many of his rites being used in other parts of the Church at an earlier date. On the other hand, while the overall pattern of his rite is typical, many details are peculiar, such as the double anointing after baptism. It is important to remember that there was no uniform liturgy of baptism universally practiced, any more than there was uniformity in the Eucharistic liturgy. The main pattern of the liturgy, inherited from the tradition, was fairly consistent, but the details of the manner of celebrating it varied, like the language of the liturgy, from one community to the next. One particular detail which is worth noticing in the baptismal liturgy of the *Apostolic Tradition* is the way in which the baptismal gift of the Spirit now appears, according to a probable reconstruction of the text, to be associated with the laying on of hands and anointing, while baptism itself is credited with the remission of sins. There is some precedent for this before the time of Hippolytus, and in the future the distinction will eventually lead to a real separation of the two rites. But here, at least, we see them together, complementary aspects of a single sacrament. Baptism is the rite of entry into the Spirit-filled Church, and that incorporation is consummated in the celebration of the Eucharist.

3. THE CLASSICAL PERIOD OF CHRISTIAN INITIATION

In the early fourth century, the conversion of the Emperor Constantine marked the end of the era of persecution and the beginning of the establishment of Christianity as the religion of the Roman Empire. With the influx of converts which followed the upturn in the Church's fortunes, the rites of initiation had a crucial role to play in the formation of a new generation of Christians whose relationships to secular life and civil authority would inevitably be closer than those enjoyed by Christians while the Church was a persecuted minority. While it is always difficult to form any very accurate impression of the general standard of Christian life in a given period—and the burgeoning monastic movement provided a vociferous commentary on the dangers of compromising with the secular world in this age—it would seem that the discipline of the Church regarding Christian initiation and the sacrament of reconciliation remained intact and vigorous.

Apostates and public sinners were barred from Communion and could still be reconciled with the Church only once in their lifetime, and that only after a lengthy period of public penance. Converts from paganism were still expected to enroll as catechumens and undergo a period of Christian formation such as described by Hippolytus before being admitted to baptism. The infant children of Christian parents were admitted to the catechumenate and then could be baptized, confirmed and given Holy Communion while still in their infancy. Nevertheless, the prospect of their children lapsing from grace as they entered adulthood and having to submit to the rigors of public penance led many Christian parents to defer the baptism of their children until they had grown up and settled down. It was not until St. Augustine, in the early fifth century, brought home to people, through his teaching on original sin, the dangers of children dying unbaptized, that this situation began to change. In the meantime, the large numbers of unbaptized catechumens in the Christian community who were prepared to defer their baptism seemingly until they were on their death beds presented a sizeable pastoral problem as time went on. Thus the rigor of the Church's discipline tended to have unwelcome side effects.

However, it is the high quality of the preaching and teaching about the sacraments which gives this age the right to be called the classical era of Christian initiation. In the century from 350 to 450, the Church was blessed with a series of teachers and theologians unparalleled in any other period of Church history: men of the stature of St. Athanasius, St. Cyril of Jerusalem, St. Basil, St. Gregory Nazianzen, St. Gregory of Nyssa, St. John Chrysostom, Theodore of Mopsuestia, St. Ambrose of Milan, St. Augustine of Hippo, Pope St. Leo the Great. What all these men have in common, besides being saints and doctors of the Church, is that they were all bishops. Their writings and sermons constitute a magnificent response to the pastoral needs of the people entrusted to their care. They defended the unity of the Church against schismatics and the integrity of the faith against heretics. They expounded the Scriptures and the Creed, provided inspiration and guidance for the moral and spiritual lives of their flocks, and commented on the profound mysteries they saw in the sacraments they celebrated.

It is mainly from the writings of these Fathers of the Church, together with the legislation emanating from various Church councils and such occasional documents as the diary of Egeria, the Spanish pilgrim whose vivid jottings portray the liturgical life of Jerusalem and the Holy Land around the year 400, that our knowledge of the rites of initiation in this period is gleaned. Of particular value are the so-called *Mystagogical Catecheses*—instructions on the sacraments of initiation preached by the bishop to those who were either about to be baptized or who had just been baptized. Chief among these are the extant sermons on initiation preached by Ambrose of Milan in the West and by John Chrysostom, Cyril of Jerusalem and Theodore of Mopsuestia in the East. They all give evidence of an intensive prebaptismal formation of candidates for baptism which culminates in the solemn annual festival of initiation held on Easter Night. Since we shall have occasion to quote them more than once, it might be useful to say a word about each of these men.

Ambrose became bishop of Milan by popular acclaim in 373, and is considered to have preached his six sermons *On the Sacraments* about the year 391. They were addressed to those who had just been baptized in a series of daily meetings held during the week following Easter Sunday, and consist of a step-by-step explanation of the meaning of the rites they had so recently undergone. Like most preachers of his time, his explanation takes the form of an appeal to the Scriptures, looking for texts or events which can shed light on the different liturgical rites. The main program of initiation does not differ vastly from that described earlier by Hippolytus, except that, instead of having two anointings after baptism, the Milanese liturgy has one anointing administered by the bishop to the newly baptized as they emerge from the font, and then, after they have been clothed in white, the bishop marks them with the seal of the Spirit. A rite peculiar to the Church of Milan and a few others is the washing of the feet of the newly baptized by the bishop in imitation of Jesus' action at the Last Supper (John 13:3ff.).

The liturgy of Jerusalem, on the other hand, was profoundly influenced by the fact that the sacraments of our redemption were being celebrated on the very spot where our redemption had been won. Cyril and his community, together with an ever growing number of pilgrims and religious, met for the liturgy in a great double basilica built by Constantine over the alleged site of Calvary and the Lord's tomb. Cyril was consecrated bishop of Jerusalem in 348. A series of sermons delivered to candidates for baptism while he was still a priest has survived, plus five *Mystagogical Catecheses* delivered to the newly baptized which, if Cyril did indeed preach them, probably date from after 348. Perhaps what most characterizes Cyril's approach to the sacraments of initiation is his sense of the awesomeness of the mysteries manifested in the liturgy of the Church and of the drama of the invisible conflict with the forces of evil which is enacted in the rites.

John Chrysostom and Theodore of Mopsuestia were both priests at Antioch, the capital of Syria, before John became archbishop of Constantinople in 397 and Theodore, bishop of Mopsuestia. John preached his *Baptismal Instructions* and Theodore his *Baptismal Homilies* while they were both still in Antioch, so they both refer to the same liturgical tradition and they both, unlike Cyril and Ambrose, explain the rites of initiation to cate-chumens who are still preparing for baptism. The approach of the two preachers, however, is quite different, probably reflecting very different temperaments. John is quite aware of the solemnity and awesomeness of the rites, but his preaching is generally full of direct pastoral practicality and marked by strong moral overtones. Theodore on the other hand is a much more speculative mind, but his rich insights are more often than not ob-scured by his garrulous and wandering manner. Of particular interest, though, is Theodore's realization that the rites of Christian initiation are really only a beginning and that the full reality they signify will only be ours in the resurrection from the dead:

> You were anointed by [the Holy Spirit] and received him by God's grace. He is yours and remains within you. You enjoy the first fruits of him in this life, for you receive now in symbol the possession of the bless-ings to come. Then you will receive the grace in its fulness, and it will free you from death, corruption, pain and change; your body too will last forever and will be free from decay, and your soul will not be liable to any further movement towards evil (*Bapt. Hom.* II, 28; Yarnold, p. 209).

A surprising thing about the Antioch liturgy of initiation is that it would appear originally to have contained no rite for conferring the Spirit after baptism. The gift of the Spirit was associated with an anointing immediately before baptism or with the act of baptism itself. On the other hand, Theodore does mention, contrary to all evidence of the Syrian rites before his time and contrary to the evidence of John Chrysostom, an episcopal "seal of the Spirit" being given to the newly baptized after they have dressed them-selves. What this suggests, though we shall look at the matter again in dealing with confirmation, is the fundamental inseparability of baptism and confir-mation and their integral unity within a single complex of initiation rites whose total effect is to free us from sin, endow us with the Holy Spirit of God and admit us to communion with Christ in the Church which is celebrated by immediate admission to the Eucharist.

4. THE BREAK-UP OF CHRISTIAN INITIATION

The creative evolution of the liturgy of Christian initiation had ceased by the end of the fifth century. From that time onwards, the forces that were to shape the process of making a Christian were generally external to the liturgy itself. Chief among these was the fact that from the early sixth cen-tury the candidates for baptism were almost exclusively infants. Coupled with that was the fact that the preoccupation of the Church in administering baptism was henceforth less that of forming Christians for life than that of saving children from dying unbaptized.

About the year 500, a Roman deacon called John (possibly the man who later became Pope John I) wrote a letter to a certain Senarius in response to some questions he had asked about the traditional practices surrounding Christian initiation. His letter gives us an outline of the rites as he knew them in Rome, together with some brief comments as to their meaning. The process of preparation for baptism has become much abbreviated, although there is no clear indication of the period of time during which the candidates are "catechized." John rightly interprets this Greek word as meaning "instructed," but associates the instruction not with any learning process, but with the rites of blessing and exorcism, undertaken so that the catechumen "may know who he is and who he shall be" (Whitaker, p. 155). The postulants for baptism are presented with the gospel and later examined as to their knowledge of it in a series of three examinations or "scrutinies" held in Lent. Baptism still takes place during the Easter Vigil. The candidates remove their clothing and are baptized by a triple immersion in the name of the Trinity (i.e., a threefold profession of faith). After baptism, the newly baptized are robed in white and their heads anointed with chrism. They are then taken to the bishop for the laying on of hands and signing with chrism for the gift of the Spirit, although John does not mention this himself for he breaks off to point out that "all these things are done even to infants who by reason of their youth understand nothing" (Whitaker, p. 157).

Indication of the sort of liturgy practiced at Rome in the period shortly after John was writing is preserved for us in parts of the so-called *Gelasian Sacramentary*. The traditional components of the extended course of preparation for baptism—the rites of inscription, the exorcisms, presentation of the creed, the gospels and the Lord's Prayer—are all to be found here. On Holy Saturday morning there is the final solemn exorcism, the renunciation of Satan, the prebaptismal anointing, the rehearsal of the creed and the dismissal of the catechumens. The vigil begins with ten readings from Scripture, each interspersed with prayer, and then the litanies are sung as the bishop, his clergy, the baptizands and their sponsors proceed to the baptistry. The blessing of the water is followed immediately by baptism, each person being baptized to the accompaniment of a threefold confession of faith. Once out of the water, the baptized is anointed on the head with chrism by a priest and then taken to the bishop for the laying on of hands, the signing with chrism and the gift of the Holy Spirit. To the accompaniment of litanies all return to the basilica and the Mass of Easter begins and the newly baptized share Holy Communion with the faithful. But by now the candidates for baptism are all infants, whereas in John's day, perhaps half a century earlier at most, there was still a mixture of adults and children.

We began by remarking that the era of liturgical creativity had long been over by the middle of the sixth century. In the liturgy, as in so many other matters, Christians were more and more inclined to preserve the past and to regard it as normative. Theology became a matter of recording what the Fathers had said and trying to reconcile their different views. Liturgy became a matter of preserving the traditional rites and prayers. The rites and texts of the liturgy of initiation were used for the Christian initiation of children without, it seems, there being any doubts expressed about their suitability. The catechetical instructions dropped out, inevitably, and what the children could not do for themselves (e.g., recital of the creed, response to questions) was simply done for them by their parents or godparents. But beyond that there was no real attempt to develop a form of Christian initiation for children, and the baptismal liturgy used in the Catholic Church until the late 1960s was this sixth century Roman liturgy, virtually unaltered.

Perhaps the most significant change in baptismal practice from the sixth century onward was the gradual abandonment of Easter and Pentecost as the annual festivals of initiation. Baptism continued to be administered only at Easter, danger of death apart, right up to the twelfth century in Rome, and Charlemagne had made an unsuccessful attempt to maintain this ancient tradition throughout his empire in the early ninth century, but there were factors at work which made it unenforceable. Chief among these was undoubtedly the high infant mortality rate, which, in view of the very widely accepted doctrine of Augustine on original sin, made it seem altogether too risky to wait until the following Easter to take a child to be baptized in the course of an all-night vigil. Original sin was not a doctrine invented by St. Augustine, but it was his defense of the infant's need for baptism which helped to anchor this belief firmly in the popular consciousness to such a degree that it was universally believed that a child who died unbaptized was eternally excluded from the vision of God and that to allow such a thing to happen through negligence was a very severe crime, punishable even in civil law.

One of the immediate effects of administering baptism outside the preferred season of Easter was the abbreviation or telescoping of the preparatory rites. St. Caesarius, bishop of Arles in the sixth century, was prepared to allow parents to have their children baptized at times other than Easter, but they were expected to bring them to the church ten days or at least a week beforehand for the initial rites and they themselves were supposed to prepare for the initiation of their children by prayer and fasting. Nevertheless, many did not turn up until an hour or so before the baptismal liturgy was due to begin, and one can imagine that this sort of practice became increasingly commonplace with the result that all the rites of the catechumenate and initiation were eventually condensed into a single ceremony. After all, these rites had originally been conceived as accompanying a process of personal conversion and spiritual growth, so there was no very clear reason for extending them over a period of time in the case of a young child who was incapable of such development.

A second effect of the unwillingness of people to postpone infant baptism until Easter was that baptism was then necessarily celebrated, not by the bishop and the whole Church, but by a priest and such people as wished to attend. Furthermore, Christianity had traditionally been a town religion until this time; so much so that to be a peasant (Latin "paganus") was the equivalent of being an unbeliever. But with the decline of the old Roman Empire and the beginning of the Middle Ages, the Church was moving out to evangelize the rural areas. For a long time the Church had known subsidiary communities founded from and dependent upon the town community with its bishop, but now the number of rural communities served by groups of priests, or even isolated priests, increased at a much faster rate, so that the character of the Church as a whole gradually changed.

Under these circumstances, increasing numbers of people were being baptized by the parish priest and not by the bishop. What had previously been done in emergencies now became a general rule. Yet, from the beginning, the bishop as head of the local Church had always presided at the initiation of newcomers to the community. He had not always and everywhere done all the water baptisms personally, often being content to baptize the first of a group of catechumens and then delegate priests or deacons to do the rest while he concerned himself with anointing the newly baptized or laying his hand on them and signing them as a sacrament of the gift of the Spirit. But what was to be done now? Obviously the bishop could not be present at every baptism.

In the East the matter was simply resolved: the bishops delegated their priests to carry out the full rites of initiation at every baptism, insisting only that the post-baptismal anointing be done with oil which they themselves had consecrated. This is probably because they tended to attribute a sacramental significance to the sacramental oil comparable to that which we attribute to the consecrated bread and wine at Mass: it was a sacrament of the Spirit's presence. In any case, the link with the bishop as head of the local Church was preserved in the East by the use of chrism consecrated by the bishop.

In the West the tradition developed differently. From the third century, the bishop of Rome had insisted that for people to be properly initiated they must receive the seal of the Spirit from the bishop. This Roman tradition was not only maintained at Rome, but spread throughout the West in the general adoption of the Roman liturgy in the eighth and ninth centuries. This meant that children who had been baptized by their parish priest within a short time after their birth were then taken to the bishop the following Easter, or later, for the rite that came to be known as "confirmation." This separation of the two parts of initiation gradually grew longer and longer, as we shall see when we discuss confirmation, until in the sixteenth century the rule came to prevail that a child should not be confirmed until it had attained the use of reason, which was generally reckoned to be about seven years of age.

It was still the custom at Rome, as we have mentioned, to admit children to the whole ritual of initiation at the Easter Vigil as late as the twelfth century; in short, they were baptized, confirmed and given Holy Communion, the latter being administered to them usually under the form of a drop of wine given them on a spoon or with a silver straw or on the priest's finger. The unified rites of initiation survived elsewhere, too, but with increasing rarity. The Middle Ages are full of episcopal complaints about parents neglecting to bring their children to the bishop for confirmation, and it would seem that for a period of time there was a real danger of this sacramental stage of the making of a Christian simply disappearing altogether.

Part of the problem was in persuading parents that this sacrament was really necessary. Once baptized, was the child not free from original sin? Theologians had to admit that confirmation was indeed not strictly necessary for salvation, and were hard put to find convincing reasons for putting parents to the trouble of getting their children confirmed. Once separated from its immediate connection with baptism, confirmation becomes, as someone once remarked, "a sacrament in search of a theology." In our own times, the much more frequent practice of admitting children to Communion before they have been confirmed makes nonsense of the sacramental process of initiation.

On the other hand, Christian initiation was never just a matter of liturgical rites, not even sacramental ones. It always was, and still remains, in the happy phrase of Vatican II, "a spiritual journey" (AG, 13). With the practice of infant baptism and its development as just described, the liturgical and sacramental framework of that journey necessarily became separated from the process of Christian formation. Throughout the Middle Ages, parents and godparents were told to ensure that they taught their children the rudiments of the Christian faith, and in particular the creed, the decalogue and the Lord's Prayer. In the Middle Ages, however, the very fact of growing up and living in a Christian society whose culture and rhythms were those of the Church and her liturgy was itself an inescapable formative influence. In modern times when such social support could no longer be relied on the problem of Christian formation has grown ever more urgent, while the rediscovery of our traditions raises the question once again of how the process of Christian initiation can best be undertaken in the very different world of the twentieth century.

5. THE RITES OF INITIATION TODAY

The results of the sort of disintegration of the process of Christian initiation which we have described include the following: loss of a sense of the local Church as an organic unity in the Spirit; an understanding of baptism largely reduced to the ablution of original sin; uncertainty about the meaning of confirmation; an understanding of faith which overemphasizes its intellectual content; widespread failure to understand the radical nature of the Christian life as a dying with Christ in surrender to God. The result of all this is that Christians today are undergoing a crisis of identity. As Vatican II recognized, we are living in one of the most critical periods in the history of the Church, one calling not only for a renewal of Church structures, but for a revitalization of Christian life at all levels.

When Vatican II set itself the pastoral task of intensifying the daily growth of Catholics in Christian living, and of making Church observances more responsive to the needs of our times (SC, 1), it was inevitable that the question of the making of Christians should come up for review. In the Constitution on the Sacred Liturgy, promulgated in December, 1963, the Council spoke of the role of the sacraments as "sacraments of faith": "to sanctify men, to build up the Body of Christ, and finally, to give worship to God" (n. 59). It linked the sacraments to "the paschal mystery of the passion, death, and resurrection of Christ" and regretted that "there have crept into the rites of the sacraments and sacramentals certain features which have rendered their nature and purpose less clear to the people of today" (nn. 61–62).

The actual revision of the liturgy of initiation was left to a commission to undertake, but the Council laid down certain guidelines for their work. These guidelines do not call for any very abrupt change of practice. What they do call for is a change of style, a reversion to the traditional celebration of initiation as a process of conversion and formation. The adult rites of initiation are to be returned to their original shape, including a period of catechumenate. The rite of baptism for infants is to be adapted to their condition as infants and the role of parents and godparents in the Christian life of the child is to be made more explicit in the rite. The connection of confirmation with baptism and the Eucharist as part of the process of initiating a person to the full Christian life is to be made clear (SC, 64–71).

The goal of Christian initiation is the formation of a Spirit-filled community of deeply committed Christian adults who can both bear witness to their faith in Christ and glorify their Father who is in heaven. What it means to lose faith in the wisdom of the world and find faith in Christ is therefore best seen in the experience of adult conversion, but the same conviction has to be engendered even in those who are born of Christian parents. For them, the sacraments of initiation may commence in infancy and be spread out over several years as they grow up, but the program of the sacraments can never divorce itself from the process of formation. The end of both is the same: the obedience of faith, whereby a person commits his whole self freely to God in Christ and the Church. In that sense, the rites of the Christian initiation of adults are normative for our understanding of what initiation is all about. It may well be the case that the Church in the future will continue her ancient practice of baptizing infants, but this will always need to be seen and understood as but the first stage in an extended program of growth towards Christian maturity. The sacraments are not magic. Grace builds on nature, and the sacraments of initiation—baptism, confirmation, Eucharist—are but milestones in the spiritual journey of the awakening child. They suppose the faith, the prayer, and the support of the individual's family and the wider family of the Church into whose life the Spirit is drawing the child.

PART TWO

BAPTISM

I

WELCOME

One of the things which makes it difficult for people today to make sense of the sacramental liturgies of the Church is the frame of mind, inherited from medieval theology and fostered by a catechesis based on that theology, which reduces all the sacraments to their indispensable element. Thus we have been led to think of the Mass in terms of consecration, penance in terms of the absolution, baptism in terms of the pouring of water with a form of words, and so forth. This is really very unhelpful, because it tends to reduce the rest of the sacramental celebration to the level of mere ceremonial "dressing." No one would think of defining a car simply in terms of its engine, difficult though it would be to make much use of a car without one. A story cannot be reduced to its ending, nor a play to its climax, for, in both cases, the culmination depends for its effectiveness on what precedes and follows it, while the other parts would be deprived of their significance if they did not lead up to some critical moment which was decisive for the future and made sense of the past.

So it is with the celebration of baptism. All that leads up to the font and what happens there is prepared for by all that goes before, while the baptism, in its turn, points to confirmation by the bishop and to the celebration of the Eucharist. The richness of the baptismal liturgy is such, however, that it does not proceed in a simple, logical progression from one point to the next. It is not a process to be gone through like a manufacturing program pared down to its absolute essentials by time and motion experts. It is more like a piece of music which makes progress by stating its theme in many different ways, elaborating it and recapitulating it, offering insights and allusions as it spills along, ever building towards the climax and finale. The opening rites of Christian baptism both set the stage and announce the theme for the drama to be enacted and they are full of rich innuendos which prepare us for the action to come.

1. *If possible, baptism should take place on a Sunday, the day on which the Church celebrates the paschal mystery* (RBC, 32).

When we call Sunday the "Lord's Day," we sometimes give the impression that it is *God's* day, as if that day were set aside for the Creator and we could claim the rest of the week for ourselves. But the Lord here is not God the Father. The Good News, according to the first Christian sermon, is "that God has made both Lord and Messiah this Jesus whom you crucified" (Acts 2:36). It was on the first day of the week that Jesus arose from the dead and was established in glory. The first day of the new week saw the "great break-through" as God in Christ broke the stranglehold of sin and death and opened the way for the human race to move into a whole new mode of exist-ence. Thereafter, the disciples of Jesus regularly met together to celebrate this "breakthrough" in the way Jesus had commanded them: by celebrating the supper, the *Lord's* supper. There they recognized his living presence and made contact with him who, having died, was now risen for the hope and joy of us all. This day of their assembly, therefore, came to be known to the early Christians as the Lord's day, i.e., Christ's day, the day for celebrating his vic-tory and ours, his resurrection and our liberation.

From the earliest times, probably even before the annual recurrence of the Sunday nearest the Jewish feast of Passover gave rise to Easter, the weekly assembly of believers to celebrate the resurrection was also the occa-sion for celebrating baptism. What, after all, did it mean to baptize someone except to admit him to the company of those who had staked their lives on dying and rising with Jesus? "Do you not know," asks St. Paul, "that all of us who have been baptized into Christ Jesus were baptized into his death? We were buried with him therefore by baptism into death, so that as Christ was raised from the dead by the glory of the Father, we too might walk into newness of life" (Rom 6:3-4).

We have already seen the Church's longstanding preference for doing baptisms during the Easter Vigil and in the seven weeks that followed until Pentecost. One of the earliest Christian writers to testify to this tradition and to its meaning is Tertullian, a priest from North Africa, writing shortly before the year 200.

> The Passover provides the day of most solemnity for baptism, for then was accomplished our Lord's passion, and into it we are baptized. . . . After that, Pentecost [i.e., the Easter season] is a most auspicious period for arranging baptisms, for during it our Lord's resurrection was several times made known among the disciples, and the grace of the Holy Spirit first given, and the hope of our Lord's coming made evident: because it was at that time, when he had been received back into heaven, that angels said to the apostles that he would so come as he had also gone up into heaven, namely, at Pentecost. . . . For all that, every day is a Lord's day: any hour, any season, is suitable for baptism. If there is a difference of solemnity, it makes no difference to the grace (*On Baptism*, 19; Evans, p. 41).

It is not essential that baptism should be celebrated on a Sunday, but it is appropriate and helps to underline the fact that to be baptized is to share in the passover of the Lord from death to life, from this world to the Father. For the same reason, the Sundays of Easter are preferable to the Sundays of

Lent for the mood of the Christian community, basking in the springtime of resurrection, will conspire with the rites of the baptismal liturgy to make a baptism a ringing and joyful affirmation of faith in our sharing the Lord's "newness of life."

2. *[Baptism] should be conferred in a communal celebration for all the recently born children, and in the presence of the faithful, or at least of relatives, friends, and neighbors, who are all to take an active part in the rite* (RBC, 32).

In all the sacraments Christ reaches out and touches the life of a person through the ministrations of the community of believers. The local congregation, gathered in his name, is the visible Body of Christ through which the Lord shares his life with us, healing and sanctifying us. For reasons we have seen, baptism, like many of the sacraments, became reduced to the status of a quasi-private affair and was carried out in the back of an empty church on a Sunday afternoon when no one was around. It is the teaching of Vatican II that "liturgical services are not private functions, but are celebrations of the Church, which is the 'sacrament of unity,' namely, a holy people united and organized under their bishops" (SC, 26). But this which is true of all the sacraments is true in a very special sense of baptism, for baptism is the sacrament of reception into the Church and it is only right that the Church should gather to receive and welcome her new members. That is why the baptismal ritual says: "The People of God, that is the Church, made present in the local community, has an important part to play in the baptism of children and of adults" (RBC, 4).

We shall see something more of this role of the local Church in the ministration of baptism later, but for the moment we might note some of the legislation concerning baptism which makes sense in this light. First, while in an emergency anyone can and should administer baptism, it has always been the right and duty, under normal circumstances, of the leader of the community to do so. Likewise, the proper place for the celebration of baptism is not the private home, or in the hospital (RBC, 12–13), or even a chapel such as might be found in a religious community. The proper place for baptism is the parish church, the home and gathering place of the local Christian community. This, the rubric says, is "so that baptism may clearly appear as the sacrament of the Church's faith and of admittance into the people of God" (RBC, 10). Or again: "In the actual celebration the People of God (represented not only by the parents, godparents and relatives, but also, as far as possible, by friends, neighbors and some members of the local Church) should take an active part. Thus they will show their common faith and express their joy as the newly baptized are received into the community of the Church" (GICI, 7). It is partly this need to express in realistic terms the dimension of baptism as welcoming a person into the Christian community which prompts the suggestion that baptism might be celebrated from time to time in the course of the Sunday Mass (RBC, 9). Also involved in this is the intimate connection between baptism and the Eucharist, but it remains true that the Sunday Mass is the main occasion when the local community gathers. Such a celebration is not a gimmick, though it may serve as a salutary reminder to the whole community that they are, after all, the community of the baptized and that they have all, at one time or another, been committed in this sacrament to a life of dying with Christ in the hope of rising with him. But a celebration such as this makes explicit what is always implicit in any celebration, namely, that baptism is the sacrament of initiation and reception into the community of the faithful, which is the Body of Christ.

In the tradition this dimension of baptism has been present from the beginning. After recounting St. Peter's sermon on that first Pentecost day, the Acts of the Apostles adds the remark that "those who received his word were baptized, and that day about three thousand were added to their number" (2:41). Just over a century later, Justin Martyr, in describing the rites of Christian initiation, makes a point of saying that "after washing [i.e. baptizing] him who has been persuaded and has given his assent, we bring him to those that are called the brethren, where they are assembled" (I *Apol.* c. 65).

It was probably the loss of this sense of baptism as a sacrament of the whole Church which made the "christening" into something which, as often as not, was a family and social occasion more than the celebration of the most profound and intimate mysteries of the Christian life and faith. To some extent that still prevails today, so that the impression often given is that this is the celebration of the *birth* of the child, rather than of its sacramental *rebirth* in Christ. Parents and families rightly want to celebrate the birth of a new child with their friends and relations, but baptism is the wrong place for this if this consideration makes them blind to the much more profound and awesome mysteries which are enacted in this sacred rite. Parents who understand this will also understand why it is a matter that affects the whole local community of believers, why the whole parish should be involved, and why the rubric suggests a communal celebration for all recently born children. For that reason, it is forbidden to celebrate baptism more than once in the same church on the same day (GICI, 27). "For just as the [human] body is one and has many members, and all the members of the body, though many, are one body, so it is with Christ. For by one Spirit we were all baptized into one body . . ." (1 Cor 12:12-13). A profound awareness of this unity of all believers in Christ—"one Lord, one faith, one baptism," as the letter to the Ephesians puts it (4:5)—pervaded the Church for centuries and governed her sacramental discipline. The authorities in the Church long resisted the indiscriminate celebration of "private baptism" just as they checked the indiscriminate multiplication of private Masses. Their fear, that the sense of the community of the Church as the "sacrament of unity" would be lost, has proven well founded. Today, if we enter into the spirit of the revised liturgy, we may rediscover that experience for ourselves.

3. *The 'dramatis personae'*

The assembled People of God is not just a crowd but a community in which different people have different parts to play and different functions to perform. Apart from the baby, who, while being the center of the community's attention, is inevitably assigned a rather passive role (and the more passive the better, from the mother's point of view, no doubt), there are a number of people who have an indispensable part to play.

It may seem a little odd to begin with the *bishop*, since most baptismal celebrations are hardly likely to be graced with his presence. Nevertheless, he remains the head and leader of the local Church community and, as such, has ultimate responsibility for the initiation of all newcomers to the Christian community. In the early centuries, when each local assembly was presided over by its bishop it was expected that he would preside over the baptismal celebrations which were among the most important events in the community's life. So Ignatius of Antioch, himself a bishop, could write to the Christians at Smyrna: "Let no one do anything concerning the Church without the bishop. . . . It is not permitted to baptize or to hold an agape without the authorization of the bishop" (*ad Smyrn., 8*). Still to this day in some countries an adult may not be baptized without the explicit authorization of the bishop; and of course, as we have already seen, when it became impossible for bishops to do all the baptisms in the communities under their care, they retained their association with Christian initiation in the West by insisting on confirming all who had been baptized, so that persons could not become full members of the Church without their bishop having laid both eyes and hands on them.

The growth of the Church made it necessary to set up other communities of the faithful which would still be part of the bishop's flock, but entrusted to the care of the pastor he gave them. The most important such grouping is the parish, and the Church leader whom most newcomers to the Church will meet is the *parish priest*. It is his duty, in dependence upon the bishop (GICI, 13), to prepare adults for baptism and to baptize children after giving the parents and godparents "appropriate pastoral guidance" (*ibid.*). In this he acts as the deputed leader of the local community. As such he is hardly expected to do everything, though he will be responsible for supervising an adequate program of preparation for the sacraments and rightly be the usual person to preside at the celebration of baptism. But Christian initiation, if it is to be initiation into a real community, must be the concern of all. Other priests in the parish, deacons if there be any, catechists and competent lay people can all be involved in the faith formation of adult converts and in helping the parents of children who are to be baptized to prepare themselves both for the baptism itself and for the responsibilities they will then assume. In a parish where such tasks are shared in a spirit of shared faith and love there is an instinctive understanding of the liturgy as a celebration of a common sacrament of faith and unity. The liturgy is defined by Pius XII as "the worship of the Mystical Body of Jesus Christ, Head and members." This is made visible in the congregation acting under the leadership of the priest and, most appropriately, the parish priest.

Among the most important people at any baptism are, of course, the *parents* of the children being baptized. In the old baptismal liturgy they were more or less passive bystanders, hovering in the background as the godparents carried the children and spoke on the children's behalf. The reason for this was quite simple. The rites of baptism which were in use until a few years ago were, as we have already seen, the ancient rites of initiation used for the baptism of adult converts whose parents, naturally, had no particular responsibility in the matter. For an adult, encounter with Christ is a matter between oneself and the Church, and the parents have no necessary mediating role to play. With the development of infant baptism the situation changed, but the ritual of baptism was not really altered to take that into account. Perhaps in medieval society the extended family played a larger role than it does today, so that the faith and practice of the parents were less crucial. Certainly in a Christian society there was far more to help a child imbibe the Christian religion and its values than can be looked for in today's world. Whatever of the past, it is certain that in our own day the personal faith and commitment of the parents are crucial. No one, not even the godparent, is going to come between a child and the parents today to supply for the defects of their faith and practice. The more prominent role of the parents in the baptismal liturgy simply reflects therefore the greater reliance which the Church—and the growing child—must place upon their personal commitment to Christ.

In the light of such considerations, the hesitation with which the Church regards the prospect of baptizing the children of uncommitted parents is understandable. In such a case the leader of the community, the parish priest, acting in accordance with the directives of the bishops who, as we saw, are "the principal dispensers of the mysteries of God and leaders of the entire liturgical life in the Church committed to them" (GICI, 12), will have to determine the time at which it is appropriate to baptize.

Put more positively, the Christian family is a living cell in the Body of Christ which is the Church. Indeed, Vatican II calls the Christian family "a domestic church" (LG, 11) and goes on to say that the parents should "by their word and example, be the first preachers of the faith to their children." As we shall see shortly, the parents will be called upon to testify to their personal faith commitment in the course of the baptismal liturgy, but lest the burden of responsibility placed upon their shoulders appear altogether too daunting, it is worth pointing out that they are not meant to be without support. This is where, once again, the community dimension of baptism comes into play, for "the child has a right to the love and help of the community" (RBC, 4). In asking to have their child baptized, parents explicitly undertake to do their best to bring their child up in the Christian way of life.

But it is also true, though it is less explicit in the rite, that the Church has responsibility for those whom she baptizes, and since it is actually the local Church which celebrates the baptism, it is the local Church or parish which implicitly accepts that responsibility and undertakes to assist the parents in their difficult and delicate task. It is for this reason that Catholic schools exist and parish CCD classes are run. It may well be that in the past parents have tended to thrust the whole responsibility for the faith education of their children onto Catholic schools and it may also be the case that the Catholic school system does not give the best possible Christian formation, given its limitations, but the instinct is absolutely right. In the future as in the past, the religious formation of the children we baptize will be the shared responsibility of both the Catholic family and the wider Christian community.

This cooperation begins even before the child is brought for baptism. "Christian instruction and the preparation for baptism are a vital concern of God's people, the Church, which hands on and nourishes the faith it has received from the apostles" (GICI, 7). Because of this, parents and parish priest should have come together some time before the baptism and perhaps even before the child is born, to make proper preparation not only for the ceremony but for the vocation to which God has called them in giving them a child. It will not be a case, then, of nameless customers for baptism turning up, relatives and friends in tow, on a Sunday afternoon to submit their child to the ministrations of whatever priest happens to be on duty, but of fellow members of the household of faith and the family of God celebrating with joy the baptism of their child into the death and resurrection of the Lord.

With the greater prominence accorded quite properly to the parents in the rite of infant baptism, the role of the *godparents* has likewise altered. No longer does the godmother have to carry the baby to the font, nor do the godparents have to speak for the children. In fact, it is true to say that their role has changed from one of caring for their godchildren to one of supporting and helping the children's parents. "Are you ready to help these parents in their duty as Christian mothers and fathers?" the celebrant asks them.

The office of godparent or sponsor originated very early in the Church's history. In the regulations governing Christian initiation in the third century document called the *Apostolic Tradition*, anyone coming to the community to ask for instruction and baptism must have someone to vouch for the individual's sincerity of motives and willingness to undergo the rigorous demands of becoming a Christian. Such a "sponsor" would have to testify before the community concerning the progress of his or her charge before the candidate could be admitted to baptism. The sponsor, then, was the candidate's contact with the community, a member of the community who would befriend, help and speak for the person. In the renewed rite of adult baptism today, the sponsor has the same role. He or she must be a member of the Christian community, a committed believer (a Catholic or at least Orthodox), able and willing to help the candidate prepare for baptism, to testify during the process of initiation, and to help the candidate to persevere in the Christian life of faith after baptism.

In infant baptism, the godparent (or godparents, if there are two) is the link between the child and parents on the one hand and the wider Christian community on the other. This is meant to set up a genuine spiritual relationship between child and godparent and to be, more than just an honor, a source of strength, support and encouragement to the parents in bringing up their children. This can only happen if the people who stand as godparents know what they stand for, i.e., if they are themselves committed Christians.

These, then, are the people who stand before the assembled community at the door of the church and who hold in their midst the children called, through no choice or merit of their own, to faith in Jesus Christ and to life in his Body, the Church.

4. *"The rite begins with the reception of the children"* (RBC, 16).

The children to be baptized wait at the entry to the church or near the back. They are newcomers waiting to be welcomed and invited in. The leader of the assembled community, accompanied by his ministers, goes down to meet them. He greets the parents and godparents, congratulating them on the children with which God has gifted them, but before he leads them into the midst of the community he has some formal questions to put to them, there at the threshold. To come into the Church and to take one's place among the faithful is what baptism is all about, so the significance of this first introduction must not be allowed to pass unnoticed, but is celebrated in a series of questions and answers and a first, tender gesture of adoption.

The meaning of all this will hopefully come home to the child in later years, long after he or she has been baptized, but for an adult convert the awareness of what it really means to enter the Church must become clear to the candidate before the baptism takes place. Today as in the past, this rite of reception is just the beginning of a long period of spiritual preparation which will culminate in the actual baptism several weeks or maybe years later. In the time of Hippolytus, whose *Apostolic Tradition* we cited earlier, three years was expected to pass between an adult's first admission to the Church as a catechumen or learner and admission as a postulant for baptism the following Easter. This period of time was a period of apprenticeship for the Christian life, a time of instruction and spiritual direction, a time for reordering life and proving conversion in good works. Even today, this period of the catechumenate is expected to last for an extended time (RCIA, 20). Before baptism, of course, the person cannot be admitted to the celebration of the Eucharist, for to take part in the Mass is the culmination of the whole long process of conversion and formation, and in the time of Hippolytus, catechumens were not even allowed to pray with the faithful or to share the kiss of peace with them, since they were not yet full members of the Church and had not yet received the gift of the Spirit who animates both the prayer and the unity of the Christian community. Even so, the catechumen does belong to the Church. Vatican II recognizes this: "Catechumens who, moved by the Holy Spirit, seek with explicit intention to be incorporated into the Church are by that very intention joined to her. With love and solicitude Mother Church already embraces them as her own" (LG, 14).

Something analogous happens here in the rite for the reception of children who are to be baptized: by their very reception they already become part of the family of the Church. In the fifth century, many children went no further for the time being. Having been received by the Church and enrolled as catechumens by their parents, their baptism was then deferred until they were old enough to make their own profession of faith—and often a good while longer! Many of the most eminent and saintly bishops of those times had been initiated into the faith in that way. The most famous of them all, of course, was St. Augustine, whose mother, St. Monica, as he relates in his *Confessions*, brought him to the church very shortly after his birth:

> I was signed with the sign of [Christ's] cross and seasoned with his salt as I came new from the womb of my mother, who had great trust in you (*Confessions*, tr. F. J. Sheed, 1944, p. 10).

Yet, despite the scare of an early illness which prompted Augustine to ask for baptism only to have it postponed again when he recovered suddenly, he grew up as a catechumen and did not enroll for instruction and submit to baptism until after his conversion at thirty years of age. Indeed, many of his contemporaries put off baptism until they were lying on their deathbeds.

Augustine mentions that he was received by the Church as an infant with the sign of the cross and with salt. The signing with the cross remains as the central gesture with which the Church receives a newcomer to the community, as we shall see, but the giving of salt was dropped in the recent revision of the rites. It probably came into the baptismal liturgy from the Middle Eastern custom of offering salt as a gesture of hospitality, but it was generally interpreted by the Church as a symbol of acquiring a taste for divine wisdom. Both in its origins and in its allegorical significance it is somewhat remote from our experience and for this reason was dropped when the rites were simplified, although it remains an option in adult baptism for those cultures where it has some significance (RCIA, 89).

5. *What name do you give your child?*

In one sense, this is no more than a practical question. The child is to be introduced to the Christian community and the priest will need to know its name. For this reason he can simply ask: "What name have you given your child?" But it is also an invitation to give the child a name, a Christian name. It is a moment which most people instinctively feel to be significant.

Naming something is an awesome thing to do. When Adam named the animals (Gen 2:19-20), he was giving each its place and significance in the human world. An explorer naming a new territory makes it accessible to other people. The scientist naming an invention or discovery extends the range of human knowledge and potential. But for one human being to give another a name is an even more awesome responsibility. To name someone is to give that person an identity, to say who he or she is and will be forever. When a pope dies, it is the custom for the senior cardinal to go to the death-bed and to verify the death by calling out the pope's name. He does not call him by his titles, or even by the name he adopted when he became pope: he calls him by the name given him by his parents at baptism. So children, grow-ing up, may well acquire other names and nicknames and perhaps honorific titles, but deep down they will only be able to be summoned by their Chris-tian names. These are the names they will always bear in life, the names in-voked to summon them to work and to play, to reward or to punishment, to joy or to sorrow; the names lisped in love and screamed in anger; the names which will be inscribed on their coffins and left to history.

The giving of a name reminds us that parenthood does not end with the child's birth, but that the parents' relationship with the child has changed. In one sense, to give the child a name is to claim him or her as their own; but it is also to recognize the child's right to exist as another person: we need a name for the child because he or she is not just a thing for us to use, but a person to whose freedom we must appeal and whose separate identity we must respect.

It is because a name identifies a person that God gave a new name to a number of the great people he enlisted in his work of salvation: Abram became Abraham, "father of many nations," and Simon, son of Jonah, became Peter, "the rock." From the fourth century onwards, and possibly even earlier, many adult converts from paganism took a new name when they became Christians, showing thereby that they were very much aware that in being baptized into Christ they were assuming a new identity, emerg-ing as a new creation, a new person. Obviously, with the baptism of infants or young children there was no point in a change of name, but in either case there was no formal provision in the baptismal liturgy for giving the baptiz-and a name, though the name was used in the formula of baptism in the East and in the invitation to renounce Satan. How is it then that baptism, in so many people's minds, is thought of as a naming ceremony? Why is it that the lovely old English word "christening"—meaning dedication to Christ—has come to mean "naming," so that people can talk of "christening" their house or their dog or their boat? In England the Book of Common Prayer has cer-tainly contributed to this. In the 1662 revision, the priest, holding the child over the font, cries: "Name this child"; and the rubric continues: "And then, naming it after them . . . he shall dip it in the water discreetly and warily, saying, "N., I baptize thee . . .""

While baptism can never be allowed to be merely a naming ceremony, the naming of the child at this point in the rite is a significant moment, for it is probably, to put no finer point on it, the first time the child is publicly named and most people would feel that from there on the name cannot be altered. It is somehow tied up, not simply with how the child is to be known in the world, but with how he or she is identified before God, so that it is rightly called his or her Christian or baptismal name. For this reason the Church has long been concerned that the name should be in keeping with the Christian identity of the child. As long ago as the thirteenth century, Archbishop Peckham of Canterbury was urging his clergy not to allow improper names to be given to children, and especially to girls, at baptism, while the former *Rituale Romanum* of 1614 ordered the parish priest to add a saint's name to those given by the parents, if the latter were not Christian names.

6. *What do you ask of God's Church for your children?*

The raising of this question gives the community and the parents the opportunity to be quite explicit about the nature and purpose of this celebration and then for the leader of the community to make quite clear to this party of parents and godparents that this is no light matter.

The answer suggested in the text is, naturally enough, "baptism." In the old rite, and still in the Rite for the Christian Initiation of Adults, the suggested answer is "faith." The change could really be quite misleading if it were to suggest that parents now seek something different for their children. Baptism, after all, has been known from the earliest times as the "sacrament of faith." The role of faith in baptism is crucial. A sacrament is a celebration in which the Church expresses her inner life as caught up in the mystery of God, saving the world in his love. It is the making visible of the Church's hidden unity with Christ. In baptism the community celebrates its own faith, expressing its trusting obedience to the God who has made himself known to us in Jesus. Baptism is thus the sacrament, or visible expression, of the community's faith in and reliance upon Jesus Christ. Baptism is the celebration of people turning to that faith: so it is the celebration of their faith, too. They and the Church together profess their shared faith. The converts turn their lives over to Christ and thus become one with the community of those who have surrendered their lives to him in the hope of sharing his glory.

Faith is defined by Vatican II as "the obedience by which a man entrusts his whole self freely to God" (Divine Revelation, 5), and baptism is the ritual commitment whereby one begins to live no longer for oneself but for Christ. To ask for baptism is to ask to make such a surrender. To ask for faith at the beginning of the catechumenate, as the convert does, is to ask the community of those who have themselves died with Christ in faith and baptism to share their grace and wisdom with this person, that he or she may learn to live by the Spirit of God and die to all that is not of Christ.

In other words, what is being asked for, whether by the adult convert or by Christian parents for their children, is the whole grace of a life hidden with God in Christ and lived out within the community of those whom his Spirit vivifies and unites. That is why the answer given in the text is not the only answer that can be given. Other suggested answers (n. 37) include "faith," "the grace of Christ," "entrance into the Church," "eternal life"—all terms expressing the same basic mystery of salvation—but the point is that the parents here give a first public testimony to their own faith and to their longing that their children should share it. Even the answer "baptism" is not a request for the *rite* of baptism so much as for the grace which baptism signifies and communicates.

This question in the Rite of Baptism for Children corresponds to the initial scrutiny of a candidate's motives for seeking admission to the catechumenate. Hippolytus, in his *Apostolic Tradition*, written about the year 215, prescribed as follows:

Those who come forward for the first time to hear the word shall first be brought to the teachers at the house before all the people [of God] come in.

And let them be examined as to the reason why they have come forward to the faith. And those who bring them shall bear witness for them whether they are able to hear.

Let their life and manner of living be inquired into whether they are slave or free . . .

Today, as in the past, there are all sorts of reasons why people might seek baptism for themselves or their children. Family and social pressures continue to operate as well as superstition and an unchristian fear of divine punishment. Yet it would be unrealistic to ask always for the purest motivation and a fully articulated sense of purpose. The Church has always recognized this and, while turning away those whose motives were clearly wrong and seemingly incorrigible—"those who cannot hear," as Hippolytus called them—she has been prepared to work with the Spirit to lead them on to a fuller appreciation of what they were asking. Such a generous policy was clearly that of Cyril of Jerusalem, the fourth century bishop who hoped that contact with the Christian community and its liturgical celebration would help such people:

We, the ministers of Christ, have admitted everyone: acting as doorkeepers, we have left the door open. This means you have been free to enter in a sinful condition and with dubious motivation. You have entered. You have passed in and been enrolled. Do you see how imposing this assembly is? Look at her order and discipline, the reading of the Scriptures, the religious who are present, the course of instruction. Let the place affect you; let yourself be changed by what you see. Go promptly away now and come back tomorrow in a better mind (*Procat.*, 4).

The Church today has the same hope, namely, that the celebration of baptism itself will bring home to the lukewarm and the half-hearted the meaning of what it is to be a Christian.

"Do you clearly understand what you are undertaking?" asks the celebrant. One is reminded of the mother of James and John, asking that they might be seated to the left and right of Jesus in his kingdom, and of Jesus' sobering reply: "You do not know what you are asking" (Matt 20:22). Jesus goes on to ask the two disciples if they can drink the cup of which he is to drink, the cup of suffering toward which his devotion to his Father's will and his love for humankind are inexorably pointing him. In less dramatic terms, indeed in a formula which is prosaic in its understatement, the leader of the Church says much the same thing. In asking to have their children baptized, Christian parents are accepting the responsibility of training them in the faith (n. 39). This means more than giving them Christian doctrine: it means initiating them into a life of Christian discipleship. Jesus sent his apostles, not simply to teach all nations, but to make disciples of them (Matt 28:19) and it is a mark of the disciples of Christ that they will abandon all things to follow their Lord, whatever the cost, even to death. Of this commitment, baptism is the sign and sacrament. "It will be your duty to bring them up to keep God's commandments as Christ taught us, by loving God and our neighbor" (*ibid.*). Again the cross looms before us, for Christ taught us what the love of God and neighbor meant above all by his own life and death. The cross of Jesus is both the revelation of God's love for us and also the last word in what it means to love God and to love one another. Yet it is not a matter of our having to prove our love for God. The very fact of infant baptism is tangible evidence that God loves us and chooses us before we know it. The Christian life is a life rooted in trust in God's love for us, a life in which that love with which God loves us flows back to unite us with him and overflows into the lives of others.

"What then shall we say to this? If God is for us, who is against us? He who did not spare his own son but gave him up for us all, will he not also give us all things with him?" (Rom 8:31-32). Yes indeed! And immediately at hand is the promise of support from our fellow Christians. The celebrant turns to the godparents: "Are you ready to help these parents in their duty as Christian mothers and fathers?" "We are." A covenant of faith and love is established between the family and the community.

7. *My dear children, the Christian community welcomes you with great joy. In its name I claim you for Christ our Savior by the sign of his cross* (n. 41).

"You are not yet born anew in baptism, but you have been conceived in the Church's womb by the sign of the cross," Bishop Quodvultdeus told his North African catechumens back in the fourth century. We have already seen St. Augustine's testimony of how people were received into the catechumenate, and so into the Church, with the sign of the cross. They were not yet fully members of the Church, for their initiation was not yet complete, but already they were marked as belonging to Christ and to his people. So it is with these children. Marked with the paradoxical sign of Christ's cross, assigned thereby both to death and to glory, they have already begun to be incorporated into the mystery of Christ's death and resurrection.

As a mark of ownership the sign of the cross is very old indeed. In the ancient world, slaves and soldiers, cattle and property were commonly branded or tattooed with the mark of the one in whose service they were employed. In the sixth century B.C., the prophet Ezekiel, surrounded by the collapse and destruction of his people, was vouchsafed a vision in which he saw God sending an angel to put a mark on the foreheads of the just, so that they might be spared and survive to form a new people (9:3ff.). The mark was the letter *taw*, last letter of the Hebrew alphabet and symbol of God himself. In the time of Christ, this letter was written X or +, so it is hardly surprising that the early Christians, regarding themselves as the new People of God foreseen by Ezekiel, should regard themselves as marked by this sign which is not only the symbol of God but the symbol of the redemption won for us by Christ's cross. In the Book of Revelation this connection is quite explicitly made: the servants of God are sealed upon the forehead to save them (7:3), but this salvation is attributed to God and to the Lamb, who saved them by his blood.

Signing with the mark of the cross has been associated with baptism from the earliest times. St. Basil claims that the practice had been handed down from the Apostles, "who taught us to mark with the sign of the cross those who put their hope in the name of the Lord" (*de Sp. Sto.*, 27). This gesture is found, in the tradition and in the present rite, at the very beginning of the process of initiation; but it is also found again at the end, when the bishop completes the whole process by sealing the newly baptized with chrism in the form of a cross traced on their foreheads. In fact, the sign of the cross has been used in different places in the rite at different times, but it always signifies the candidates' growing likeness to Christ as they are drawn more and more into his Body, the Church. So important is this sign in Christian initiation, that the whole process could be summed up in the phrase "giving the seal," i.e., marking with the cross. So St. Paul, for example, tells the Ephesians: "In [Christ] you also, who have heard the word of truth, the gospel of your salvation, and have believed in him, were sealed with the promised Holy Spirit, which is the guarantee of our inheritance until we acquire possession of it . . ." (1:13). It is this idea of the baptismal seal or mark of the cross giving us entry into the heavenly kingdom which lies behind the prayer for the dead in the Roman Canon of the Mass, when we commend to God those who have gone before us "marked with the sign of faith."

From its initial use in baptism, the sign of the cross becomes a constant part of the Christian's life, an indispensable reminder of who he is and under whose protection he lives. In the second century Tertullian wrote:

With every undertaking and enterprise, with every coming in and going out, putting our shoes on, washing ourselves; when at table, or lighting the lights; when lying down or sitting down; whatever business may engage us, we trace the sign of the cross on our forehead (*De corona*, 3).

We still do this at Mass as we prepare to hear the gospel, and those who say the Office make a small sign of the cross on their lips as they begin the day's prayer. The larger sign of the cross, made from forehead to breast and shoulder to shoulder, came in in the Middle Ages.

Whatever form it takes, and whenever it is used, the meaning of this gesture is the same: it identifies us as belonging to Christ. The effect of this is twofold. First, as the cross is the sign of Christ's victory, it reminds us that we have been remade in his likeness and that the glory of his new life shines through our faces (2 Cor 3:18). Secondly, if we share in the victory of Christ this can only be because he has delivered us from all evil. Thus the sign of the cross is made to invoke the protection of the Risen Lord. So Cyril of Jerusalem told his converts:

Let us not be ashamed of the cross of Christ, but even if someone else conceals it, do you carry its mark publicly on your forehead, so that the demons, seeing the royal sign, trembling may fly far away. Make this sign when you eat and drink, when you sit down, when you go to bed, when you get up, when you speak—in a word, on all occasions (*Myst. Cat.* 4:14).

And again:

Let us not be ashamed to confess the Crucified. Let us make the sign of the cross with assurance on our foreheads with our fingers, and so do in all circumstances . . . Here is a great protection that is free for the poor and easy for the weak, since the grace comes from God. It is a sign for the faithful and a terror for the demons. On the cross, he triumphed over them: and so, when they see it, they remember the Crucified; they fear him who crushed the heads of the demons (*Myst. Cat.* 13:36).

It is as a sign of adoption and of protection, then, that the Christian community traces the cross upon the foreheads of the children to be baptized. In the old Roman baptismal liturgy, it was accompanied by a prayer which expressed this perfectly:

Hear our prayer, Lord God, and guard these chosen servants of yours. May your strength never fail them now, for we have traced upon them the sign of Christ's cross. May they always remember what they learn of your greatness and your glory. May they keep your commandments; and may they, too, be found worthy of glory, the glory of new life in you.

This tender and loving gesture is made first of all by the priest as leader of the community, and then by the children's parents and godparents, for they, after all, are the members of the community who will be most directly involved in training the children to be faithful to the Lord in whose service they are now enrolled. It is to be hoped that this will not be the last time that the parents sign their children in this way. It used to be a regular practice for parents to bless their children, and what better way to do it than to trace the cross gently on their foreheads?

8. Welcome

The theme of baptism as rebirth led, in the ancient tradition, to the elaboration of a whole series of images extending this theme. Thus the local community, in whose midst the baptized came to new life, was seen not only as the virgin spouse of Christ, but as "Mother Church." The waters of the baptismal font, overshadowed by the Holy Spirit, was her womb from which her new offspring came forth. Little wonder, then, that the celebration of baptism was understood as the local community conceiving new and divine life, as Mary did, through submission to the Word and through the action of the Spirit. This could well come to mind as the baptismal party makes its way through the welcoming assembly of the faithful to take its place for the Liturgy of the Word.

This entry procession is quite important in the Adult Rite, but in the Rite of the Baptism of Children it is played down. This is largely out of practical considerations. If the Word of God is to be read and listened to intently and the faith of the baptizing community stirred up, it will usually be advisable to give the children over to other members of the community who will look after them in a room nearby until the Liturgy of the Word is over. Such provision would be the kind of hospitality a Christian child would need at this stage, so it is by no means a matter of going back on the solemn welcome. In the meantime, the parents and godparents and the whole Christian community prepare to hear the Word of God, so that hearing they may believe, and believing they may celebrate the sacrament of faith.

II

CELEBRATION OF GOD'S WORD

1. *The celebrant invites the parents, godparents and the others to take part in the Liturgy of the Word.*

Baptism is the sacrament of faith. But faith, St. Paul reminds us, comes from what is heard, and what is heard comes by the preaching of Christ (Rom 10:17). The preaching of Christ remains alive in the Church through the reading of the Scriptures and the preaching of the Church. In this way, God speaks to the assembled people, calling them to share his life, inviting them to respond. "The liturgy of the word is directed towards stirring up the faith of the parents, godparents, and congregation" (RBC, 17) so that the baptismal celebration will be an expression of their own faith and the faith of the Church. So important is this that we would do well to pause for a moment and think about what it involves.

2. *Hearing the Word*

The various New Testament accounts of different people's conversions give the very distinct impression that little or no time elapsed between the preaching of the gospel, coming to faith and submitting to baptism. St. Peter's proclamation of the death and resurrection of Jesus at the feast of Pentecost in Jerusalem seems to have been followed immediately by the baptism of three thousand converts. The deacon Philip shared a chariot ride with an Ethiopian court official who was reading the prophet Isaiah. No sooner was he convinced of Philip's explanation that the text he was reading referred to Christ than he was saying, "See, here is water! What is to prevent my being baptized?" They stopped the chariot, went down to the water and the man was baptized. Paul baptized his jailer after what could not have been more than a few hours of instruction (Acts 8:26ff.; 16:31ff.). But no matter how short the time, there was always a preaching of the word and instruction, designed to awaken faith, and only after a person had taken that word to heart and believed it could the person be baptized.

The *Didache*, or Teaching of the Twelve Apostles, is a very early collection of texts, probably written about the same time as St. John's Gospel. The first six chapters give a summary of the instruction to be given to those who sought baptism and is proposed as a choice between two ways, the Way of Life and the Way of Death, between faith and refusal of faith. Chapter 7

39

begins: "Regarding baptism, baptize as follows: after first explaining all these points, baptize in the name of the Father and of the Son and of the Holy Spirit, in running water." Half a century or so later, St. Justin is writing in Rome, explaining Christian initiation to the Emperor. "Those who are convinced and believe what we say and teach is the truth, and pledge themselves to be able to live accordingly, are taught in prayer and fasting to ask God to forgive their past sins, while we pray and fast with them. Then we lead them to a place where there is water, and they are regenerated in the same manner in which we ourselves were regenerated . . ." (*I Apol.* c. 61).

In the early texts, there is little or no indication of any lengthy period of prebaptismal instruction in the faith. It was simply that when a person was convinced of the truth of the Christian message and ready to submit to the lordship of Jesus, baptism was administered. On the other hand, the practice was already coming in of restricting the celebration of baptism to the feast of Easter. This had the advantage of emphasizing the fact that to be baptized was to share in the dying and rising of the Lord, and also of making the celebration of baptism an event of special festivity for the whole community. But it also meant that there was time to embark upon a systematic preparation of the candidates, which, given that the converts to the Church were now more often pagans and rarely Jews, meant having to sketch in the whole background of the salvation history of the Old Testament with which the converts from Judaism would be familiar. Not that this extended catechumenate was only a matter of instruction; it was, as we have seen, a matter of an all-round formation in the Christian faith as a way of life. But then faith is not just a matter of doctrine, and the response of faith to the Word of God includes both coming to belief and undergoing conversion of life. By and large, people do not experience such a transformation as a once and for all event, but rather as a process of struggle and growth. By the time of Hippolytus (c. 215), there was a three-year catechumenate program at Rome, which consisted of instruction, prayer with laying on of hands, and initiation into the charitable and apostolic life of the community. But the total transformation of a person's life and life-style was considered the result of taking the word of God to heart: "But if there is one who is not purified let him be put to one side because he did not hear the word of instruction with faith." To celebrate baptism, then, it is necessary to hear the word of God with faith. But what is the word of God?

3. The Word of the Lord

In the Scriptures, the word of God is not in the first instance a spoken word. It means something wider than that and includes any significant event whereby God communicates with human beings. So, for example, the shepherds on the Bethlehem hillside are reported, in the Douay translation of the Bible, as saying to one another: "Let us go to see this word that has come to pass" (Luke 2:15). This rather strange phrase captures quite well the scriptural notion of the word of God as something—an event, a dream, a message, a person—through which God acts among people and so makes himself known to them. It is in this sense that we speak of Jesus, par excellence, as the Word of God made flesh. He is already the self-communication of God even before he says anything. Even as an infant lying in the manger, the very form of his presence and manner of his coming already speak volumes. We reflect upon the kind of life he lived and the sort of things he did because his whole presence and activity, as well as his words, reveal God to us and call us to reconciliation with God. So it has been all through history. God has communicated with people through significant events whose meaning has been grasped and proclaimed and clarified by those gifted with faith. In fact, it was in the light of what God had done in the history of the Old Testament that the first believers were able to recognize that Jesus was, indeed, the promised Messiah. Time and again the evangelists underline this continuity by remarking of some words of Jesus or event of his life that "this was so that the Scriptures might be fulfilled." Just as we learn from our experience of the past to make sense of the things we come across in our lives, so, too, as believers the presence and action of God in the lives of people today are discernible in the light of what we know of him from the past.

We shall have to return to this point about the continuity between past events of salvation history and our own experiences later, but already we have seen enough to understand that the word of God to us is to be found primarily in the events of our own lives. As you read this page, you recognize words you have met before and this enables you to make sense of them now. You have an experience of baptism to draw on which makes what you see at your next celebration of baptism intelligible. So, in a somewhat similar way, the faith interpretation of past events enables us to make a faith interpretation of present experiences and to recognize them, too, as significant, as a word of God addressed to us in our present life and circumstances. For this reason, in preparing people for baptism, the Church has always presented them with the events of salvation history as recorded in the Scriptures and understood by the faith of the Church.

The Spanish lady, Egeria, who went on pilgrimage to the Holy Land in the early fifth century, was most impressed by the way this was done in Jerusalem. Each day during Lent:

> The bishop's chair is placed in the Great Church, the Martyrium, and all those to be baptized, the men and the women, sit round him in a circle . . .
>
> His subject is God's law; during the whole forty days he goes through the whole Bible, beginning with Genesis, and first relating the literal meaning of each passage, then interpreting its spiritual meaning. He also teaches them at this time about the resurrection and the faith. And this is called *catechesis*. After five weeks teaching, they receive the Creed, whose content he explains article by article in the same way as he ex-

plained the Scriptures, first literally and then spiritually. Thus all the people in these parts are able to follow the Scriptures when they are read in church, since there has been teaching on all the Scriptures from six to nine in the morning all through Lent, three hours of catechesis a day (46:1-3; Wilkinson, p. 144).

In Rome, this integral part of the preparation for baptism was celebrated in a ritual Presentation of the Gospels, in which the postulants for baptism were introduced to the four gospels in the presence of the faithful. Even when those being prepared for baptism were no longer adults but young children and infants, still the practice was retained of reading the beginning of each gospel and giving an explanation of the sign of each evangelist. By this time it had become simply a traditional custom, but its roots are to be sought in the preparation of adults for baptism and in the Church's concern to enable them to discover in their own conversion experience the same pattern of faith as Jesus revealed in the events of his own life, death and resurrection. Later, the readings dropped out of the celebration of baptism altogether only to be restored when the present rite was published in 1969.

When, today, the Scriptures are read at the liturgy of baptism, the purpose is the same. It is to help the faithful make sense of what they are presently experiencing, by recalling such interventions of God in the historical past as his deliverance of the Israelites from Egypt via the waters of the Red Sea or the promise, made through the prophets, that he would gather a new people to himself. Above all, it is by recalling the words and actions of Jesus himself, recorded and interpreted through the writings of the New Testament, that we are enabled to trust in the continuing effectiveness of God's promises and to look for, and discover, his active presence in our midst today. That generous, life-giving presence will be discerned in many different facets of life: in our own election by God as believers, for example, or in the very birth of a child which is seen not simply as the fruit of two people's love but as a gift of God who inspires that love and has blessed it with fruitfulness. But above all it is in the assembly of the people of God and in their celebration of baptism that God's faithfulness will be recognized.

Baptism is no mere ceremony. It is yet another significant event, another "word of God" in which God acts among us and makes his goodness known. It is this which makes baptism a sacrament: an outward sign, a visible celebration, which discloses the hidden, invisible reality of God's compassionate love and healing activity toward those who receive the sacrament. Thus the whole celebration from first greeting to final dismissal mediates the presence and gentle embrace of Christ himself, the word of self-communication of the Father. One could therefore say of the whole liturgy: "This is the word of the Lord"—a word expressed in the human words and gestures of an assembled group of believers, but a word which, like all God's words, effects what it signifies, carries out what it says.

For as the rain and the snow come down from heaven and return not thither but water the earth, making it bring forth and sprout, giving seed to the sower and bread to the eater, so my word that goes forth from my mouth; it shall not return to me empty, but it shall accomplish that which I purpose, and prosper in the thing for which I sent it (Isa 55:10-11).

Hence the importance of the homily. If the celebration were to pass directly from the reading of an ancient scriptural text to the performance of ancient ritual gestures, the whole thing could seem no more than a quaint old ceremony. So the leader of the celebration is called upon at this point to stand up and testify to his faith and the faith of the Church. His message will be that of Jesus to the people who had just heard him read a passage from the prophet Isaiah in the synagogue: "Today this scripture has been fulfilled in your hearing" (Luke 4:21). In other words, he will stir up the faith of the people to recognize the presence of Christ in their midst so that they will act in his name, their prayers becoming his prayer, their actions his actions. In this way, the merciful promises of God, who is faithful from age to age, will be seen to be made good, here and now, in respect of those whom the Church baptizes. This is what the Church has always believed and taught about baptism. Centuries ago, in his *First Catechetical Instruction*, St. Augustine recorded for us a sample of his own preaching and this is what he told his hearers:

All the things you now see happening in the Church of God, and in the name of Christ all over the world, were already foretold long ago. And just as we read about them, so we see them too, and in this way we are built up in faith.

4. *The Obedience of Faith*

What is this faith? If the word and sacrament of God need to be interpreted and understood, then faith is obviously the God-given ability to do this. In that sense, faith is the gift of being able to see in the events of life, and particularly in the Scriptures and the sacraments of the Church, the continuing presence and action of God. It is thus a sort of "second sight" which enables the believer to see what the unbeliever cannot acknowledge. But it is not an intellectual gift, simply. "It is only with the heart that one can see rightly," said the fox to the Little Prince. "What is essential is invisible to the eye" (*The Little Prince*, Antoine de St. Exupery). So faith, concerned with seeing what is essential, is more a matter of the heart's than of the mind's eye. The believer, then, is one who takes these things to heart and is enabled to understand the things of God because one has given one's heart to God. Thus faith is very different from opinion, as St. Paul makes clear when he speaks of faith as an obedience. The Latin word from which our English word is derived (*obedire*, from *ob-audire*) meant originally an attentive listening: to obey means giving oneself over to listening to someone, thus submitting to that person's word.

This understanding of faith, which is so much deeper than giving credence to the incredible, is what Vatican II means when it talks about faith, and it is this understanding of faith which underlies so much modern talk about faith. The Constitution on Divine Revelation (n. 5) quotes St. Paul's expression, "obedience of faith" (Rom 16:26), and defines it as "an obedience by which man entrusts his whole self freely to God, offering the full submission of intellect and will to God who reveals, and freely assenting to the truth revealed by him." This emphasis on the gift of self wholly to God corrects a tendency to see faith as a matter of believing certain doctrines to be true. To have faith in God is first of all to entrust oneself to him and secondly, as a consequence of that, to assent to what is discovered in the course of such a relationship to be true.

We have always spoken, quite properly, of the "gift" of faith, wondering perhaps why it is that some people have it and others have not been given it. But it is a gift in an even deeper sense than that. It is a gift because, in the first place, to come to faith is to come to share in the faith of Christ himself.

The epistle to the Hebrews goes to great pains to show Jesus really was one of us: "he had to be made like his brethren in every respect" (2:17); he is one "who in every respect has been tempted as we are, yet without sinning" (4:15); "he learned obedience through what he suffered" (5:8). He even subjected himself to the common human destiny of death by becoming one of us: "He himself likewise partook of the same nature [of flesh and blood], that through death he might destroy him who has the power of death, that is, the devil, and deliver those who, through fear of death were subject to lifelong bondage" (2:14-15). The way Jesus made this breakthrough, then, was by living a full human life with all that we experience, but living it, unlike us, in complete dependence upon God his Father. He lived in this world; but he lived, not for himself, but for his Father and for us. It was this total surrender of his whole life which reached its fullest expression when it came to its climax on Calvary, as he continued to trust God even in the face of failure, desolation and death. "Although he was a Son, he learnt obedience through what he suffered; and being made perfect, he became the source of eternal salvation to all who obey him" (5:8). Thus Jesus died with faith as he had lived by faith; and God, who is faithful, vindicated his faith by raising him to glory, so opening the glory of God to the human race.

Now this is the only faith that counts: by no other name can we be saved. But anyone who obeys Christ by making Christ's submission to God the basis of one's own life will be saved from bondage to Satan and from fear of death. A person will share the life of Christ because, like Christ, one will entrust one's whole self freely to God; and God has already vindicated such a way of life in raising up Jesus to a new kind of life, abundant and invincible. There is no other way to live except to abandon our own lives to God. What this means, we, like Jesus himself, will have to learn in the circumstances of our own life and times.

When we speak of the faith of the Church, then, it is primarily to faith in this sense that we refer. The Church is the community of believers, the community of those who, in baptism, have made the faith of Jesus their own and been baptized with the baptism with which he was baptized: his own suffering, death and glorification. It is, in that sense, an alternative society, founded on entirely different suppositions from those by which people normally shape their lives. In proclaiming the lordship of Jesus, the community of his disciples maintain, in word and in manner of life, the wisdom of God revealed in Jesus; that wisdom which was revealed to us most explicitly in "the word of the cross" (1 Cor 1:18). This is nonsense to those who do not believe, but proves itself in the lives of those committed to "one Lord, one faith, one baptism."

The faith of the Church, then, is far more than beliefs held in common. It is the faith by which Jesus lived in submission to and love of his Father. That faith is communicated to the Church by the Spirit of Jesus who both enables believers of every generation to accept that in Jesus the Word was made flesh, and to understand what the Word is saying about God and what it is calling us to. The Spirit of Jesus, living in the Church, forms the Church into the Body of Christ, an organic unity sustained by the same faith, love, hope and obedience which animated Jesus himself. In baptism, individuals are incorporated into the community of the Church, professing the faith of Jesus and the Church as their own. It is not that they profess a faith of their own, for they are professing that they now no longer live for themselves, but for God: and this is the meaning of their identification with Christ. So they can say as St. Paul said: "I have been crucified with Christ. It is no longer I who live, but Christ who lives in me; and the life I now live in the flesh I live by faith in the Son of God who loved me and gave himself for me" (Gal 2:20).

The Spirit of God, dwelling in the Church and in the individual within the Church, leads both the community of the Church and the individual believers into an ever deeper understanding of the mystery of faith. He is able to do so because both the word of God and the faith of the believing faithful are his work. The Spirit is given us so that we might recognize the work of the Spirit who is operative in human history, turning the events of that history into signs or words of God. It was because Mary was overshadowed by the Spirit that the Word was made flesh in her womb; and wherever the Spirit of God is at work, there God is revealing himself as present among us and calling us to union with him. But just as it is only in the Spirit that a person can say "Jesus is Lord," acknowledging the Word made flesh (1 Cor 12:3; 1 John 4:2), so it is only in the Spirit that one can recognize the word of God coming to one today in the signs of the times. The Spirit brings about what St. Thomas calls "connaturality," an instinctive ability to recognize and respond to the word and call of God. Thus, from age to age the Church glorifies the God who has called her into existence in Christ and proclaims to every generation the Good News of the Word made flesh among us. In both these ways, she gives expression to the faith by which she lives.

5. Baptism—the Sacrament of Faith

The Introduction to the Rites of Christian Initiation says quite explicitly that "baptism is, above all, the sacrament of that faith by which men and women, enlightened by the Spirit's grace, respond to the gospel of Christ. That is why the Church believes it is her most basic and necessary duty to inspire all, catechumens, parents of children still to be baptized, and godparents, to that true and living faith by which they adhere to Christ to enter into or confirm their commitment to the new covenant" (GICI, 3).

When a group of people get together for a celebration, they show that they are a group of people with something in common. The gathering and the way of celebrating show what kind of a group they are and what it is that they have in common: a family celebrating a birthday, a group of workers celebrating a new contract, a city celebrating its charter, a nation celebrating its independence. With the Church it is no different. When the local Christians gather to celebrate they show themselves to be the Church in that place, and the way they celebrate shows what it is they have in common, namely, their faith. They are a community of brothers and sisters, united by the one Spirit who animates them all, identified with Christ in his love and in his faith. The regular form of celebration in the Church is that which is called the Eucharist, or Mass. There they express their unity by sharing the one bread and drinking from the one cup; but the meaning of this eating and drinking is made clear only by the proclamation of the mystery of faith which is made over the bread and the cup. In the Great Prayer of Thanksgiving, the Church expresses her faith in the great acts of God with gratitude and joy, before going on to plead with hope for the completion of God's work of reconciliation. Then, in eating and drinking together, the partakers proclaim by their very action the mystery of their faith, their faith in the death of the Lord as the basis of their common life.

The celebration which marks the admission of a newcomer to this community of faith is likewise a celebration of that faith in words and gestures. The whole rite of baptism gives expression to the faith by which the Church lives; it is a sacrament of faith, the visible expression of an invisible reality. In the readings, the hymns, the ritual acts and the prayers, the Body of Christ which is the Church expresses the faith which is the faith of Christ himself: his loving dependence upon and submission to his Father. Thus baptism, too, is a proclamation of the death of the Lord, for it is by dying with Christ to live to God that the Church lives. And so, in baptism, as in the Eucharist, there is a solemn profession of faith in the great acts of God in the past, especially in the acts of God in Christ, and an affirmation of faith and hope in the continuing faithfulness of God. This we shall see when we look at the creed.

Adult converts who come to the Church have to be helped to understand more deeply the action of God in their lives calling them to this fullness of faith, to this total commitment of their lives to God. When they see this and show themselves ready to respond to the word of God spoken in their own lives, then the Church will admit them by celebrating with them her sacramental celebration of faith. This celebration will be the celebration, then, both of the faith of the community and of the faith of the individual converts themselves: their faith, the faith by which they live, is the same faith by which the Church lives—or perhaps one should really say, the community and the newcomers both give expression to their sharing the faith of Christ. Because this is, as we have seen, not just a matter of expressing shared opinions but of being committed to a total way of life, the expression of faith is not simply a matter of saying "I believe," but a ritual death: the candidate is plunged into the water.

When we come to the individual rites which make up the ritual of baptism, we shall see how each of them contributes to the celebration of faith by making explicit one or more aspects of coming to live by the faith of Christ. In each act of the baptismal drama, the community which celebrates baptism gives visible and audible expression to the faith commitment by which it lives, and the adult who is baptized actually surrenders step by step to that life of faith lived with God in Christ. It is in this sense that baptism may be called the sacrament of the faith of the Church and the sacrament of the faith of the person being baptized. It is both because it is ultimately the sacrament, or making visible and effective, of the faith of Jesus himself.

6. *The Baptism of Children*

Obviously the situation is going to be different when an infant or young child is baptized. Infants will not only be unable to speak for themselves, but they will be unable to commit themselves to God in faith, which is what the rite of baptism is about. Indeed, babies can do very little for themselves at all, being dependent for almost everything upon the love and care of their parents. Yet it would seem that from the very earliest days, the Church has been quite prepared to allow infants to be baptized and at times has encouraged it very strongly indeed, as she still does today. But what sense does this make? Is there any point in celebrating the sacrament of faith for one who, in virtue of age and condition, is humanly incapable of making any commitment to faith?

The Church's answer to this question, elaborated by many bishops and theologians, but especially by St. Augustine, is well summed up in the Introduction to the Rite of Baptism for Children:

Our Lord said: "Unless a man is reborn in water and the Holy Spirit, he cannot enter the kingdom of God." The Church has always understood these words to mean that children should not be deprived of baptism, because they are baptized in the faith of the Church. This faith is proclaimed by their parents and godparents and those who are present, who represent both the local Church and the whole society of saints and believers: "The Church is at once the mother of all and the mother of each" (RBC, 2).*

Such children, who cannot have or profess personal faith, are baptized in the faith of the Church. But what does this mean?

There is an opinion abroad—and it has been around so long and is so commonly shared that it is almost part of our mental framework, and hence rarely adverted to—that being a Christian is a matter for the individual's private decision. Many people, in consequence, appear to live their Christian lives very much with the conviction that this is something we decide to do for the salvation of our own souls or at best as a favor to God. It must be said, however, that this is not a Christian perspective. The Christian life and Christian faith are not, in the first instance at least, something we do for God, but something God does for us. Both faith and the life of grace are essentially the work of the Spirit within us, a Spirit freely given by God to those whom he chooses. Thus the first and primary characteristic of our Christian commitment is that it is a response to God's initiative. Faith, prayer, the works of love are all ascribed in the Scriptures to the Spirit of God. They are primarily God's work within us coming to visible expression in a way of life as we make them our own. Christians are those who discover and accept the invitation and gift of God and cooperate with them to allow them to transform us into the creatures we are thereby capable of becoming, for his glory, not for ours.

This is the case in adult baptism. However much the experience of witnessing an adult come to the faith may make us aware of the struggle and the sacrifice involved (and these are very real), most people who have actually undergone that experience will be the first to admit that becoming a Christian is something they have undergone rather than undertaken. Somehow, beneath all the struggle of personal crisis and within all the confusion and hesitation, there is finally a sense of having been "graced." Faith is not so much a matter of knowledge which can be acquired, but of insight which is given or understanding which dawns on a person. The same is true of faith as submission to God. It is not purely the individual's decision alone, but the discovery of being discovered, loved, and called to faith. The very freedom with which we surrender to God is itself God's gift and grace. Thus the decision to become a Christian, or to remain a Christian, springs from a person's discovery of the grace of God and is not simply the person's own decision, much less a mere matter of opinion.

* Author's translation: the official English text is inaccurate and misleading at this point.

One would have thought, perhaps, that after centuries of infant baptisms, we would have developed a much greater sensitivity to the initiative and graciousness of God in our lives, and yet there are those who ask whether it is not "unfair" to baptize such children. The Fathers of the Church suffered no such meanness of spirit, but saw the sacrament of faith given to children as a precious sign of God's unconditional and extravagant love. They were fond of citing the instances in the gospel where Jesus is recorded as having given new life and strength to people who were themselves beyond asking for it. Did Lazarus ask to be raised from the dead? Did Jesus or anyone else ask the son of the widow of Naim whether he wanted to live? Nor was the centurion's servant consulted about whether he wanted to be snatched back from the jaws of death. All these were simple instances of the compassion of God.

Yet in each instance—and in such other instances as the cure of the man born blind, the healing of the paralytic, the cure of the daughter of Jairus and of countless others who were brought to Jesus—there were other people involved. They were brought to Jesus by their families, friends and acquaintances: by anyone who cared about them. And an important aspect of all these stories is that, not only were the people cured, but they were given back to their loved ones. And so it is with infants who are baptized: they are given the gift of life and entrusted to the care of the Christian community, Mother Church.

The Fathers also emphasized that we owe our baptism ultimately not to our parents who had us baptized, nor even to the Church who baptized us, but to the Holy Spirit of God. Certainly, the Church is ready to baptize their child, but she does so, not so much because the parents ask for it, but because the parents' desire to have the child baptized is a likely sign that the Spirit has, as it were, earmarked this child: the child is chosen by God. Obviously, parents may bring their child for baptism for all sorts of motives, not all of them compatible with the working of the Spirit. For this reason, as we have seen, the parish priest, as representative of the bishop, has to practice a certain "discernment of spirits." The Church can only baptize those who are sent to her by the Spirit. If the parents are living a life marked by obedience to the Spirit of God, then the Church will unhesitatingly and joyfully embrace the child as, literally, a God-send. But if their lives are marked by indifference to the things of God, then the Church will be hesitant.

Put more positively, the desire of Christian parents to have their child baptized is already the beginning of the child's grace of baptism. The same Spirit who acts in the pouring of the water is already active in the hearts of the parents, for both the desire and the water mark only the initial stages in the transformation of this child into an adult believer, a mature, Spirit-filled disciple of the Lord.

For this reason, St. Augustine taught that the child is presented for baptism not so much by the parents as by the Church. It is the Church who brings the child to Jesus, and the parents are moved to do so insofar as they, too, are members of the Church which is "the community of saints and believers united in the Holy Spirit" (Ep. 98). Although the parents have an indispensable role in the baptism of their child insofar as they are the members of the Church particularly entrusted with this child, infant baptism is the concern of the whole local community. For this reason, the title "Mother Church" was first applied to the local congregation and St. Augustine can say: "Mother Church lends infants the feet of others that they might come to baptism, the hearts of others that they might believe, the tongues of others that they might confess their faith" (Sermon 176, 2).

This last text from St. Augustine points to an involvement of the local Church in the baptism of infants which goes beyond bringing them to the font. We have already seen that baptism is the sacrament of the faith of the Church. The celebration of the sacrament gives voice to the faith which binds the Christian community together and makes them one body in the Spirit. In this sense, too, infants are baptized in the faith of the Church, for it is the faith of the community expressed in word and gesture which provides the Holy Spirit, dwelling in the community, with the visible sacrament through which he enters into the lives of the infants. Theologians talk of baptized infants being given the gift of "infused faith." This is nothing more nor less than the gift of the Spirit of Jesus himself. With the continuing support of the community of faith, and the atmosphere of their own family, the "domestic Church," the children will learn as they grow to live increasingly by this spirit of faith and so grow more and more Christ-like in their trust and devotion towards their heavenly Father.

One can only feel that people who argue that it is unfair and unreasonable to commit a child, in baptism, to a life he or she has not chosen must be seriously unappreciative of the meaning of "grace": God's free gift to those whom he loves. Eusebius of Caesaria, the fourth century Church historian, tells a story about Origen, a theologian he much admired:

> It is said that often when the boy was asleep [his father] would bend over him and bare his breast, and as if it were a temple of the divine spirit would kiss it reverently and count himself blessed in his promising child (*History of the Church*, 2.15; Williamson, p. 241).

On the other hand, the fact that we now have a rite of infant baptism as well as accommodated versions of the rite for the Christian initiation of adults for use with older children does point to the inescapable fact that God works with people as they are; or, in the language of the theologians, grace builds on nature. Being baptized at six days or six weeks is not the same as being baptized at six years or sixteen years of age. St. Gregory Nazianzen (c. 390) favored deferring baptism until children were about three years of age, so that "they can hear the mystic words and answer them: even if they do not understand them properly, they will be impressed, and the memory will remain with them." In this he was something of a lone voice, but he does have a point which is being taken up again in our own day. It is argued that, danger of death apart, it would be pastorally more effective to defer the baptism of children until they were old enough for it to be something they could actively participate in. The idea behind this is not that they would then be uncommitted until they were old enough to choose for themselves, because, unbaptized or baptized, we are all confronted with the choice of what we are going to make of our lives. We know only too well that the fact that a child is baptized in infancy does not dispense with one's giving or refusing assent to that baptism later. It is rather that a postponed baptism would, as St. Gregory pointed out, make it psychologically more effective. There would be need and occasion for a careful program of preparation for baptism culminating in the solemn celebration of the full rites of initiation and issuing immediately into admission to the community celebration of the Eucharist.

Arguments such as these cannot be brushed aside as "merely psychological," for grace seizes the whole person yet does not do violence to the condition of that person. Clearly, the grace of baptism is seriously limited as far as its immediate effectiveness is concerned when it is given to an infant. For this reason, it might be sufficient and, in the face of widespread lapsing by those baptized in infancy, more effective, simply to receive the newborn child into the Church as a catechumen, signed with the sign of Christ's cross, as was the custom in the fourth and fifth centuries. The only argument against infant baptism which is really unacceptable to a Christian is that it is unfair to the child. Baptized or received as a catechumen, that child is still chosen by God for membership in the community of faith, and it is hardly fitting for a Christian to call God's election to grace "unfair."

7. The Celebration of the Word

This long excursus on word and faith was occasioned by the need to reflect on the place and purpose of the reading of Scripture and the subsequent homily in the liturgy of baptism. Their function could well be described as that of "consciousness-raising": bringing the assembled community to a focussed awareness of the awesome mysteries which are about to be celebrated, the mysteries of the Lord's death and resurrection by which the community itself lives and into which these newcomers are about to be introduced. The reading and homily are meant to stir up the hearer so that, to borrow a phrase from St. Augustine's work on Christian instruction, "he to whom you speak may by hearing come to faith, by believing come to hope, and by hoping come to love" (*First Catechetical Instruction*, n. 4). This is not a time, then, for giving instruction in Christian doctrine, but for awakening the faith, hope and love of the people of God that they may proclaim, in word and ritual, the mystery of faith.

This "mystery of faith" is the plan of God for his people that was made known to us in and through Christ and is even now operative in this celebration of baptism. It is a plan God had from the beginning, a plan to unite all things in Christ (see Eph 1:3ff.), and it is realized now as yet more people, adults or children, are brought into the community of the Church and incorporated into the Body of Christ. The newly baptized, then, represent the latest stage in this unfolding history of salvation and what is happening to them is only intelligible in the light of what God has already done in the past to accomplish this plan and of what he has promised to do in the future to complete it.

The occasion, *par excellence,* for the celebration of baptism is, of course, Easter Night. This is the night when the community of the faithful assembles in a mood of great festivity, not simply to celebrate the resurrection of Jesus as a historical event, but to celebrate it as something in which we, too, are involved. We are the people who live in what St. Peter calls "the end of the ages" (1 Pet 1:20), in the final stage of God's unfolding plan, the time between the glorification of the Lord and his second coming. On Easter Night, then, the liturgy puts the present times into their proper perspective in a long series of readings from the Old Testament, culminating with Paul's reminder of what has happened to us in baptism (Rom 6:3-11) and the proclamation of the gospel of the resurrection, the dawn of the new era to which we belong (Matt 28:1-10; etc.).

It is always a little odd when baptism is not celebrated at the Easter Vigil, because baptism is what all the readings are about. They begin with a reading from Genesis (1:1–2:2) in which God is portrayed as having brought his original creation forth from the waters of chaos. Then there is the story of how Abraham, "our father in faith" as the Church calls him, was called upon to sacrifice his son and how his faith in God was rewarded by the promise that he would be blessed with countless descendants: a story foreshadowing that other Son whose faith-unto-death brought into existence the countless multitude of the baptized of every age. The story of the exodus of the Israelites from Egypt tells of how God rescued a population of slaves to form a people who would witness to him, saving them, as he saves the new people of the baptized, through water. The four readings from the prophets look forward quite explicitly to the new covenant we now enjoy with God, a covenant established by Christ and which we enter by baptism.

Some of these readings are to be found among those listed for the baptism both of children and of adults, and there are many more besides, taken from the Old and New Testaments. Normally, there would not be as many readings at any other celebration of baptism as there are at the Easter baptismal vigil, but there must be at least a reading from the gospel so that the sacramental celebration is seen for what it really is: the continuing action of the God of history, reaching out through Christ in the Holy Spirit in his holy Church to embrace this man, this woman, this child whom, in his love, he has chosen for himself and gathered into his people. "They are the ones he chose specially long ago and intended to become true images of his Son, so that his Son might be the eldest of many brothers" (Rom 8:29).

III

PRAYER AND EXORCISM

"The word of God is living and active, sharper than any two-edged sword, piercing to the division of soul and spirit, of joints and marrow, and discerning the thoughts and intentions of the heart. And before him no creature is hidden, but all are open and laid bare to the eyes of him with whom we have to do" (Heb 4:12-13).

Anyone who takes the word of God to heart cannot fail to be soberly realistic about the truth of life, aware of the ambiguity which marks existence: "ambiguity" because one finds oneself in need of salvation and yet standing before a God who wants nothing other than to save that person. The word of God reveals our poverty and sin by its very offer of reconciliation and new life. We are shown what is ultimately at stake in our lives, and we are given a choice: "See, I have set before you this day life and good, death and evil. . . . I call heaven and earth to witness against you this day, that I have set before you life and death, blessing and curse; therefore choose life . . ." (Deut 30:15, 19).

It is to this realization that we come in hearing the reading of the Scripture and the homily, and we let it sink in in the silence that follows until the word sown in the receptive silence of our hearts rises to our lips and bursts forth in a prayer of supplication. "God speaks to us in his readings; we speak to him in our prayers," says St. Augustine. But underlying these prayers—the petitions, the litany, the prayer of exorcism—is a vivid awareness of how divided our hearts are, how we are pulled in different directions, how we are constantly called to respond to the call and grace of God and slough off the sin that clings so closely to every fiber of our being. Small wonder, then, that the New Testament speaks of the Christian life in the images of warfare, struggle and the endurance of the long-distance runner. We know enough of what this is about from our own experience, recognizing perhaps wrily enough that the doctrine of original sin is one of the most obvious truths of the Christian faith.

Although clearly the whole rite of baptism is about the deliverance of a person from bondage to original sin, these prayers, and particularly the prayer of exorcism, probably serve as the best context in which to think about it, not least because they help us to see it, not in terms of a despairing pessimism about the human condition, or in terms of a sort of supernatural handicap with which every child is unfairly burdened to the risk of his or her eternal salvation, but through the calmer and clearer perspective of the believing and praying Church.

1. *The Church at Prayer*

When Jesus spoke of the baptism with which he was to be baptized (Mark 10:39; Luke 12:50) he was, as we have seen, referring to his own suffering and death. In St. John's Gospel, the crucial importance of this event is implied in Jesus' recurrent references to the "hour" which is coming. It is an hour for which he and his disciples must brace themselves, so he takes them with him out to Gethsemane to watch and pray as the crisis breaks over them.

The disciples of Jesus in every age must be baptized with the baptism with which Jesus was baptized, thereby experiencing, not simply in ritual form but in their own flesh and in the carrying of their own cross, the crisis of that hour when he gave himself up to death that we all might be lifted up with him. To this does baptism commit us, so that in this simple ritual a whole lifetime of suffering and joy, of failure and victory, of despair and hope is focussed in a concentrated moment of anticipation. And not only a lifetime as yet unlived, but the person's death, too. There is a special poignancy here at the baptism of children. So recently arrived in this world, their death is already being celebrated as the culmination of a life story which has as yet hardly begun to unfold. Yet, in a sense, the particular details of that story are comparatively insignificant. Already, in the celebration of baptism, the meaning which those details will flesh out is already being disclosed. The ultimate test of whether one's life will have value or not is whether one will grow to be the person God is giving that individual the possibility of becoming. Will he or she live by the Spirit of Jesus, with faith and love such as Jesus himself so triumphantly manifested and vindicated in his "hour"?

Since the whole meaning and purpose of a person's life is summed up in this moment of crisis, the Christian community has never underestimated its importance, but has always marked it with insistent prayer to God on behalf of those to be baptized. They were not left to themselves. The Church associated itself with them in prayer and in fasting even before they had associated themselves with the Church in baptism. Two of the earliest Christian documents dealing with baptism make this point quite explicitly. The *Didache* (ch. 7) orders: "before baptism, let the baptizer and him that is to be baptized and such others as are able first fast." St. Justin records the practice of his day:

> As many as are persuaded and believe that these things which we teach and describe are true, and undertake to live accordingly, are taught to pray and ask God, while fasting, for forgiveness of their sins: and *we pray and fast with them* (*I Apol.*, c. 61; Whitaker, p. 2).

The purpose of the prebaptismal fast was undoubtedly, as of all fasting, to bring the faithful to a heightened state of awareness of spiritual realities, but the *Didache* goes on to order that those being baptized should fast for one or two days before baptism. This extended (total) fast is probably best understood as a form of the paschal fast, i.e., the fast kept by the faithful from Good Friday to the end of the Easter Vigil as a way of participating in the death of the Lord and showing solidarity with him, as it were, as he lay buried in the tomb.

With the virtual cessation of adult baptism, the fast lost its association with baptism and came to be regarded as part of the ascetical fast of Lent, although the liturgical books of the Middle Ages still contained indications that the Church frowned on infants being suckled during the baptismal vigil! Still, this owed less to the old prebaptismal fast than to the fact that they were going to receive Communion at the Mass that followed.

Nevertheless, the prayer of the Christian community on behalf of those being baptized remained. At Rome, the pope and most of his assistants went to the baptistry at the end of the long series of readings on Easter Night to bless the baptismal water and to administer the sacraments of baptism and confirmation. Meanwhile, the body of the faithful remained in the church and stormed heaven, while the rites of initiation were in progress, with multiple litanies on behalf of those being baptized.

This, in reduced form, is what is still done in the present rite. The ritual for the baptism of children provides a series of petitions, followed by an abbreviated litany of the saints. But it is an indication of the community's awareness that it, too, is making a commitment in undertaking to baptize these children when we find that the prayers are offered not only for the children themselves, but for their parents and godparents and for the whole community. In fact, taken together, the petitions provide quite a full picture of the meaning and implications of infant baptism.

For the children to be baptized we pray that they may become living members of the Church of God, with all that that implies. It implies in the first instance that they be brought into a whole new set of relationships with the triune God: sons and daughters of the *Father*, reborn in the likeness of Christ, the *Son of God*, to be his faithful witnesses and loyal disciples; united to him and adopted by the Father through the power of the *Spirit*, given to them as a gift to transform their lives. Conscious that baptism is but the first stage of initiation, the Church also prays that what has been begun in them will be brought to completion when "they come with joy to the table of your sacrifice" (RBC, 220). Unfortunately, there is only one petition of this kind, and that is tucked away among the alternative forms in an appendix. Finally, there are a number of prayers which look forward to the glorious consummation of our life in Christ, when we pass from the world of sacramental signs to the vision of his glory: may they share his resurrection and enter into eternal life amid the joys of the Kingdom, for we believe that "if we have died with Christ, we shall also reign with him."

The community prays, too, for the parents of the children and for their godparents, asking that God keep them always in his love and enable them to lead their children, by word and the example of their own Christian lives, to the knowledge and love of him.

Finally, the community prays for itself, the people of God. Every celebration of baptism is a reminder and a renewal of the local community's own identity, derived from baptism: for "Christ loved the church and gave himself up for her, having cleansed her by the washing of water with the word . . . that she might be holy and without blemish" (Eph 5:25-26). So we pray that the grace of baptism may be renewed in all who are present; that we may be preserved in the unity of faith and love into which we were baptized; that we may so live as to inspire all persons to seek the baptism of rebirth and so show forth our faith as to provide the children as they grow up with models of holiness and wisdom.

But even this is not enough. There is more here than meets the eye. The Church into which these children are being baptized is more than just this little congregation of families, friends and acquaintances. It is more even than the world-wide Catholic Church on earth. The sacramental celebrations of the Church, while celebrated by the local community, are nevertheless "surrounded by a great cloud of witnesses," to borrow a phrase from the epistle to the Hebrews (12:1). This is something of which the Eastern Churches particularly are aware, and which they express in their luminous icons of the saints and in the constant invocations of the saints which punctuate their liturgies. The Church on earth and the Church rejoicing in the glory of heaven are one Church.

Becoming part of the Church at baptism, then, we become "fellow citizens of the saints" (Eph 2:19). As such, we may confidently call upon them to join their voices with ours as we pray for these children at the "hour" of crisis which is their baptism. We turn first, naturally enough, to Mary the Mother of God and to St. Joseph, in whose care the child Jesus himself "grew in wisdom and stature and in favor with God and with men" (Luke 2:52). We invoke St. John the Baptist, whose baptism of Jesus in the Jordan marked the beginning of our salvation and provided the pattern of our own baptism in Christ. We ask the intercession of Ss. Peter and Paul, witnesses to the Lord's resurrection and founders of the community of faith in Rome, from whence in the course of history, the Good News of salvation was brought to us. To these we may freely add the names of local saints and patrons; and the names, too, of the patron saints of those being baptized. Every baptism is the concern of the whole Church in heaven and on earth, for the newly baptized becomes part of that living communion which is bonded and transformed by the Holy Spirit into a single body in Christ. "All you saints of God, pray for us!"

2. *The Prayer of Exorcism*

The wide publicity given to a number of bizarre cases of alleged "diabolical possession" in recent years, together with the popularity of such films as *The Exorcist*, may make it somewhat disquieting to find that exorcism forms part of the Church's rite for the baptism of children. On the other hand, a good number of Christians today will admit quite frankly that they simply do not believe in the devil anyway. So what are we to make of this prayer of exorcism, particularly in view of the fact that it is provided for use even with new-born babes?

Historically, exorcisms have been an integral part of the rites used for preparing people for baptism from the earliest times. What the Fathers have to say about such exorcisms in their commentaries on the baptismal liturgy makes it quite clear that they envisaged the unbaptized person as being quite definitely under the power of Satan if not possessed by him. The old Roman liturgy addressed itself quite explicitly to Satan: "Depart from him, unclean spirit, and give way to the Holy Spirit, the comforter."

Even though such rites were used until quite recently even for the baptism of children, it is worth recalling once again, that they developed as rites for the initiation of *adults* and that, until our own day, no thought was given to the possibility, indeed the need, of altering them to take the condition of children into account. Moreover, the adults who were being baptized in the period when our ancient liturgies were in process of development were all converts from Judaism or paganism. There were very few totally "secular" people such as we know today. If the Church took a pessimistic view of other religions, regarding them as works of Satan, this is hardly surprising either. After all, for the first three hundred years of her existence, the Church had clung tenaciously to life in the face of persecution first by the Jews and then by the Roman Empire.

In the face of such hostility and hatred, Christians were hardly likely to forget the warning of Jesus himself that the world, under the control of the prince of darkness, would hate them and persecute them as it hated him and would compass his death. Nor would they forget the words of Jesus to the Jews who would not accept him: "Why do you not understand what I say? It is because you cannot bear to hear my word. You are of your father the devil, and your will is to do your father's desires. He was a murderer from the beginning, and has nothing to do with the truth because there is no truth in him" (John 8:43-44). Given this verdict of Jesus and their experience of the savage persecution meted out to all who would not worship the gods of the state, it is hardly surprising that the early Church regarded all its converts as needing to be liberated from their enslavement to Satan before they could be set free, in baptism, to serve the living God. Regarding the postulants for baptism, therefore, the *Apostolic Tradition* made this regulation:

> And when the day draws near on which they are to be baptized, let the bishop himself exorcise each one of them, that he may be certain that each is purified.

But if there is one who is not purified let him be set on one side because he did not hear the word of instruction with faith. For the strange spirit remained with him (ch. xx, 3–4; Whitaker, p. 4).

Major exorcisms, those which call upon Satan directly to quit the person God has called to baptism, may still be used in the Christian initiation of adult converts who have, as pagans, been involved in witchcraft, voodoo and suchlike practices. That is left to the discretion of the local bishops. Today, however, we are able to see more clearly than in the past that not everyone who is unbaptized is thereby to be convicted of bad faith or presumed to be possessed by the devil. We are, in short, able to make a distinction which the early Church could not easily see, namely, a distinction between those who are possessed or have exposed themselves to the risk of demonic possession, and those who, not being baptized, belong to the world of unbelief, and hence to the dominion of Satan. This latter presupposes no personal guilt, no decision against Christ. Indeed, it is the natural state of everyone born into this world. It is what we generally call "original sin."

3. Original Sin

It is not unusual to hear people talking about original sin being "forgiven" or "washed away." Such, however, is not the language of the Church's liturgy and since the doctrine of original sin developed out of the Church's reflection on her baptismal practice, it is to that practice that we should go to understand what the doctrine means. The faith of the Church is expressed in the two prayers of exorcism offered for use in the Rite of Baptism for Children:

A.
Almighty and ever-living God,
you sent your only Son into the world
to cast out the power of Satan, spirit of evil,
to rescue man from the kingdom of darkness,
and bring him into the splendor of your kingdom of light.
We pray for these children:
set them free from original sin,
make them temples of your glory,
and send your Holy Spirit to dwell within them.

B.
Almighty God,
you sent your only Son
to rescue us from the slavery of sin,
and to give us the freedom
only your sons and daughters enjoy.

We now pray for these children
who will have to face the world with its temptations,
and fight the devil in all his cunning.

Your Son died and rose again to save us.
By his victory over sin and death,
bring these children out of the power of darkness.
Strengthen them with the grace of Christ,
and watch over them at every step of life's journey (RBC, 49).

Through both prayers there run two sets of images each describing a state of being. The prayers beseech God to bring those being baptized from the state in which they find themselves now to a new and different state. Baptism is thus presented as a transition ritual, or "a rite of passage" as anthropologists would call it. This idea is fundamental to the whole concept of salvation and the images used are all taken from the New Testament. For example, the first letter of Peter addresses the baptized as follows:

> You are a chosen race, a royal priesthood, a holy nation, God's own people, that you might declare the wonderful deeds of him who called you *out* of darkness *into* his marvellous light. *Once* you were no people but *now* you are God's people; *once* you had not received mercy but *now* you have received mercy (2:9-10).

Looking at the texts of the two prayers more closely, we see that the state of the unbaptized is expressed by three kinds of images. At one level, this state is a state that they simply find themselves in: the kingdom of darkness, the slavery of sin, the world. At another level, this state can be said to bring influence to bear upon them: it enslaves them, they face a world with its temptations. At a third level, this state is one which is experienced as having an autonomous power, even a personality of its own; they are in the power of evil, under the dominion of Satan, spirit of evil, and they will have to fight the devil in all his cunning.

There is no suggestion here that the unbaptized children are in any sense "possessed" by Satan and it seems to be the experience of the Church that such possession can only occur, in any case, when people lay themselves open to such diabolical manipulation. A possessed person is one who in some way surrenders his or her freedom, and an infant is in no position to do that for the same reason that the child cannot make an act of faith. We shall return to the question of the devil when we look at the renunciation of Satan. For the moment we can concentrate on the state that all flesh is naturally heir to, that of being in the world, dwelling under the slavery of sin.

What sort of experiences do these images conjure up? If we start with the image of the "world" we have to bear in mind that here, as with the other images, we are dealing with an experience colored by faith in Christ and therefore by the knowledge that things need not be and should not be as they are. It is a world in need of redemption that is meant here: not the physical world of nature, created good by God, but the human world, the man-made world and the society that inhabits it. It is the world as the human collectivity, where the lowest common denominator consistently triumphs over ideals of excellence; where initiative too often is stifled and penalized; where the individual walks in fear of the judgment and condemnation of one's neighbors; where the desire for a quiet life makes cowards of us all. It is the world pervaded, in Tennessee Williams' phrase, by "an air of mendacity" because pretense rules over honesty in the name of kindness or convenience. It is a world which fears change and tolerates only a limited freedom. It is the world of the Israelites in the desert who were quite willing to surrender their new-won freedom for the security of knowing where their next meal was coming from in Egypt. It was this world which was threatened by the truth and freedom which Jesus exhibited, and which succeeded in squeezing him out, as it has done with all prophets before and since. Into this all too familiar world every child is born, only to grow up and be broken in and become part of it—unless the grace of Christ prevails in that child.

From another angle, this same world is the "kingdom of darkness," a human society pervaded by ignorance, suspicion and fear. This darkness haunts our inner life and our relationships with others. We act without knowing why we do what we do and are afraid of what we may discover if we know ourselves too well. We hide ourselves from others and even from ourselves. We act without knowing what the effect of our actions will be and pretending not to care. Too often the face we present to the world is simply a mask molded by our own fears and other people's real or supposed expectations, so that we become more and more identified with the mask and less and less living out of our real identity, so that the sense of inner loneliness, isolation and desolation must either become unbearably acute or be constantly suppressed with techniques of self-deceit learned from our earliest years.

All this adds up to a sense of frustration and a feeling of being caught in a stifling web of untruth which we are impotent to dispel. This the faith of the Church identifies as the "slavery of sin." The slavery is everyone's experience, both at the personal and at the social level. As individuals and as a race we reach for the moon only to find our feet still stuck in the mud. All sorts of miracles of human progress occur in our times, yet we are dogged by our inability to cope effectively with the perennial problems of peace and war, personal conflicts and social injustice. However much the conditions of human life may change, human nature itself seems incorrigible. Our material progress is continually undermined by our moral flaws. Nero's recipe for civil order was to provide the people with bread and circuses. Camus, twenty centuries later, writes: "One sentence will suffice for modern man. He fornicated and read the papers."

To call such human experience the "slavery of sin," however, is to interpret that universal experience through the eyes of faith. Note that the word used is "sin" in the singular, not sins in the plural. It refers to the human condition as such, anterior to the sins of individuals. For this state of sin in which the world finds itself, the word most frequently used in the Scriptures is *hamartia*, which means "missing the mark." And this is significant, for it presumes there is a mark to miss. It presumes there is a state in which human beings could find themselves, or towards which they could be moving, but from which they have in fact gone astray. Thus, to call our negative experience of the human condition "sin" is at the same time to say that there is hope for us. This is precisely the Good News, revealed in Jesus Christ and preached by the Church: that our condition is not irredeemable, that we need not "miss the mark." The ground of this hope is given by God himself. The Father has loved the world so much that he sent his only Son to bring the world back to himself. The human race is "off the mark" until it begins to do the works of God by the obedience of faith, submitting to God's plan for the world.

It is thus very important to realize that when we talk about original sin, we are talking about the human condition, which we inherit simply by being born. Most people have a fairly resigned view of it: "That's human nature," they'll say. Some, like Camus cited above, write human life off as a meaningless absurdity. Others believe still in the ability of people to better themselves continually, though this sort of attitude was probably more common in the early days of the scientific revolution than it is today.

A conflict of views such as this led the Church to clarify her thinking about the human condition in the first place. Pelagius was a British monk who flourished in the late fourth and early fifth centuries. He was an immensely popular and influential spiritual director, and a dominant factor in his whole approach to the spiritual life was his belief in the complete freedom of the human will. The doctrine associated with his name held that, with sufficient will power, human beings can save themselves, so that although they will need grace in order to be saved, they need it only as an aid to salvation, not as a condition for salvation. This, of course, called into question the necessity of Christ's whole redemptive work and indeed Pelagians held that it was not really necessary, that Christ has really come simply to give us an example of how to live.

One consequence of this sort of teaching was that it made the whole question of grace irrelevant for infants. Since sin is a matter of our free choice against God, children who died in infancy died before they could sin and consequently did not need baptism. It was because Pelagius, or his followers, attacked the Church's practice of baptizing infants that they first came to the notice of the Church authorities and were eventually condemned at a council of North African bishops at Carthage in 418. The great opponent of the Pelagian doctrine was St. Augustine. His defense of the necessity of salvation for all was based upon the practice of the Church in baptizing infants, and this argument was widely followed. Certainly, in teaching that baptism meant the forgiveness of sins, the Church had always meant the sins committed by adults, for the vast majority of her newly baptized had hitherto been adults for whom baptism meant a profound conversion of life. But was it only personal sins that made it impossible for individuals to be saved without the grace of God? Had not the Church been accustomed from the earliest days to baptize, along with adults, infants and small children who had not reached the age where they could be guilty of personal sin?

In this way, the Church, by reflecting on a practice which she had hitherto practiced more or less by instinct and by reliance on Christ's welcome of little children recorded in the gospel (Mark 10:14; etc.), began to see that even before a person commits any personal sin, that individual still needs the redemptive grace of God to be saved. The life and death of Jesus were for all. He is the savior of the world, not just a model of the good person. There is something out of joint in the world itself, something amiss to which individuals contribute by their own sinfulness, but which precedes such personal guilt and makes it inevitable unless God saves them with his gracious intervention.

Thus the Church neither goes along with those who hold a facile and optimistic view of human perfectibility, nor with those who attribute the problems in the world to the sum of individual failings. Equally important, though, the Church also believes with St. Paul that "where sin abounded, grace abounded all the more" (Rom 5:17). Without God's intervention in Jesus Christ, human prospects were indeed bleak and the dark picture of human experience we have given above would have been left as one of ultimate hopelessness. But the Church can face realistically the worst manifestations of human weakness and failure because she believes they are more than compensated for by the Good News of our salvation in Christ.

Original sin continues to define our actual human condition and hence to be the state of every newborn child. Yet we can never just say that without also saying immediately that we are not left unaided. Jesus Christ is the savior of the world (John 4:42), the true light that enlightens every person coming into this world (John 1:9), the one who takes away the sin of the world (John 1:29) and gives life to the world (John 6:33). It is God's will that everyone should be saved through him (Acts 10:34ff.), and his Spirit is now poured out over the whole earth.

Still, in freeing us from the slavery of sin, God has not enslaved us again. Christ *offers* us freedom, because one cannot force a person to be free or compel a person to love. Consequently, salvation is offered to everyone in one way or another, but the acceptance of salvation is still one's free choice. Obviously, many people pass through this life without being confronted with this gospel, and presumably the universal salvific will of God works in their regard in its own mysterious ways. But it is equally obvious that anyone who hears the gospel and refuses faith and baptism thereby refuses the offer of salvation and thus cannot be saved. Jesus' saying that "unless a man be born again of water and the Spirit he cannot enter the kingdom of God" (John 3:5) supposes and does not destroy this freedom.

What the work of Christ has done, therefore, is to break through the vicious and despairing circle of our powerlessness to save ourselves. He has, by opening up the way to his Father, offered us the possibility of "hitting the mark," of finding everything that the images of freedom, truth, light, life and peace conjure up.

> For we ourselves were once foolish, disobedient, led astray, slaves to various passions and pleasures, passing our days in malice and envy, hated by men and hating one another; but when the goodness and loving kindness of God our Savior appeared, he saved us, not because of deeds done by us in righteousness, but in virtue of his own mercy, by the washing of regeneration and renewal in the Holy Spirit, which he poured out upon us richly through Jesus Christ our Savior, so that we might become justified by his grace and become heirs in hope of eternal life. The saying is sure (Titus 3:3-8).

As "heirs in hope of eternal life," the full reality of salvation is not yet ours. Indeed, Paul in his letter to the Romans can still complain that although "I delight in the law of God, in my inmost self . . . I see in my members another law at war with the law of my mind and making me captive to the law of sin which dwells in my members" (7:22-23). He speaks of himself, even after baptism, as "carnal, sold under sin" so that "I do not understand my own actions, for I do not do what I want but I do the very thing I hate" (7:14-15). We know the experience well enough, but what does it mean in the light of all we have said?

The Church at the Council of Trent has understood St. Paul to be speaking here not of the state of sin and powerlessness in which he found himself before baptism, but of the effects of sin, sometimes called "concupiscence," which in turn continue to incline a person to commit sin. The original sin has been overcome, but the effects of it are still felt. So what has altered? Everything and nothing. Nothing has altered in the sense that the believer is not necessarily going to be less subject to temptation than anyone else, nor is the believer guaranteed to remain sinless. But on the other hand, everything has altered. When Christ delivers someone from what the prayers call "the kingdom of darkness" and the "slavery of sin" it means the situation is no longer the hopeless, despairing plight it was. There is now, thanks to the saving grace of Christ, the possibility of breaking through the natural limitations of humanity to truth, to love, to life itself. Baptism does not put a person beyond the possibility of sinning, nor even beyond the possibility of condemning oneself to eternal despair, but it does open up the doors of eternal life, and it does give the inestimable gift of the Spirit of God to guide and transform one's existence. The baptized is no longer a slave of sin, but a child of God led by the Spirit of God, who helps us in our weakness, giving us the freedom of the children of God and prompting us to cry out "Abba! Father!" (Rom 8, passim).

Rather than talking of original sin being "forgiven" or "washed away" in baptism, then, we would do better to stick close to the terminology of the Church's liturgy. In baptism we are "rescued," "set free" and "brought out of the power" of original sin, so that we may enjoy the freedom of the children of God and be inhabited by the Holy Spirit who is the grace of Christ which strengthens us against the effects of original sin and brings us eventually to "the splendor of [God's] kingdom of light." It is not simple pessimism about humanity which prompts Christians to speak of the state of a newborn child in such stark, dark images as we find in these prayers. It is rather the awareness which faith gives of the dramatic contrast between people as they naturally are and as they might be when they take to heart the gifts and promises of God. It is a reflection upon the great love and compassion of our God, rather than a despising of self. Indeed, the Church can even rejoice that things are the way they are, for the very depth of our distress has only served to bring out the extraordinary bounty of our God. Recalling this at the great baptismal vigil of Easter Night, the Church sings:

Father, how wonderful your care for us!
How boundless your merciful love!
To ransom a slave
you gave away your Son.

O happy fault, O necessary sin of Adam,
which gained for us so great a Redeemer!

4. The Anointing

Closely associated with the preceding prayer of exorcism, and still dominated by the sense of crisis provoked by the word of God and expressed in the prayer, there follows the anointing of those to be baptized. In the rite of adult baptism, the anointing is tied to the renunciation of Satan immediately before baptism because, for an adult, that personal repudiation of the kingdom of darkness demands an immediate response of protection and care on the part of the Church. In the case of infant baptism, however, the renunciation of Satan is made by the parents and godparents as a renewal of their own baptismal commitment, not in the name of the child. For this reason, the prebaptismal anointing now follows the exorcism-prayer spoken over the child, since this is the moment at which the child's baptismal liberation is most clearly expressed.

The use of oil in the rites of Christian initiation dates from the second–third centuries, and may be even older. The ways in which it has been used and the importance and significance attached to it have varied greatly in different parts of the Church at different times, suggesting that it has a secondary role in the complex of baptismal symbols, serving to highlight the meaning of Christian initiation as a whole. In fact, its use in the liturgy was probably derived from the association of oil with bathing in ordinary every-day life in the ancient world. In ancient Greece and Rome, oil was used much as we use soap today: you went to your bath with your oil and your towel!

But, in fact, oil had a great many uses: as medicine, as a cosmetic, as pro-tection for the skin, as a liniment, as well as all its other uses in cooking, light-ing and so forth. In the context of baptism, therefore, it was capable of all sorts of associations which made it a helpful symbol of the interior trans-formation which the baptized person was undergoing. But throughout the history of the Church there have been two sorts of oil used in initiation: plain oil, such as is used before baptism in our rite, and chrism, or perfumed oil, which is used after baptism. Each of these has its own associations and its own symbolism.

Various names have been given to the oil used before baptism: "oil of ex-orcism," "oil of sanctification," "oil of consecration." These terms suggest the ways in which the anointing itself has been understood. Today it is known simply by its old name, "the oil of catechumens," after those for whose benefit it is used.

The way of administering it has also varied. In Jerusalem it was evidently poured quite liberally over the naked candidate for baptism and smeared all over the body, for St. Cyril reminds his congregation that "when you were stripped, you were anointed with exorcised oil from the very hairs of your head to your feet . . ." (*Myst. Cat.* 2:3). In St. Ambrose's liturgy in Milan something of the same kind presumably happened, for he compares the naked candidates to wrestlers, and wrestlers used to grease themselves all over to make it difficult for their opponent to get a grip on them. On the other hand, in fifth century Rome it appears that the candidates were anointed on the ears, the nostrils and the chest: the ears to enable them to listen to the gospel and remain deaf to temptation; the nostrils, as a reminder to serve the Lord as long as they draw the breath of life and to remain insen-sitive to the sweet smell of worldly pleasure; and the chest because it is the seat of the heart, where Christ now dwells after driving out the devil.

Later, in the Middle Ages, there was just a double anointing, on the chest and on the back, in the form of the cross. This was the rite in use until recent years. Now the celebrant anoints the children to be baptized simply on the breast, and the words he uses gives the sense of the gesture:

We anoint you with the oil of salvation
in the name of Christ our Savior;
may he strengthen you with his power,
who lives and reigns for ever and ever.
Amen (RBC, 50).

The rubrics say quite explicitly that where there are a large number of children, the anointing may be omitted. The celebrant stretches his hands out over them all and says: "May you have strength in the power of Christ our Savior, who lives and reigns for ever and ever" (RBC, 51). Nevertheless, the anointing is an ancient and still powerful symbol of protection and care. Used somewhat generously and rubbed in (and applied to the chest instead of to the lower neck as too often happens!), it is still a recognizable gesture, a manifestation of the care Christ extends to these children through the ministry of his priest and people.

A baby, particularly, needs to be touched and handled and held and tended, not only for its physical well-being but for its happiness and for its later psychic health. The ministrations of a parent, if developmental psychologists are to be believed, have a critical importance far beyond the baby's immediate needs. If it is to grow up free from the torments of inner anxiety and able in its turn to show and accept love, then the attitude of the parent in the early months and years must be one of warmth, love and reassurance. This is because the child has just undergone the trauma of moving from the womb to the outer world and needs to know he or she has not just been thrust out into empty space. This is a paradigm of the rebirth of baptism where, likewise, the baptized is brought from one world to another and needs the assurance and support and love of those who are bringing that person forth. If the loving care which a parent lavishes on the child in all sorts of tender gestures and little services has a significance which goes beyond what is immediately apparent and is so important for its long-term effects, the same may be said of the gestures of Mother Church in baptism. Out of many quite functional human gestures of care and protection, the anointing with oil has been traditionally selected by the Church to express the care with which she embraces the children God sends her. Oil, with all its associations as a protective ointment, embodies the protection which the Christian community extends to the children. But the Christian community is the sacrament or sign of the presence of Christ himself. It is ultimately the power and strength of the risen Lord himself, victorious over sin and death, which this lowly oil conveys.

And so the drama of initiation unfolds. The themes announced in the opening welcome—the children being accepted into the Church, the community's acceptance of its responsibilities towards them, their being put under the protection of the cross of Christ—have been highlighted in the reading of the word of God and brought into sharper focus in the prayers. Faith aroused by the hearing of the word has erupted into prayer. A lively realization of what is at stake in the making of a Christian has led to exorcism and anointing. All is now ready. The community rises from its knees and turns to the baptistry, where the children are being led to the font.

IV

REBORN OF WATER AND THE SPIRIT

Assembled around the font, in the company of their families, godparents and the ministers of the Church, the children stand at the threshold of immortality. For adult converts this will be the culmination of months and perhaps years of spiritual journeying, whose pace has intensified through the weeks of Lenten discipline and prayer. For the last two days they will have lived through the events of the Lord's giving himself up to death, his crucifixion and death. They will have shared his death and burial in silence, prayer and fasting until the Great Vigil began and, in the midst of the faithful assembled around the paschal candle, symbol of the risen Christ, they will have just heard of the great acts of God through human history. The climax of that history was not the solemn proclamation of the gospel of the resurrection, but the realization that they would, this very night, become part of that ongoing history and sharers in that resurrection itself. But for the whole community of faithful this moment is a poignant reminder of the blessings received by each in his or her own baptism. It is a moment of particular poignancy for those parents and godparents who are presenting children at the font that they might enter into the life by which they themselves live—the deathless life of the risen and glorified Christ.

1. *The Blessing and Invocation of God*

The first generations of Christians were baptized by being plunged into whatever water was available—in lakes or rivers, in spring water or sea water—or, if there was no body of water at hand, water was poured over their heads as they professed their faith. The custom of blessing water first appears in the late second century and seems to have been envisaged as invocation of the Holy Spirit and as an exorcism of the water itself. Thus St. Cyprian, writing c. 256, held that "the water should first be cleansed and sanctified by the priest, that it may wash away by its baptism the sins of the one who is baptized" (*Ep.* 70). The invocation of the Holy Spirit is understandable enough, given that the water ritual is but the sign and vehicle of the interior renewal wrought by the Spirit. But why an exorcism of the water?

In the time of Christ and for centuries after, it was commonly believed that the world which belonged to God had been taken over and perverted by

67

Satan. It was against this background, as we shall see later when we come to the renunciation of Satan, that the whole redemptive work of Christ was understood. He is the one who broke Satan's grip on humanity and made it possible for those who believe in him to live under the rule of God instead of under the rule of the Evil One. But material creation, too, had been affected by this situation. Instead of speaking to us of the glory of God, it had been usurped by Satan to serve his own perverted ends. The acuteness with which such an awareness was felt has varied very much in the Church according to different cultures and different historical periods, but where it was felt strongly exorcisms have tended, naturally enough, to multiply.

Water is, in any case, dangerous and can easily be envisaged as having a life and even a will of its own, not being easily tamed, as experience discovers. In angry mood the stormy sea and rushing torrent can sweep frail craft away and suck their equally frail passengers down into the deadly and murky depths. Storms and floods can be experienced as remorseless and superhuman enemies, the sheer physical phenomena being just the terrifying manifestation of the hidden, unpredictable and wanton forces that drive them on. It is hardly surprising then to find that, even in the Scriptures, the waters are portrayed as the dwelling place of primordial powers and forces of evil. St. Cyril of Jerusalem refers to a text from the Book of Job in one of his instructions, using the description of the monster Leviathan to illustrate the work of Christ:

> According to Job, there was a dragon in the waters who actually sucked the Jordan into his mouth. When it came for this dragon's head to be crushed, Christ went down into the water and bound up the strong one, so that he himself might be given power to trample serpents and scorpions under foot. No small monster was this, but huge! "Fishing boats could not withstand the thrash of his tail; and devastation stalked before him," spreading its contagion wherever it went. Then Life comes to bring Death under control, so that all of us who have attained salvation might say, "O death, where is thy sting? O hell, where is thy victory?" For by baptism, the sting of death is destroyed (*Myst. Cat.* 3:12).

Small wonder, then, that the traditional Roman blessing of the font on Holy Saturday used to beg God to drive away all unclean spirits and all the evil of Satan's trickery.

For such images really to speak to us today we would probably need a more lively imagination than our rational age encourages and a more immediate relationship to natural phenomena than most of us enjoy. But in any case, as is quite clear from Cyril's words above, the assertion of the saving work of God in Christ is more important than the mental pictures with which believers of any given age have experienced it. Turning to the present rite, therefore, it is hardly surprising to find that the exorcistic passages of the old Roman prayers have been excised.

What we find in the present text is in fact the most ancient form of a prayer of blessing and one which many scholars believe preceded the introduction of the exorcism of evil spirits from the water. It is a prayer which is best described not as a blessing of the water as such, but, as the title has it, as a "blessing and invocation of God" pronounced over the water. It recalls the great moments of salvation history associated with God's use of water. These are usually referred to as "types" of baptism and it might be good to pause here for a moment to look at what is involved in the whole notion of typology.

2. *Typology*

We have already had occasion to remark, in discussing the word of God, upon the continuity that exists between the saving actions of God in history and our own experience of salvation. We saw how the word of God is something living and active now, being recognizable and intelligible today in the light of the history of salvation in the past. Christianity is an historical faith, then, not only in the sense that it is inescapably rooted in certain critical events of history, but that it continues to witness to the further unfolding of that history from one generation to the next. The Christian Church both acknowledges what God is doing in the world today and furthers his work. In that way it furthers salvation history by actively shaping the lives of individuals and the history of our times.

For this very reason, precisely because it is the vocation of Christians to cooperate in the ongoing history of God's redeeming work in the world, we have to look to the historic interventions of God in past ages to find there the key to understanding what is happening to us and recognizing what we are called to do. God, who is faithful from age to age, is never inconsistent. However different the circumstances of our lives from the lives of our forebears, certain basic patterns still recur in human affairs which can be found to appear in widely different situations. Some of these can be discerned by the believing community to bear the stamp or imprint of God's presence and redemptive action. Our English word "type" comes from the Greek word "tupos" meaning a stamp or pattern, so that when we talk of events or figures of the Old Testament as being "types" of Christ and of the Christian sacraments as being "antitypes" of the saving work of Christ, we mean that there is a pattern common to the Old Testament events, the work of Christ and the sacramental experience of the Christian community today.

Thus the meaning of what we undergo in our sacraments can really be understood only in reference to the past. This recognition explains the constant appeals of the Fathers to the history of the Old and New Testaments to explain and clarify the meaning of the sacramental symbols. In fact, it was the basis of their whole approach to understanding the Scriptures. Its fullest development is seen in the tradition associated with the Church of Alexandria where the Scripture text was interpreted at four levels: the literal sense of the text; its reference to Christ (messianic sense); the light it sheds on our present situation (moral or tropological sense); what it tells us about the final consummation of God's plan for the world (eschatological sense). In every text, therefore, clues were sought about each of the four stages of the unfolding "mystery of salvation": the Old Testament stage, the new era inaugurated in the person of Jesus, the final goal of the history of salvation, and finally, somewhere along the road between these last two points, our own present historical situation.

We can thus situate ourselves, and render our present experiences intelligible, by reference on the one hand to what God has already achieved in the past, and on the other to what he has promised for the future. So St. Augustine writes:

> At this point we should begin our narration starting out from the fact that God made all things very good, and continuing, as we have said, down to the present period of Church history, in such a way as to account for and explain the causes and reasons of each of the events we relate, and thereby refer them to that end of love from which in all our actions and words our eyes should never be turned away (*First Catechetical Instr.*, 6).

Ultimately, as Augustine says, it is the love of God, who wills to gather all to himself, which accounts for the fundamental unity of the different stages of the history of salvation, so that the acknowledgement of what he has done in the past opens our eyes to what he is doing in the present.

This provides the basic structure of Christian prayer. The prayers of the liturgy, and especially the Great Prayer of the Mass, begin by thankfully recalling what God has achieved in the past and move from there to intercession for the present, asking God to further and to bring to completion the saving work he has begun in our history. Thus the Eucharistic prayer at Mass begins with thanks and praise for all that has been and ends on a note of longing as we pray for the final establishment of his kingdom in Christ, when we shall be united with him, with his saints and with all who have died. The prayer of the Church is never far removed from the prayer of the prophet Habakkuk:

> Lord, I have heard of your fame,
> I stand in awe at your deeds.
> Do them again in our days,
> in our days make them known (3:2).

The solemn prayer of blessing and invocation of God with which the rite of baptism proper opens deserves our careful attention, for both its overall shape and its different parts have much to tell us about the meaning of the baptism which is shortly to follow. It is a confession of faith in the God of the ages, acclaiming what he has done in former times, confident of his love being effective now, and looking forward to the resurrection which will be the joyful lot of all who are buried, through baptism, with Christ in death.

3. *The Prayer of Blessing*

Father, you give us grace through sacramental signs,
which tell us of the wonders of your unseen power.

In baptism we use your gift of water,
which you have made a rich symbol
of the grace you give us in this sacrament (RBC, 54A).

The prayer opens with an act of faith in the God who communicates with us through signs, sharing his life with us and raising us up through visible events and the spoken word. As Vatican II said of the whole work of God: "the deeds wrought by God . . . manifest and confirm the teaching and realities signified by the words, while the words proclaim the deeds and clarify the mystery contained in them" (Divine Revelation, 2). Thus what we see and hear is only half the story: it points to the hidden work of God of which it is but the sign. This is what defines a sacrament as "an outward sign of inward grace." The prayer also uses the term "symbol" which means, not something standing for something else, but something which makes visible and tangible that which is of its nature beyond perception. "Symbol" in its original meaning meant literally "half a sixpence": it was a token broken in two and shared between two lovers, or two parties to a contract, as a sign and a pledge of their relationship. In this case, the unseen reality, the relationship, is that of "grace." But grace is such an all-embracing term—meaning simply the loving initiative of God towards us—that it does not mean too much unless we have some inkling of what form that grace is taking on this occasion. But that is precisely the role of the sign. The nature of the sign indicates the nature of the grace and in commenting upon each of the different parts of the liturgy of baptism we are trying to make explicit the grace which they both signify and mediate. The "types" of baptism recalled in this prayer serve to give us further insight into this mystery of our salvation.

At the very dawn of creation your Spirit breathed on the waters, making them the wellspring of all holiness.

The reference here is clearly to the account of creation, and to the Spirit of God hovering over the waters of the primordial chaos (Gen 1:2), from which dry land was brought forth. This image of the world's origins is very common indeed among primitive peoples. Nothing can live without water for long. When the rains come to put an end to the drought, life revives and a barren land is reborn; plants, animals and humans begin to live again. So basic is water to life that it seems to be the very principle of life itself; formless water is breathed into shape by the spirit and word of the creator. In becoming a Christian, however, a person becomes, in St. Paul's phrase, "a new creation" (2 Cor 5:17), thanks to the creative Spirit moving once again over the face of the water, now the water of the baptismal font. Taking up this theme, St. Ambrose comments:

> We read: '"Let the earth produce from herself vegetation" and the earth produced vegetation yielding seed.' You have read the same about the waters: '"Let the waters produce living things:" and living things were born.' These were born in the beginning, at the creation; but this gift was kept for you: that the waters should regenerate you into grace, just as those other waters generated into life (*Sacr.* 3:3; Yarnold, p. 121).

Both in creation and in baptism water is involved, but whereas in creation God brought forth natural life, here in baptism he remakes his people, as it were, giving them a totally new kind of life—a share in his own life.

The waters of the great flood you made a sign of the waters of baptism, that make an end of sin and a new beginning of goodness.

The story of Noah's ark is still well enough known to appear in children's books and popular songs, though the appealing image of animals going in two by two generally manages to obscure the stern point of the whole story, which is one of judgment. Here water appears, not in its benign life-giving role, but as a savage instrument of destruction. The ancient myth of a universal flood, common to many Middle Eastern peoples, is adapted by the sacred authors of Israel to express the historical plan of God to destroy evil and rescue those who put their trust in him. "[God] did not spare the ancient world, but preserved Noah, a herald of righteousness, with seven other persons, when he brought a flood upon the world of the ungodly" (2 Pet 2:5). "Is not this flood baptism," St. Ambrose asks, "by which all sins are wiped out and only the spirit and the grace of the righteous are revived?" (*Sacr.* 2:1).

Elaborating this parallel further, the Fathers point to the ark as a figure of the Church, a ship of salvation with the cross for its mast, to which comes the dove of peace, the Holy Spirit, carrying the olive branch of reconciliation from God (see Tertullian, *On Baptism*, 8:18). The rescue of Noah and his family meant a new beginning for the human race, a new people who would look to the God who had saved them, by means of the flood waters, from a world of wickedness and corruption. Likewise the baptized: for them, too, baptism marks "an end of sin and a new beginning of goodness" as God forms a new people for himself.

Through the waters of the Red Sea you led Israel out of slavery, to be an image of God's holy people, set free from sin by baptism.

The exodus from the slavery of Egypt is the most important event in the whole of the Old Testament, for it was in the exodus that God revealed himself as a savior, and created a people for himself. Everything that happened subsequently was interpreted in the light of it and even the ancient myths and traditions of the people were henceforth colored by their experience of God as the one who had delivered them from the Egyptians, when he let his people pass through the sea dryshod and then turned the waves back again to drown and destroy the pursuing army of the Pharaoh. These events served, in later Jewish history, to offer an interpretation of the traumatic experience of the exile and return, as well as grounds for hope that God would do something similar in the future when he would once more deliver his people from oppression and establish them in peace for ever.

These expectations were seen by the early Christians as having already been fulfilled in the passing of Jesus from this world to the Father. His suffering and death, by which he entered into his glory, were understood as his "passover" from death to life, from the kingdom of death to new and immortal life. Thus baptism, in which we are marked with the pattern of Jesus' death and burial, is our participation in the passover of the Lord, a participation which will be completed in our own physical death. But even now all the elements of that original passage from slavery to freedom are realized in our own experience.

When Pharaoh, that most savage and cruel tyrant, afflicted the free and noble people of the Hebrews, God sent Moses to lead them out of their debasing slavery at the hands of the Egyptians. Their doorposts were smeared with the blood of a lamb so that the destroyer might avoid the houses bearing the bloodstain, and thus against all expectations the Hebrews gained their freedom. But when they had been liberated they were pursued by the enemy, who saw the sea miraculously part to afford the Hebrews a path. Yet even so the Egyptians pressed on in their footsteps, and at once they were submerged and drowned in the Red Sea.

Now turn your mind from past to present, from symbol to reality. Of old, Moses was sent into Egypt by God, but in our era Christ is sent into the world by the Father. As Moses was appointed to lead his afflicted people from Egypt, so Christ came to deliver the people of the world who were overcome by sin. As the blood of the lamb served to avert the destroyer, so the blood of Jesus Christ, the blameless lamb, had the effect of routing demons. The tyrant of old pursued the ancient Jewish people as far as the sea, and here and now the devil, bold and shameless, the source of all evil, followed you up to the waters of salvation. Pharaoh was submerged in the sea, and the devil disappears in the waters of salvation (Cyril, *Myst. Cat.* 1:2-3; Yarnold, p. 69).

The Church is the new Israel of God (Gal 6:16), a people he has redeemed for himself, and all who belong to it must have passed through the waters of deliverance.

In the waters of the Jordan your Son was baptized by John and anointed with the Spirit.

From the Old Testament we move now to the new covenant between God and his people inaugurated by Jesus himself. And first we recall his baptism in the Jordan. This is important for several reasons. In the first instance, he who was himself without sin identifies himself thoroughly with us in answering John the Baptist's call to repentance in view of the coming kingdom of God (Mark 1:4ff.). It was the occasion for him to be recognized as the one who was to come, the anointed servant of God (i.e., the Christ). It thus marks the real beginning of the mission of Jesus "for us and for our salvation." The descent of the Spirit upon him as he emerged from the waters of the Jordan was a sign of his consecration to the work of God, and hence eventually to the suffering and death which awaited him and which he spoke of, in fact, as "the baptism with which I am to be baptized" (Mark 10:38). In all these ways, too, baptism consecrates us. It makes us like him who became as one of us, committing us to do the works of God in fidelity to the guidance and consolation of his Spirit.

Your Son willed that water and blood should flow from his side as he hung upon the cross.

This gospel episode is mentioned only by St. John: "One of the soldiers pierced his side with a spear, and at once there came out blood and water. He who saw it has born witness—his testimony is true, and he knows that he tells the truth—that you also may believe" (19:32-33). The way St. John underlines the truth of his testimony indicates the importance he attaches to this event as a vivid expression of what St. John's Gospel is about: namely, that Christ is still with his Church. He clearly sees the water and the blood as symbols of the sacraments of baptism and the Eucharist, by means of which Christ is present to the faithful of every generation and communicates his own life to them. Through our participation in the sacrament of water and the sacrament of his Body and Blood we are enabled to share the life of him who gave himself up to death for us, thereby opening for us the way to life. The Fathers recognized this symbolism and took it further, seeing the Church herself being born at this moment of the Lord's death. According to the book of Genesis, God put Adam into a deep sleep and, while he was asleep, took a rib from his side, from which he created Eve (Gen 2:21-22). While Christ was in the sleep of death, God formed the Church from his side, as his bride and partner. The Church, not Eve, is now "the mother of all the living" (Gen 3:20) and she derives her life and her fruitfulness through the constant sharing in his life which the sacraments of baptism and the Eucharist make possible. He is the Lord of glory, whose death inaugurates a new era of freedom and life: "Dying you destroyed our death, rising you restored our life. Lord Jesus, come in glory!"

After his resurrection he told his disciples: "Go out and teach all nations, baptizing them in the name of the Father, and of the Son, and of the Holy Spirit."

Like the institution narrative in the Eucharistic prayer of the Mass, this reference to the Lord's command makes it clear that when we baptize we are doing what he told us to do, confident that he will do for us what he intended when he ordered us to do it. It is thus a way of saying that what we do now has value because of what he did and because he told us to do it. Notice how Jesus only gave this command *after* his resurrection. Apart from passing references in John (3:22; 4:1) to an abortive early mission, there is no evidence that Jesus himself ever baptized anyone, or ordered his disciples to baptize at any time before his death. Baptism therefore belongs to the era of the Lord's triumph over death and it is the way in which those who accept him and follow him in his obedience to the Father can share his triumph and his risen life. It is a pity that the text of the prayer is a translation from the Latin text of St. Matthew's Gospel. The Greek text has "go and make *disciples* of all nations," which better expresses what it means to render to Christ the obedience of faith. Baptism goes, not with simply being taught, but with becoming a disciple of the Lord, a follower heart and soul.

Father, look now with love upon your Church, and unseal for her the fountain of baptism.

From recalling the past wonders of God, and confident that God is faithful from age to age, we turn now in prayer to the present. "Look now upon the face of your Church," is a literal translation of the Latin text, and it reminds us of the Song of Songs, that passionate canticle of love between a man and a woman which has traditionally been understood as symbolizing the strong and undying love of Christ for the Church which is his bride: "Let me see your face, let me hear your voice, for your voice is sweet, and your face is comely" (2:14). Given that this prayer is probably about 1500 years old it is hardly surprising that there should be occasional evidence of its antiquity, despite its being revised for the present rite of baptism. The prayer asking God to unseal the fountain of baptism probably reflects the practice, common in many parts of the Church from the fourth century, of not only limiting the celebration of baptism to the annual baptismal festival of Easter, but of actually locking the baptistry and putting the bishop's seal on its gates. To open the baptistry, therefore, was to invite God to show his mercy and grace to all who waited upon him. Nor is the reference to "the fountain of baptism" a mere metaphor. From the earliest days, the Church preferred to baptize in "living" (i.e., running) water, and when baptistries began to be built, efforts were made in many places to maintain that practice; from which, of course, the "font" got its name.

You created man in your own likeness: cleanse him from sin in a new birth to innocence by water and the Spirit.

The reference here is to the contrast drawn by Jesus in his conversation with Nicodemus (John 3:1-15) between the old creation and the new, between human nature ("flesh") in its powerlessness to save itself and human nature "reborn" by the power of the Spirit of Christ. The whole creation was made to mirror the glory of God, and humanity, as its crown, was made to image the free, creative love of God himself. But as the doctrine of "original sin" so vividly conveys, everything has gone out of joint and only God can restore his world by inviting humanity to accept his help, the gift of his own Spirit. As the prayer of Christmas puts it: "Our human nature is the wonderful work of your hands, made still more wonderful by your work of redemption. Your Son took to himself our humanity. Grant us a share in [his] godhead."

The celebrant touches the water with his right hand and continues:

We ask you, Father, with your Son to send the Holy Spirit upon the water of this font. May all who are buried with Christ in the death of baptism rise also with him to newness of life. We ask this through Christ our Lord. All: *Amen.*

The stirring of the water says it all: the water moves, ripples with life and energy as the Spirit passes over. It is reminiscent of the curious detail reported in some versions of St. John's Gospel concerning the pool of Bethsaida, where Jesus healed a man who had been lying there crippled for thirty-eight years. Around the pool "there lay a crowd of sick people, blind, lame, and paralyzed, waiting for the disturbance of the water. For from time to time an angel came down into the pool and stirred up the water. The first to plunge in after this disturbance recovered from whatever disease had afflicted him" (5:3-4). The point that St. John is making in recounting this miracle is that the healing and restoration of God's people now comes through Christ. This is explicitly connected in the gospel account with liberation from sin and with the declaration, as it were, of an "open season"; for, as Christ says, "My Father is working still, and I am working" (5:17). Through Christ, the Father sends forth the Spirit, "the Lord and giver of life" as the creed calls him, for the redemption of the human race.

It is also John who associates the outpouring of the Spirit most closely with the death of Jesus. The climax of his life among us is reached when, hanging on the cross, "he said 'It is finished'; and he bowed his head and gave up his spirit" (19:30). It is by being drawn into the death of Jesus by baptism that we are able to receive his Spirit, his dying gift, and so enter with him into a new kind of existence. "We were buried therefore with him by baptism into death, so that as Christ was raised from the dead by the glory of the Father, we too might walk in newness of life" (Rom 6:4).

If baptism takes place within the fifty days of the Easter season, which ends with Pentecost (meaning simply "the fiftieth day"), the water used is that which was blessed at the Easter Vigil and the prayer for the descent of the Spirit is replaced by a simple request that the sacrament of baptism may be effective in the lives of those whom God has called to it. But the blessing of God and the prayer for the baptized remain an important part of every baptismal celebration. During the Easter season, the use of water blessed at the vigil points to the unity of all baptismal celebrations—"one Lord, one faith, one baptism" (Eph 4:5)—and their inescapable reference to the paschal mystery of the Lord's passing from death to life. Outside the Easter season, "it is desirable that the water be blessed for each occasion, in order that the words of blessing may clearly express the mystery of salvation which the Church recalls and proclaims" (GICI, 21). Thus in every baptism, this "blessing and invocation of God"—either in the classic text we have just looked at, or in one of the two alternative forms provided—is both an expression of the fact that the sacrament of baptism is God's work rather than ours and an important statement of the Church's convictions about what happens in baptism. It is both a profession of faith and a prayer; or better, it is a hymn of faith which naturally and necessarily leads into intercession. "Lord . . . I stand in awe at your deeds. Do them again in our days . . ." (Hab 3:2).

4. Renunciation of Sin and Profession of Faith

We have already had occasion to remark in more than one context that baptism is best understood in terms of a transition from one life-style, one set of values and loyalties to another. The summons of the gospel is not only to faith but to repentance, not only to belief but to conversion; or rather it is to a life of faith which cannot express itself but in conversion of the whole person. "Put away your old nature which belongs to your former manner of life and is corrupt through deceitful lusts, and be renewed in the spirit of your minds, and put on the new nature, created after the likeness of God in true righteousness and holiness" (Eph 4:22-24). "Repent . . . and turn again, that your sins may be blotted out" (Acts 3:19) was the appeal preached by the apostles. To say that baptism is the sacrament of faith, then, is to say that it is the sacrament of conversion, whereby a person rejects one obedience to adhere to Christ in an obedience of faith.

The profession of faith has always been at the heart of the sacrament of baptism, and with it, as its inseparable counterpart, goes the renunciation of sin. To be converted means literally to turn one's back. In the Eastern Churches to this day, the renunciation of sin and the turning to Christ are expressed in gestures as well as words as the candidate faces the west, where the night sky is still dark, and renounces Satan. In some churches, for emphasis, the candidate spits to the west before turning around and, facing the east where the first light of dawn is creeping over the horizon, makes his or her profession of adherence to Christ. Evidence of this particularly dramatic ritual is found in the Church of Jerusalem around the year 400:

> You began by entering the forecourt of the baptistry. You faced westward, heard a voice commanding you to stretch out your hand, and renounced Satan as though to his face . . . So when you renounce Satan, you trample underfoot your entire covenant with him, and abrogate your former treaty with Hell. The gates of God's Paradise are open to you, that garden which God planted in the east, and from which our first parent was expelled for his transgression. When you turned from west to east, the region of light, you symbolized this change of allegiance (Cyril of Jerusalem, *Myst. Cat.* 1:2, 9; Yarnold, p. 68).

Our own Roman rites are not quite as colorful as this Eastern tradition, but the immediate juxtaposition of the renunciation of Satan against the profession of faith sets up a quite unmistakable contrast. It also symbolizes the tension which runs continually through our lives for, despite the once-for-all impression which the baptismal liturgy gives, we find ourselves in fact to be people of two minds, people of divided heart. Consequently, this rite should be understood less as the last word than as a first commitment which needs continually to be renewed. Our identification with Christ and the acceptance of his Spirit is something which demands continual conversion, for it is something which, in virtue of our baptism, we are able to grow into.

Traditionally, this ongoing life of conversion has been kept alive in the Christian community by the weekly celebration of the Eucharist, sacrament of the Lord's death and of our participation in it, and the celebration of the sacrament of penance, which the Fathers liked to regard as a second baptism. In recent years we have been encouraged to make an explicit renewal of baptismal promises before being confirmed, every year at the baptismal vigil of Easter, and occasionally in the course of a mission or some such thing. It is important to notice, then, that in the context of infant baptism, it is not the child who makes any baptismal promises, nor the parents or godparents who make promises for the child. On the contrary, they speak for themselves and for themselves alone. They are invited to renew their *own* baptismal vows, to make public profession before the assembled people of God of their continuing will to renounce sin and to cling to Christ. This is the faith by which the Church lives, the faith in which the children are to be baptized and raised. How can they foster the life of God in their children if they are living a different kind of life altogether? So the celebrant urges them: "Renew now the vows of your own baptism. Reject sin; profess your faith in Christ Jesus. This is the faith of the Church. This is the faith in which these children are about to be baptized" (RBC, 56).

5. *Do you reject Satan?*

In commenting upon the prayer of exorcism, we deliberately passed over the references in the text to "Satan, spirit of evil" in order to reflect upon the doctrine of original sin. In actual fact, it is hardly possible to deal adequately with original sin without also mentioning the devil, but in any case we now come to a point in the rite where the question of Satan has to be faced. What is implied in the promise to "reject Satan, father of sin and prince of darkness"?

It must be said, first of all, that the New Testament, even more than the Old, is haunted by the presence of Satan and his demons. Belief in the devil provides the framework within which the redemptive work of Christ is very largely presented. The world which God has made is experienced as being in the power of an alien ruler, "the ruler of this world" (John 12:31), from whom Christ has come to wrest it back. His miracles are acts of liberation:

Satan is cast out and the kingdom of God appears whenever Jesus frees people from the illnesses and diseases which afflict them, from destructive spirits which control them, or from death which has overtaken them. His whole life and ministry and death are presented in terms of a dramatic struggle which culminates in apparent defeat by the powers of evil only to be irreversibly vindicated in his own resurrection from the dead. St. Paul attributes Christ's death to the malevolence of the mysterious "rulers of this age" who "crucified the Lord of glory" (1 Cor 2:8); but God "disarmed the principalities and powers and made a public example of them, triumphing over them in [Christ]" (Col 2:15).

It is tempting to dismiss such language as mere metaphor, or perhaps as the superstitious mythology of a culture more primitive than our own. We would also have to say the same about centuries of Christian faith, for the prayers and writings, the art and liturgies of Christians the world over—not least the classical baptismal liturgies—take the reality of Satan and his minions very seriously indeed. Precisely because such beliefs conflict so sharply with the rational spirit of our own age, it is important that we do not dismiss them out of hand, but try at least to recognize the experience to which such language relates, even if we cannot unself-consciously adopt it in its entirety.

When looking at the prayers of exorcism, we pointed out that three kinds of image are to be found there: those which refer to what we might call simply "the human condition"; those which suggest that we are positively influenced by the world in which we live; and those, finally, which suggest that we are actually the victims of some mysterious power with a will and personality of its own. Thus the prayers speak not only of a world which tempts and enslaves us, but of "the devil with all his cunning," whom they also call "Satan, spirit of evil." In other words, the prayers, in keeping with the Scriptures and the traditions of the liturgy, suggest that the evil we encounter in our experience of the world is something more than merely neutral and unhelpful living conditions and more than the effects of other people's wickedness. Indeed, the suggestion is that the difficulties which the material world poses for us and the fact of widespread human corruption and degradation are both related to some sinister, superhuman power from which we need to be delivered, and which lies behind the evil that people do.

Obviously there is a danger here, not always avoided in the past, of inventing a figure onto whom we can project our own moral evil in an attempt to escape responsibility and guilt. But, even admitting this danger and thus guarding against it, we are still left with the impotence of the individual and of society in the face of self-destructive tendencies.

Perhaps the proper place to start is at the level of the collectivity, with the ancient adage that "the whole is more than the sum of its parts." Every family, group, society, nation is more than the sum of its constituent members: it has a life, an *esprit de corps*, a character of its own. In ancient times, this recognition was expressed in the veneration shown to the 'genius' of the family, to the ancestors and household gods, to the tutelary deities of cities and armies of guilds. Interestingly enough, the Israelites shared this belief. Their acceptance of Yahweh as the one God did not exclude their believing in a host of lesser and dependent powers who ruled various human collectivities and institutions. On the contrary, they saw this as an integral part of God's arrangement of the universe: "When the Most High gave the nations their inheritance . . . he fixed the bounds of the peoples according to the number of the sons of God" (Deut 32:8). Here the sons of God are not men, but the powers of the nations of the world, the "angels" of each nation.

This seems to have been the earliest stage of a Jewish theology of angels: each nation had its "angel" appointed by God; but Israel was God's own people, whom he kept for himself. Satan himself was originally one of the "sons of God" (Job 1:6), but one entrusted with the task of reporting disloyalty; hence his name, which means simply "the Adversary." He was a kind of public prosecutor. The change of role from servant of God to enemy of God reflects the change in the fortunes of the people of Israel in the centuries leading up to the time of Christ. As one disaster and disappointment followed on another, it seemed as if the order fixed by God was getting twisted out of shape. The "powers" had rebelled. They had claimed from human beings the allegiance due to God alone. Everything was beginning to fall apart. A strange and ancient story found in Genesis told of the sons of God intermarrying with the daughters of men (Gen 6:4), and this now became the point around which a whole series of speculations about the fall of the angels and the beginning of calamity developed.

This brief summary of the theology of Satan and his angels must suffice for our purposes, but it does make us hesitate before identifying Satan with absolute evil. The teaching of the Church has never defined anything about the devil, except to condemn those opinions which set him up as a sort of anti-god, a God of Evil eternally co-existing with the God of Good. There is only one Supreme God, and he is the creator of all that is and all that he created he created good. Whatever is evil in the world is the perversion of what was good in itself. Perhaps we can now return to our own experience of life in the world and see what sense it makes for us to talk of the devil and of rejecting Satan.

We saw that the experience of "angels" is the experience of the collectivity as having an identity, one might almost say a personality, of its own. This in itself is a good thing. It provides the individual with a sense of one's own identity while enabling each to achieve more and to be more than one could ever be as an isolated individual. But, at the same time, it is open to perversion if it is accorded more importance and loyalty than is its due. The sense of nationhood, if accorded absolute value, becomes the diabolical spirit of nationalism, spawning fear and hatred of foreigners, unholy alliances with the strong, and aggressive exploitation of weaker nations. The spirit of the race becomes perverted into racism; the *esprit de corps* of a group becomes an excuse for dispensing with the rights of the individual. Institutions are necessary for all levels of human living, but there is the constant tendency for them to degenerate into "the system," at best reducing the value of the human person, at worst destroying the person. The news headlines of this century would probably, taken together, provide an exhaustive list of the crimes committed by the "devils" who rule our collectivities: the genocides of Nazi Germany and Soviet Russia, the campaigns of victimization, terror, murder and brutal savagery conducted in the name of "the cause" in Ulster and the Congo, in Cambodia and Brazil, and all those other places whose names are indelibly inscribed in the annals of infamy.

The individual is not only the victim of such evil but also, wittingly or unwittingly, its perpetrator. A person becomes the tool of the angel of the institution, the cause, the system, so enslaved that one is incapable of thinking or acting outside its terms of reference. This happens, more often than not, quite unnoticed. A person imbibes the false values, the petty lies, the shabby compromises with falsehood and injustice, the concern for expediency, security and all other false gods. The world's fascination with the events of Watergate was a fascination not with what was strange, but with what was strangely familiar: decent men giving to an institution the type of total loyalty which it has no right to. This is, perhaps, something like what was meant by the sons of God intermarrying with the daughters of men: human beings selling their souls to the collective institution, giving the kind of total service to which God alone has claim. The fall of the angels is inseparable from the fall of humans; rather the fall of both lies in their unholy alliance which disrupts the proper order of values and constitutes a rebellion against the Most High.

Rare is the person who can even see what is involved in such situations and in the spirit of the age, let alone stand out against it. In fact, no one can do so except by the grace of God, which is both enlightenment and deliverance. "And you he made alive, when you were dead through the trespasses and sins in which you once walked, following the course of this world, following the prince of the power of the air, the spirit that is now at work in the sons of disobedience" (Eph 2:1). Where the other New Testament writers might speak of Satan and evil spirits, Paul talks of "the rulers of this age," of "rule and authority and power and dominion" (Eph 1:21). "Put on the armor of God, that you may be able to stand against the wiles of the devil. For we are contending not against flesh and blood, but against the principalities, against the powers, against the world rulers of this present darkness, against the spiritual hosts of wickedness in the heavenly places" (Eph 6:11-12).

The many different names given to this experience of evil in the New Testament are themselves indication that this is something more easily felt than defined. And yet while the net effect is one of disruption and the corruption of what is meant to be whole and wholesome, and while the manifestations of it are manifold, yet there sometimes seems to be a conspiracy of evil abroad, especially when that evil is challenged. This was the experience of Jesus, who came into the world, the world he had made, and the world would not receive him (John 1:10). It is hardly an accident that he who came to liberate people from evil should have had to be destroyed to protect the power of the collectivity: "It is expedient for you that one man should die for the people and that the whole nation should not perish," Caiaphas told the council of Pharisees (John 11:50). Because of this conspiracy of evil, enslaving the weak and crushing the strong, irrational, wanton, and apparently wilful in its destructiveness, St. John talks of "the prince of this world" (John 12:31; 14:30; 16:11). He appears as the archenemy of God and therefore of Christ, the adversary of both God and humanity. It is he who leads and coordinates the "angels" of the world who are in rebellion against God and who hold God's people in thrall. In that sense he is, as the liturgy calls him, "father of sin and prince of darkness." The terrible visions of the Book of Revelation, with their graphic descriptions of tyranny and persecution, of the rise and fall of empires, of devastation and plague and bloodshed and death, were a reflection of the early Church's experience of bitter persecution. They continue to be read because the visions are still valid, both in terms of the continuation of the conflict and in terms of the promise they hold that the prince of darkness will be overthrown.

The resurrection of Jesus was the turning point in human history, for by it the domination of the principalities and powers who rule this world (and who crucified him) has been broken. The decisive victory has been won, yet the war drags on from one generation to the next. Everyone who hears the gospel becomes aware of what is at stake. We have to choose: either to enlist with Christ and become part of the solution, or to refuse and thereby contribute to the problem; either to surrender to the Spirit of God who raised Jesus from the dead, or to sell ourselves to the service of the prince of this world and condemn ourselves to perdition.

We do right to laugh at images of Satan as an imp with a tail, whispering impure thoughts into our ear. When we have experienced the frenzy of a blood-crazy mob or the frightening immorality of self-justifying institutions; when we have seen people beside themselves with rage or driven to their destruction with a lust for wealth or power or success; when we have seen the terrible horrors which ordinary men and women can find themselves committing for an ideology; when we view the madness that passes for sanity in the accumulation of instruments of global destruction for the purposes of preserving peace, then we can look again with respect at the demonology of the Scriptures and the liturgy and recognize what they mean when they speak of the spirit of evil and the father of lies.

Every man and woman yearns for life and for fulfilment; all temptation is the temptation to seek it where it cannot be found, to put one's trust in the creature instead of the creator. That is what St. Paul calls "deceitful lusts"

(Eph 4:22) and what the baptismal liturgy calls Satan's "empty promises": "He was a murderer from the beginning, and has nothing to do with the truth, because there is no truth in him. When he lies, he speaks according to his own nature, for he is a liar and the father of lies" (John 8:44). To come to faith in Jesus is to accept him as the way, the truth and the life (John 14:6) through whom alone we can have access to the Father. "By his great mercy we have been born anew to a living hope through the resurrection of Jesus Christ from the dead, and to an inheritance which is imperishable, undefiled, and unfading" (1 Pet 1:3).

Baptism necessarily means rejecting all that Satan stands for. It means doing the works of God instead of cooperating with the works of Satan, which are described in the Book of Revelation as blasphemy, violence, misuse of authority, and the undermining of all that Christ stands for (13:5-8). It means making the obedience of faith one's rule of life and standing fast against the seductiveness of evil and against the easy compromise which enables the "masters of this age" to begin to bend us to their will. It means taking to heart the words of St. Paul: "You did not receive the spirit of slavery, to fall back into fear, but you have received the spirit of sonship. When we cry 'Abba! Father!' it is the Spirit himself bearing witness with our spirit that we are children of God, and if children, then heirs of God and fellow heirs with Christ, provided we suffer with him in order that we may also be glorified with him" (Rom 8:15-17). The matter is well expressed in the baptismal liturgy celebrated by St. John Chrysostom in fourth century Antioch:

> I renounce you, Satan,
> your pomp, your worship, and your works.
> And I pledge myself, Christ, to you (see Yarnold, p. 166).

6. *Do you believe in Jesus Christ?*

Baptism is the celebration of a person's passing from outside the Church to inside the Church, from not belonging to Christ to becoming a member of his Body, from being enslaved to the spirit of evil to the freedom of the children of God who are animated by his Spirit of holiness. In short, it marks the withdrawal of a person from being counted among the "sons of disobedience" (Eph 2:1) and one's public commitment to the "obedience of faith." This is of the essence of baptism, the sacrament of faith, and of the justification (the new relationship with God) which it mediates. For this reason, the profession of faith has been a constitutive part of the baptismal liturgy from the beginning. Although in our liturgy, as in others, the renunciation of Satan precedes the profession of faith, it is secondary to the profession of faith and serves merely to make explicit what is implied in any act of faith in Christ.

In the New Testament, baptism is given to all whom God has chosen and the sole indication of God's choice of a person is the gift of the Spirit who enables him to acknowledge Jesus as the one whom God had sent and had glorified, for the salvation of the world. "No one can say 'Jesus is Lord' except by the Holy Spirit" (1 Cor 12:3). To say that Jesus is Lord is to say everything. It is to identify him with the God of the Old Testament, and to say that he is from that God and reveals him: "He who sees me, sees the Father" (John 14:9). To call him "Lord" is to acknowledge his resurrection and glorification at the right hand of the Father: "This Jesus God raised up," Peter told the Jews at Pentecost, "and of that we are all witnesses. Being therefore exalted at the right hand of God, and having received from the Father the promise of the Holy Spirit, he has poured out this which you see and hear . . . Let all the house of Israel therefore know assuredly that God has made him both Lord and Christ, this Jesus whom you crucified" (Acts 2:32-33, 36). To call him "Lord" is to submit to the whole economy of salvation which he ushered in by his life, death and resurrection.

To call Jesus "Lord," therefore, is not so much to concede a title or admit to belief in his divinity. It is to acknowledge the significance of what he has done for us. God, it has been said, is a verb and not a noun. Certainly he allows us to experience him, but never to define him. We know what God is like only from what he has done. For this reason, the Christian creed is not a set of doctrines so much as the summary of a history embracing past, present and future; and to profess one's faith in baptism is to make public acknowledgement of what God has done, is doing and will yet do. It is to acknowledge the unfolding plan of God in history, a plan in which one is included by the celebration of baptism.

For this reason, the profession of faith in the lordship of Jesus ("I believe that Jesus Christ is the Son of God": Acts 8:37) was generally accompanied by some explicit reference to the events in which our salvation was effected and his glory manifested. Thus Paul can say: "If you confess with your lips that Jesus is the Lord and believe in your heart that God raised him from the dead, you will be saved" (Rom 10:9). This was simply to accept and profess the faith of the Church as the apostles preached it. In various places in the Acts of the Apostles we are given a synopsis of such apostolic preaching. Here is one example:

> The God of our fathers raised Jesus whom you killed by hanging him on a tree. God exalted him at his right hand as Leader and Savior, to give repentance to Israel and forgiveness of sins. And we are witnesses to these things, and so is the Holy Spirit whom God gives to those who obey him (Acts 5:30-32).

Thus the profession of faith made by those who accepted this preaching was an acknowledgement of what God had done in Christ and of what this meant for our salvation. It is no simple admission of "facts," therefore, but a confession of gratitude that all this was undertaken, as St. Irenaeus puts it, "because of his surpassing love for his creation" (*Adv. haer.* III, iv, 2); or, as we say in the Creed, "for us and for our salvation."

In the second and third centuries, this original baptismal profession of faith in Christ was elaborated in response to the need to clarify the relationship of Christ to the God of the Old Testament, to include a profession of faith in "the God and Father of our Lord Jesus Christ," the creator of the universe. Because of the need to emphasize that Christ's saving work continues in the Church, a further section was soon added spelling out the implications of the abiding presence of the Spirit of Christ in his Church: the unity and holiness of the Church (which is the communion of saints), the forgiveness of sins and the resurrection of the body to everlasting life.

In the early centuries this threefold confession of faith was the sole baptismal formula in almost all the Churches, and it remained so in the Church of Rome for seven hundred years. The earliest witness to this Roman practice is the *Apostolic Tradition* of Hippolytus:

> The person to be baptized goes down into the water, and the one baptizing lays his hand upon him saying:
> Do you believe in God the Father almighty?
> And the one being baptized shall say:
> I believe.
> Let him forthwith baptize him once, laying his hand upon his head.
> After this let him say:
> Do you believe in Christ Jesus, the Son of God
> who was born of the Holy Spirit and the virgin Mary,
> who was crucified in the days of Pontius Pilate,
> and died, and was buried
> and rose the third day living from the dead
> and ascended into the heavens
> and sat down at the right hand of the Father,
> and will come to judge the living and the dead?
> And when he says: I believe, let him baptize him the second time.
> And again let him say:
> Do you believe in the Holy Spirit, in the holy Church and the resurrection of the flesh?
> And the person being baptized shall say: I believe.
> And so let him baptize him the third time (XXI, 12-18).

This baptismal profession of faith, here so intimately linked with the very act of baptism itself but later moved back to its present position immediately before baptism, was central to the life and unity of the Church. This "one rule of faith, unchangeable and unalterable," professed by every member of the Church, was cited by preachers and theologians, and served as the touchstone to which appeal could be made in the doctrinal controversies about the person and work of Christ which so vexed the Church of the fourth and fifth centuries. The so-called "Nicene Creed" was originally the baptismal profession of faith used in the Church of Jerusalem and adopted and expanded by the fathers of the Council of Constantinople in 381. Instead of saying, as the person being baptized would, "I believe," they adapted the formula to make a common profession of faith: "We believe."

Not only did the baptismal faith serve to guide the teaching authorities in the Church and to inspire the lives of individuals who had committed themselves to that faith in baptism, but it bound Christians everywhere into a common bond of unity. St. Irenaeus, in the second century, testifies to this in a beautiful and important passage:

> The Church, although scattered throughout the whole world, even to the ends of the earth, has received the faith from the apostles and their disciples. This is the faith in the one God, the Father almighty, who has made heaven and earth and sea and all that is in them . . . Since the Church has received this preaching and this faith, as we have said, although she is scattered throughout the whole world, she preserves it carefully, as one household; and the whole Church alike believes in these things, as one in soul and heart, preaching these beliefs in unison, teaching them and handing them on as with one mouth. For though there are many different languages in the world, still the meaning of traditions remains one and the same. And there are no different beliefs or traditions in the Churches established in Germany or Spain, or among the Celts, or in the East, or in Egypt or Libya . . . But just as God's creature the sun is the same the world over, so the preaching of the truth shines everywhere and enlightens all who wish to come to the knowledge of the truth (Adv. haer. I, x, 1-2; Bettenson, pp. 126-127).

Irenaeus, bishop of Lyons, was one of countless Christians who have died refusing to renounce this faith, putting their trust, not in the doctrine (which would have made them simple fanatics), but in him of whom the formulae of faith speak. Right beliefs about Christ are important because they make possible a proper relationship with him. Thus the time of the catechumenate was spent both in doctrinal instruction and in spiritual formation, as the candidates for baptism grew in their knowledge and understanding of Christ and his Church. The Church shares her faith with all who hear the call of Christ, leading them on until the point at which they can say with conviction that the faith of the Church, received "from the apostles and their disciples," is their own. In the ancient Roman liturgy, this handing on of the faith was given ritual expression in the "presentation of the gospel" and the "presentation of the creed." The candidates were presented with the gospels and heard the creed recited in the midst of the assembled church. They had to learn the creed by heart and then return to recite it in public shortly before their baptism. In the Roman liturgy of presenting the creed, the candidates for baptism were told: "With quiet and steadfast faith you must believe that the resurrection, which in Christ became a fact, must be completed in us all, that what started in 'the head shall follow in the whole body' [see Col 1:18]. Moreover, the very sacrament of baptism which you are to receive expresses the form of this hope. For in it is celebrated a kind of death and resurrection" (*Gel. Sacr.*, Whitaker, p. 176).

Like the renunciation of Satan, the profession of faith in Christ is not something which can be made once and then forgotten. An ancient and healthy Christian instinct has included the Apostles Creed—which is basically the baptismal profession of the Roman Church—among the daily prayers of the faithful. Its recitation is a renewal of our baptismal identity as the people whom Christ redeemed and who form the community of believers living by faith in the Son of God and in his cross. It is only fitting, then, that such a profession of faith should be demanded of those who are undertaking to foster the faith-life of the children they bring to baptism.

Like the candidates for baptism in the rites of adult initiation, the parents and godparents speak for themselves as they make public profession before the gathered community of their faith in Christ. Asked whether they believe, each of them says, "I do." But that faith is precisely what makes them members of the Church. It is our common faith, so that each person's own faith statement is greeted at the end with a cry of recognition: "This is our faith. This is the faith of the Church. We are proud to profess it in Christ Jesus our Lord" (RBC, 59).

The significance of this acclamation is well expressed in the Introduction to the Rite of Baptism: "During the rite . . . the community exercises its duty when it expresses its assent together with the celebrant after the profession of faith by the parents and godparents. In this way it is clear that the faith in which the children are baptized is not the private possession of the individual family, but is the common treasure of the whole Church of Christ" (RBC, 4). This treasure is the shared obedience of faith, the common submission to God in Christ which makes us one people, a faithful people, into whose ranks the children are about to be admitted in a rite which both flows from and shows forth that faith.

One by one, the children are brought to the font at the invitation of the celebrant by their parents and godparents. "Is it your will that N. should be baptized in the faith of the Church, which we have all professed with you?" he asks. "It is," they reply; and the child is thus baptized in the faith of the Church.

7. Baptism with water . . .

There is always a kind of divine understatement involved in the sacraments of the Church; the very simplest things, the most ordinary gestures, become the medium of God's activity for us and among us, as if to warn us that even the most solemn, impressive, extravagant and costly human productions would inevitably fall short of the unfathomable mysteries which they are called upon to convey. The touch of a hand, the breaking of a piece of bread, a gentle anointing . . . a brief and simple washing with water: through such things is the world remade. Tertullian was one of the many writers who have remarked upon this disparity, and what a stumbling block it is to those who do not believe that we should make such claims for such unprepossessing rites:

There is nothing which so hardens men's minds as the simplicity with which God's works are accomplished in action as compared with the magnificence of the effects promised. So in this case, too; because a man is sent down into the water with such simplicity, without ceremony, without special equipment, and not least without it costing him anything, and is dipped with but a few words; and because he emerges little or no cleaner than he went in, it is thought unbelievable that he should have attained everlasting life (*On Baptism*, 2).

So it may be with us as we come to the heart of the process of initiation. The gesture is so simple that it is difficult to remember that the rest of the entire rite, and even the multiple rites and disciplines of the extended catechumenate and the season of Lent, are nothing more than a making explicit of what is given in the water. Indeed, here is contained the whole pattern of our Christian life and future hope. "Do you not know that we who have been baptized into Christ Jesus were baptized into his death? We were buried with him therefore by baptism into death, so that as Christ was raised from the dead by the glory of the Father, we too might walk in newness of life" (Rom 6:3-4).

The Greek word "baptizein" means literally to dip repeatedly, to dip under the water, and hence to bathe. Such total washing had a place in ancient Judaism and was the rite adopted by John the Baptist as a sign of moral conversion in preparation for the coming kingdom of God. Taken over by the Church and carried out in the name of Christ, the action remained the same although, in conjunction with the profession of faith, it took on new significance. Still, the Church has always retained a preference for the immersion which the name "baptism" implies and the pouring of water over the candidate's head will always have to be understood as a modified version of the complete bath.

Since the washing with water is a sign of the mystical sharing in the death and rising of Christ, by which believers in his name die to sin and rise to eternal life, it achieves its full importance in the celebration of baptism. The rite of immersion or of infusion or of pouring is chosen according to what is more suitable in individual cases, so that, according to various traditions and circumstances, it may be understood that the washing is not merely a rite of purification but a sacrament of union with Christ (RCIA, 32).

There, in a sense, is the rub. For centuries we have for the sake of convenience been practicing baptism by pouring, with the result that the sacrament of baptism has been understood for the most part merely in terms of a kind of moral or legal purification. Yet it is clear from the teaching of the

New Testament and of the Church, from the practice of the classical liturgies and from what we have seen of our own rite, that what is involved is nothing less than a transformation of the whole person so radical that it has to be described in terms of death and rebirth. This is only adequately expressed when those being baptized are really plunged into the water, and the present rite continues to encourage this practice as being "more suitable as a symbol of participation in the death and resurrection of Christ" (GICI, 22).

We have no direct evidence of how the apostolic Church baptized— though a preference for immersion can probably be detected in the way the New Testament speaks of baptism—but at the end of the first century the *Didache* gives clear instructions:

> Concerning baptism, baptize in this way. Having first rehearsed all these things [i.e., prebaptismal instruction], baptize in the name of the Father and of the Son and of the Holy Spirit, in living water. But if you have not living water, baptize into other water; and, if thou canst not in cold, in warm. If you have neither, pour water thrice on the head in the name of the Father, etc. (n. 7, Bettenson, p. 62).

This seems to have been the rule throughout the Church for centuries: that baptism was by immersion unless lack of a sufficient body of water— and possibly cold weather!—made it impossible. Baptism by infusion (the pouring of water over the candidate's head) was generally used only in emergency baptisms, when a catechumen was in danger of death. Probably the tendency to baptize infants at an even more tender age also contributed to the gradual disappearance of immersion, although even there baptism by immersion was considered preferable under normal circumstances. Thus in England, for example, the Sarum Rite which was in use right up to the Reformation ordered that the child should be dipped in the water three times: once on the left side, once on the right, and once face down!

Of course, the rite of immersion meant that the candidates had to be naked, and this led to various provisions being made to secure the dignity and decency of the proceedings: baptistries built separate from the main church, or else curtained off; separate disrobing rooms for men and women; deacons to accompany the men into the water and deaconesses to assist the women. The need to build baptistries provided an occasion for underlining the symbolic dimension of baptism as a death and burial with Christ. Baptistries were designed to look like mausoleums and the font inside often took the shape of a sarcophagus. Not that this was in any way morbid, as the decoration of the baptistries and the mood of the liturgy revealed. On the contrary, it was precisely victory over death which was being celebrated as the practice of entering the font on one side and emerging from it on the other showed. "Blessed and holy is he who shares the first resurrection! Over such the second death has no power, but they shall be priests of God and of Christ, and they shall reign with him a thousand years" (Rev 20:6).

Judging from the evidence of pictorial representation of baptism, it is likely that in many places the candidate stood up to his or her knees or waist in water and then was either pushed under (as the *Apostolic Tradition* suggests) or else had water poured over the head three times. Theodore of Mopsuestia, describing the Syrian practice familiar to him, indicates that there the bishop stood at the edge of the font, while the candidate stood in the water. He laid his hands on the candidate and bent the head forward into the water. "You obediently follow the signal he gives by word and gesture, and bow down under the water. You incline your head to show your consent and to acknowledge the truth of the bishop's words." This is done three times, in the name of Father, Son and Holy Spirit. "If you were free to speak at this moment you would say 'Amen.' . . . But since at the moment of baptism you cannot speak, but have to receive the sacrament of renewal in silence and awe, you bow your head when you immerse yourself to show your sincere agreement with the bishop's words" (*Bapt. Hom.* III, 18; Yarnold, p. 201).

However the details of the operation may vary, the meaning of the rite is essentially the same and is invariably explained by the Fathers with reference to Romans 6:3-11. There are many passages in the patristic writings which deal with this theme, but one of the most vivid is found in one of Cyril of Jerusalem's sermons to the newly baptized, preached in a church built over the site of the Lord's own tomb:

Then you were conducted by the hand to the holy pool of sacred baptism, just as Christ was conveyed from the cross to the sepulcher close at hand . . . You made the confession that brings salvation, and submerged yourselves three times in the water and emerged: by this symbolic gesture you were secretly re-enacting the burial of Christ three days in the tomb. For just as our Savior spent three days and nights in the hollow bosom of the earth, so you upon first emerging were representing Christ's first day in the earth, and by your immersion his first night. For at night one can no longer see but during the day one has light; so you saw nothing when immersed as if it were night, but you emerged as if to the light of day. In one and the same action, you died and were born; the water of salvation became both tomb and mother for you. What Solomon said of others is apposite to you. On that occasion he said: "There is a time to be born and time to die" [Eccl 3:2], but the opposite is true in your case—there is a time to die and a time to be born. A single moment achieves both ends, and your beginning was simultaneous with your death.

What a strange and astonishing situation! We did not really die, we were not really buried, we did not really hang from a cross and rise again. Our imitation was symbolic, but our salvation was a reality. Christ truly hung from a cross, was truly buried, and truly rose again. All this he did gratuitously for us, so that we might share his sufferings by imitating them, and gain salvation in actuality. What transcendent kindness!

Christ endured nails in his hands and feet, and suffered pain; and by let-
ting me participate in the pain without anguish or sweat, he freely
bestows salvation on me (2:4-5; Yarnold, pp. 76-77).

St. Cyril is here enlarging upon the statement of Paul in Romans 6:5 that
"we have been united with [Christ] in a death like his," or more literally, "we
have been united with him in the image of his death." The drama of "going
under" is the ritual imitation or likeness of the Lord's own death. It is a
watery grave that we go into, rather than an earthen one, and we are spared
the terrible sufferings of Christ and the agony of physical death. Yet something has happened which makes this a real death, undergone in the hope of
being "united with Christ also in the image of his resurrection" (*ibid.*).

This is rightly called a mystery, the "paschal mystery," not in the sense of
a riddle or problem which cannot be solved, but in the sense in which I might
speak of another human being or of myself as a mystery: something which
can be experienced but never really defined, into which I may catch insights,
but which I shall never understand exhaustively. And death is a mystery, for
what does it mean to die? Certainly it means the radical break with all the
various ties of affection and claims of responsibility that make up each person's world; it means breaking with life as it is known, leaving the past
behind; it means going beyond the reach of the law, abandoning the security
of the tried and the familiar, escaping the claims of unpaid debts and un-
finished business. But it also means going into the darkness of the totally
unknown, abandoning oneself to one knows not what. For most of us, this
fear of the unknown weighs more than the burden of past and present or
the hopelessness of an uncertain future. Of all terrors, death, not simply as a
physical event but as a human experience, is the ultimate and greatest threat,
"the last enemy" as St. Paul calls it (1 Cor 15:26).

It is not primarily as a physical occurrence that the death of Jesus is important, but as a human event. Most people hope that death will just happen
to them, so that it will not be a human experience for them. But Jesus "gave
himself up to death," making it a significant gesture, the climax of a life of
self-giving. He abandoned himself in death, as he had given himself in life, to
his Father. Just by doing that, he transformed the human significance of
death. No longer need it be an inescapable defeat against which we can only
struggle despairingly. It can now be the last act of love, a final, total, un-
reserved act of commitment to the will of the Father, the consummation of
the obedience of faith. This is the pattern of Christ's life and death to which
we are conformed by the sacramental act of baptism. God has validated this
way of death in raising his Son from the dead: "If we have died with Christ,
we believe that we shall also live with him. For we know that Christ being
raised from the dead will never die again; death no longer has dominion over
him" (Rom 6:8-9). The cross which overshadows the baptismal font is both
death and life: "By your cross and resurrection you have set us free: you are
the Savior of the world!"

This transformation of death does not spare us from the inevitability of death as a physical event, but it both takes the sting out of death and is already a foretaste of the resurrection of the body. "Death is swallowed up in victory," it is overcome in every way. "O death, where is thy sting?" cries St. Paul. And he continues: "The sting of death is sin, and the power of sin is the law" (Rom 15:55-56). While we live under the rule of the law, we are constantly trying to prove ourselves to be law-abiding and constantly being found wanting. But when we live, not by the law, but by faith in Christ and under the power of his Spirit, our union with God and our hope of life are guaranteed, not by our deserts, but by God's love for us manifested in the life and death and resurrection of Jesus. Thus the Christian, conformed in baptism and in life to the pattern of Christ's own death, can say with Paul: "I have been crucified with Christ; it is no longer I who live, but Christ who lives in me; and the life I now live in the flesh I live by faith in the Son of God, who loved me and gave himself for me" (Gal 2:20).

The sacrament of faith, as we described it earlier, is thus identical with baptism as the sacrament of the Lord's cross and resurrection. To live that life of faith is to live with that same mind which was in Christ, who "emptied himself, taking the form of a servant, being born in the likeness of men. And being found in human form he humbled himself and became obedient unto death, even death on a cross. Therefore God has highly exalted him . . ." (Phil 2:5-9). This is the life-style of every baptized person, marked as we are with the sign of Christ's cross and sustained by our hope of resurrection with Christ.

Still, resurrection remains a matter of hope. In a certain sense we already share the risen life of Jesus and this is experienced whenever his victory over sin and death shines through the Christian's life. Whenever evil is resisted, truth upheld, adversity born patiently and cheerfully, injustice resisted, love cherished and violence turned aside by the strength of non-violence, there God's kingdom breaks through and the victory of Christ appears. But such transformations of human life will always be precarious. They are the flickering presentiments of a new era which, because of Christ's resurrection, is now in the most literal sense a foregone conclusion. The glory that is Christ's is yet to break definitively over the face of our earth, and as long as human history continues, every man and every woman will still be free to make their own decision. We live now by faith; what the fulness of the risen life will mean we do not yet know. So Paul is careful to say, not "we have been buried with him and we have been raised with him," but "if we have died with Christ, we believe that we shall also live with him" (Rom 6:8). The life of faith is a life of dying with Christ; it is the basis of our hope in the resurrection.

It is important to realize this because otherwise the sacraments might appear somehow magical or else totally unrealistic. For baptism does not make us sinless or immortal or free or loving, as we know only too well. What it does is enable us to *become* all these things. It opens the way for us to become free, loving, spirited and victorious over death. It is the crucial break: the offer to us by God in Christ of a way out of the vicious circle of defeat and powerlessness. But it is an offer which we have to take very much to heart and live out day by day. Baptism is an initiation into a different way of life, a way of life which we have to make our own in this world if we are to experience the power of the resurrection within us. Baptism sets us free to be free. As an ancient Greek writer put it: "He who daily rises from his own past will not be surprised by the resurrection from the dead." For such a person, the waters of death have proved to be the waters of life, as that person clings to the cross of the Lord.

A person comes into this world as a frail child, not as a ready made adult. Similarly with the newly baptized. They are not full-grown Christians. The first letter of Peter, generally reckoned to be an early homily to the newly baptized, addresses its readers as "new-born babes," as does Paul in his first letter to the Christians of Corinth (1 Pet 2:2; 1 Cor 3:1). Like a child, the newly baptized person has a capacity for life, for the life of Christ, which has to be nourished, strengthened and developed. The image of rebirth, therefore, expresses well the delicate and precarious nature of the grace received, as well as its radical newness. Being baptized means no more than simply being born into the world unless the baptized person lives out the baptismal life and grows from strength to strength. It is not an achievement, but a gift; not something over and done with, but a beginning. The Church is not a mother who abandons her child. We have already seen how the community is committed to being responsible for those whom it baptizes. This is expressed in a small and discreet rubric with a long history: "If baptism is by immersion, the godmother or godfather lifts the child out of the font" (RBC, 60). The child's parents put the baby into the water (or hold the child if baptism is by infusion); but the godparents, representatives of the Church, deliver the child into the new life which is God's gift to him or her. They are rightly called God-parents: in terms of the new life the child is now beginning, they are closest kith and kin. So conscious has the Church always been of this that she has extended to this relationship the sort of incest taboos which prevail between a person and one's natural family. But this impediment to marriage is just the negative side of what has surely been a very close tie in the past. If relations between godparents and godchildren had not been warm and familiar, how can one account for the fact that our English word "gossip" is but the corruption of "godship" and originally served as a term of address and endearment between a person and those who had received the child when he or she was brought forth from the font?

It used to be the custom, a custom the present rite would like to see restored (RBC, 60), to acclaim the newly baptized with songs or chants. Here is one given in the Appendix to the rite, and taken originally from the baptismal liturgy of the Christians of East Syria:

Holy Church of God, stretch out your hand
and welcome your children
newborn of water
and of the Spirit of God (RBC, 243).

8. . . . and a form of words

According to the letter to the Ephesians, Christ made the Church whom he loved clean "by washing her with water and a form of words" (5:26). It is not the water alone that is the sign of baptism, but the bathing in water together with the word of faith. "Word and element come together to form a sacrament, which is, as it were, a visible word," says St. Augustine. Like the whole history of salvation in the past, the sacrament too is realized "by deeds and words having an inner unity" (Divine Revelation, 2). Like the caption on a photograph, the words of baptism point to the significance of the ritual being enacted: both together constitute a single sacramental sign, a visible medium for the hidden work of God.

While we have been at pains to emphasize the role and importance of faith in the celebration of baptism, it must nevertheless be remembered that in the last analysis the whole celebration is at the same time the work of God. It is he who calls us to faith, he who pours out his Spirit to prompt us to faith and to prayer. Thus while the whole rite is a form of prayer and an expression of the Church's faith, it is also the vehicle through which God continues to reach out to his people.

We have already seen that the more usual way of administering baptism in the early centuries was for the person being baptized to make a three-fold profession of faith while standing in the water. In Syria, however, the words of Matthew 28:19, "Go therefore and make disciples of all nations, baptizing them in the name of the Father and of the Son and of the Holy Spirit," seem to have been adopted as a formula for baptism from the beginning. It gradually spread through the East and came into Europe through Spain, being finally adopted at Rome in place of the ancient interrogations in the eighth century. One of the reasons for the adoption of this formula must almost certainly have been its suitability for infant baptism, since it did not demand the active cooperation of the person being baptized.

In the East, the form used is: "N. is baptized in the name of the Father and of the Son and of the Holy Spirit." Such an objective declaration sounds somewhat strange to our Western ears, but its meaning is well explained by Theodore of Mopsuestia, who points out that the priest, using this impersonal form, proclaims himself to be "simply the obedient minister" and that "the Father, the Son and the Holy Spirit are the cause of the gifts we receive at baptism" (Bapt. Hom. III, 15). On the other hand, when the priest in the Roman rite says "I baptize you in the name of the Father, etc.," he is expressing the conviction that when the Church acts in the sacraments it is Christ who acts through her. Although St. John Chrysostom used the Eastern formula for baptism, his comments on the role of the priest express perfectly the meaning of our text: "No angel or archangel can be effective in the things which come from God. The Father, the Son and the Holy Spirit do everything; the priest simply lends his tongue and his hand" (*On John*, 86:4). Thus in either form the conviction is the same: that when baptism is administered in the name of Christ, it is Christ himself who baptizes through the ministry of his Church.

But what does it mean to be baptized in the name of the Trinity? Justice may be administered "in the name of the law," that is to say, under its authority and with all the rights and sanctions that law provides; but here all this is implied, and something more. Before he died, Jesus prayed for his disciples: "Holy Father, keep them in thy name, which thou hast given me, that they may be one even as we are one" (John 17:11). God has revealed his name to us and shown who he is through Jesus. To believe in the name of Jesus is to commit oneself to the God who has come close to us in him. To live, to pray, to assemble in the name of Jesus is thus to live, to pray and to assemble in a way which is characterized by a relationship of intimacy with the Father through Jesus in the Holy Spirit. The Acts of the Apostles talks simply of "baptism in the name of Jesus," but the meaning is the same (see Acts 8:16; 10:48; 19:5). To believe in the name of Jesus is to be able to call God, "the Father of our Lord Jesus Christ" (Eph 1:3), "our Father." It is to be animated by the Spirit of Jesus, a Spirit who prompts us to cry out: "Abba! Father!" (Rom 8:15). In other words, by faith in Jesus we discover God to be our Father and by being baptized in that faith we are adopted as children, being drawn into the very life of God by the "Spirit of adoption" (*ibid.*).

Thus the formula "N., I baptize you in the name of the Father and of the Son and of the Holy Spirit" indicates that through this rite of baptism we are drawn into a new set of relationships with Father, Son and Spirit. Baptism unites us with Christ, who said, "The Father and I are one" (John 10:30), reconciling us with him for the forgiveness of sin through the Holy Spirit. In this way we are caught up into the intimacy of God's own life. Our God may live in "unapproachable light," but he is a God who has come in search of us by sending his Son in history and together they send the Spirit now that we might share the unity that they enjoy.

In this brief formula, all the effects of baptism are implicitly contained. Being incorporated into the Church, the Body of Christ, we are incorporated into Christ himself. With Christ, we become children by adoption of his Father, whom Christ teaches us to address confidently as "our Father." As sons and daughters of the Father, we are co-heirs with Christ to the Kingdom of God (Gal 4:7). This adoption and transformation are effected by the gift of the Spirit. It is the Spirit who is the bond of love between Father and Son, so that when we receive him we are drawn into that union in such a way that the Father looks at us and sees the likeness of his beloved Son. This gift of the Spirit means the forgiveness of sin, for all that separates us from God is overcome and the distance between us is reconciled. This is what we have traditionally called "sanctifying grace," the grace that makes us holy; it is nothing less than the presence in our lives of the Spirit of Jesus himself. The Eastern Churches, speaking of the same reality, prefer to use the term "divinization" which expresses very forcibly the transformative potential of the gift of the Spirit.

All this has been made possible by the cross of Christ. "Do you believe in our Lord Jesus Christ and in his cross?" St. Ambrose used to ask those being baptized. The water is poured over the child's head three times in the form of a cross as the child is baptized in the name of the Father and of the Son and of the Holy Spirit. The child was first welcomed to the Christian assembly with the sign of the cross and throughout life will learn to begin each day, each prayer and every serious undertaking with the sign of the cross made "in the name of the Father and of the Son and of the Holy Spirit." With that the baptized will center on the presence of the saving God who has sought this person in the past, who seeks this one yet, and who will not fail to deliver and bring this person into his glory. "Beloved, we are God's children now; it does not yet appear what we shall be, but we know that when he appears we shall be like him, for we shall see him as he is. And everyone who thus hopes in him purifies himself as he is pure" (1 John 3:2-3).

The Father's voice calls us above the waters,
the glory of the Son shines on us,
the love of the Spirit fills us with life (RBC, 242).

9. *Anointing with Chrism*

The Roman baptismal liturgy is unique in the way it uses anointing after baptism, for the newly baptized are anointed first by a priest and then by the bishop. The pattern dates from the earliest times and is clearly seen in the instructions given in the third century *Apostolic Tradition:*

And afterwards, when he comes up out of the water he shall be anointed by the presbyter with the Oil of Thanksgiving, saying: "I anoint you with holy oil in the name of Jesus Christ.
[The newly baptized then dress and are led to the bishop who lays his hands on them and invokes the Spirit.]
After this, he pours the consecrated oil from his hand and laying his hand on their heads he shall say: I anoint you with holy oil in God the Father almighty and Christ Jesus and the Holy Spirit.
And sealing them on the forehead, he shall give them the kiss of peace . . . (*Ap. Trad.* xxi, 19-xxii, 3; Whitaker, p. 6).

How this double anointing originated is impossible to say, but with the breakup of the unity of the rites of initiation this second, episcopal anointing became identified as a separate sacrament of confirmation. In the liturgy of

St. Ambrose of Milan and in the Syrian liturgy of Theodore of Mopsuestia we find but one anointing after baptism and that is administered by the bishop. This too became identified with confirmation even when, in the absence of a bishop, it was administered by a priest; and this seems to have been the general pattern outside those rites where the Roman tradition made its influence felt. Interestingly enough, the priestly anointing is omitted in the revised Roman rite if, as in the rite of adult initiation, the sacrament of confirmation is conferred in the same celebration (RCIA, 223–224).

What is the meaning of this anointing? First, we need to distinguish it quite clearly from the anointing which has already taken place before baptism. The first was administered on the breast as a gesture of protection; this is oil poured out upon the head as a celebration of joy. The first was plain olive oil; this is "chrism," a perfumed oil. The first was what Hippolytus called "the Oil of Exorcism," or what we call "the Oil of Catechumens"; this chrism, however, is "the Oil of Thanksgiving," sometimes called, in a reference to Ps 45:7, "oil of gladness." This oil is not a liniment, but a cosmetic, called in the East "myron" or "myrrh." "The myrrh is for the bride, the oil for the athlete," says St. John Chrysostom.

It is clear from the references to it given by the Fathers, that this was not something dabbed on and rubbed off again. It was a heavily scented oil, poured out lavishly over the newly baptized: the after-bath lotion of the ancient world, the heady perfume of the new bride.

> Was not David speaking of this when he said,
> 'It is like the precious oil upon the beard,
> running down upon the beard,
> upon the beard of Aaron,
> upon the collar of his robes!' (Ps 133:2)
> This is the ointment Solomon spoke of,
> 'Your name is oil poured out,
> therefore the maidens love you' (Song of Songs 1:3).
> How many souls reborn today have loved you, Lord Jesus, saying, 'Draw us after you, we hasten after the perfume of your robes, that they may drink in the odor of your resurrection!'
>
> (Ambrose, *On the Mysteries*, VI, 29).

A further indication of the lavishness with which this oil was applied is the fact that the newly baptized needed a band of linen, known in medieval England as the "chrisom," wrapped around their head, presumably to keep the oil out of their eyes.

The significance of the anointing is indicated by the words addressed to the child beforehand:

> God, the Father of our Lord Jesus Christ,
> has freed you from sin,
> given you a new birth by water and the Holy Spirit,

and welcomed you into his holy people.
He now anoints you with the chrism of salvation.
As Christ was anointed Priest, Prophet, and King,
so may you live always as members of his body,
sharing everlasting life (RBC, 62).

The effect of baptism is that we are reconciled with God in Christ and enter into a new kind of life, the life of the Spirit, which is the life by which Christ himself lives. It is this Spirit-given identity with Christ which the anointing celebrates above all, for the name "Christ" (Greek: christos) means "one who has been anointed."

In the Old Testament, kings were anointed to set them apart for the service of God, for they were to rule the people of God in his name and with his authority. This made them sacred to God, so that it was considered a sacrilege to strike a blow against the anointed king. Priests, too, and sacred objects and vessels used for the worship of God were also consecrated with oil to set them apart from profane use and thereby to indicate that they were at the service of God in his dealings with his people. In the prophetic tradition, the image of such an anointing was used to suggest the way in which the Spirit of God could seize men or women, making them messengers of God to others. Looking to the day when God would re-establish his people in peace and security forever, the Jews expected God to raise up and anoint for himself a king (Isa 9:1-6; 11:1-9; etc.) or a priest (Ps 110:4) or both (Zech 6:12-14). Jesus is the Christ, the anointed one, because he is the one sent by God with divine authority (Matt 28:18; John 5:43). But he also identifies himself with the mysterious Suffering Servant, the prophetic figure whose words he quotes and applies to himself: "The Spirit of the Lord is upon me, because he has anointed me to preach the good news to the poor" (Isa 61:1ff.; Luke 4:18-20).

This "anointing" of Jesus to undertake the work his Father gave him was made manifest in his baptism in the Jordan (Mark 1:9-11 and par.) when the Spirit was seen to descend upon him. This event, together with the ancient association of bath oil with bath water, must have suggested our present rite. Certainly, the Fathers explain this anointing by reference to this incident:

Now that you have been 'baptized into Christ' and have 'put on Christ,' you have become conformed to the Son of God. For God 'destined us to be his sons,' so he has made us like to 'the glorious body of Christ.' Hence, since you 'share in Christ' it is right to call you Christs or anointed ones . . .

Christ bathed in the river Jordan, and having invested the waters with the presence of his body, he emerged from them, and the Holy Spirit visited him in substantial form, like resting upon like. In the same way, when you emerged from the pool of sacred waters you were anointed in a manner corresponding with Christ's anointing (Cyril of Jerusalem, *Myst. Cat.* 3; Yarnold, pp. 79–80).

Thus the anointing with perfumed oil is the joyful acknowledgement that we are one with Christ, living members of his body, members through whom he continues to live in the world and to act among us for our salvation and for the Father's glory. "You are a chosen race, a royal priesthood, a holy nation, God's own people, that you may declare the wonderful deeds of him who brought you out of darkness into his own wonderful light" (1 Pet 2:9). In and through Christ, the baptized proclaim the works of God in the liturgy, in the assembly of his people, and bear witness to his name in the world by word and by the testimony of their lives. It is by baptism, then, that a person is given the right to take part in the liturgy of the Church and to share in her sacraments, for "the sacred liturgy . . . is the whole public worship which our redeemer, the head of the Church, offers to the heavenly Father and which the community of Christ's faithful pays to its founder, and through him to the eternal Father" (Pius XII, *Mystici Corporis*, 20).

The baptized person shares in the kingship of Christ, too, insofar as one submits to the rule of God in all that is done. Wherever there is a Christian, there should the rule and kingdom of God be visible in the world. Such a one owes allegiance now, not to the kingdom of darkness but to the kingdom of light; and in this kingdom the baptized is no mere lackey, but a member of the royal family. "His head is anointed," says John the Deacon (c. 500), "with the unction of sacred chrism, that the baptized person may understand that in his person a kingdom and a priestly mystery have met" (Whitaker, p. 157). "To him who loves us and has freed us from our sins by his blood and made us a kingdom, priests to his God and Father, to him be glory and dominion for ever and ever. Amen" (Rev 1:5-6).

10. *Clothing with the White Garment*

In the days when adult baptism was common and baptism by immersion was the rule, the inevitable taking off and putting on of clothes was invariably attributed with symbolic meaning. "Upon entering [the baptistry] you took off your clothing, and this symbolized your stripping of 'the old nature with its practices' [Col 3:9]. Stripped naked, in this too you were imitating Christ naked on the cross, who in his darkness 'disarmed the principalities and powers' and on the wood of the cross publicly 'triumphed over them' [Col 2:15] . . . This was a remarkable occasion, for you stood naked in the sight of all and you were not ashamed. You truly mirrored our first-created parent Adam, who stood naked in paradise and was not ashamed" (Cyril of Jerusalem, *Myst. Cat.* 2:2; Yarnold, pp. 74–75).

Perhaps this baptismal experience of undressing and dressing lies behind the Pauline imagery of casting off "the works of darkness" (Rom 13:12), sins (Col 3:8), in short, "the old man" (Eph 4:26; Col 3:9), in order to put on "the Lord Jesus Christ" (Rom 13:14; Gal 3:27), the "new man" (Eph 4:24; Col 3:10), "immortality" (1 Cor 15:53-54), "the breastplate of faith and love" (1 Thess 5:8). Certainly it was this sort of awareness of the new identity of the baptized which made it unthinkable that one should just put old clothes back on after drying off. At least, this is true of the fourth century, when people began to look for meaning in every detail of the rite.

"As soon as you come up out of the font, you put on a dazzling garment of pure white. This is a sign to the world of shining splendor and the way of life to which you have already passed in symbol," writes Theodore of Mopsuestia (*Bapt. Hom.* III, 26). Just as the apostles were given a glimpse of the glory of Christ when they saw him transfigured, "and his face shone like the sun, and his garments became white as light" (Matt 17:2), so now the newly baptized, dressed in pure white, their faces glistening with oil, catch a glimpse of their own future transfiguration, when the time comes for them to take their places in that innumerable multitude of people "from every nation, from all tribes and peoples and tongues, standing before the throne and before the Lamb, clothed in white robes, with palm branches in their hands" (Rev 7:9).

At the baptismal vigil of Easter, the newly baptized would be led into the church where the community was assembled and where the faithful had been occupied with prayer on their behalf. One can imagine the impact of their arrival: these figures who had been on the fringe of the community for so long, now being brought into its midst in their shining white robes. In the East, the community would strike up a chant, greeting them in the words of Paul: "In Christ Jesus you are all sons of God through faith. For as many of you as were baptized into Christ have put on Christ. Alleluia!" (Gal 3:26–27).

Here the community would be reminded not only of their own baptism and of their present baptismal identity, but of their future glory:

> All the neophytes are arrayed in white vesture to symbolize the resurgent Church, just as our Lord himself in the sight of certain disciples and prophets was thus transfigured on the mount, so that it was said: 'His face did shine as the sun; his raiment was made as white as snow' [Matt 17:2]. This prefigured for the future the resurgent Church, of which it is written: 'Who is this that riseth up' [Cant. 3:6] all in white? And so they wear white raiment so that though the ragged dress of ancient error has darkened the infancy of their first birth, the costume of their second birth should display the raiment of glory, so that clad in a wedding garment he may approach the table of the heavenly bridegroom as a new man (Letter of John the Deacon; Whitaker, p. 157).

The last lines of John's commentary on the baptismal garment touch on two other references. The first is to the theme of the Church as bride of Christ, a theme based upon the letter to the Ephesians 5:21–32 and developed by the interpretation of the Song of Songs as being a dialogue of love between Christ and his bride. Dressed in white, the newly baptized represent the Church in her wedding dress, a bride that Christ presents to himself "in splendor, without spot or wrinkle or any such thing, that she might be holy and without blemish" (Eph 5:26-27). At the same time, given that the newly baptized are about to take part for the very first time in the Eucharistic meal, if they are adults, their white robes remind us of the parable told by Jesus of the king who gave a marriage feast for his son and required that his guests come dressed in appropriate wedding garments (Matt 22:11).

This rite, together with the anointing which precedes it and the giving of the lighted candle and the 'Ephphetha Rite' which follow, is numbered among the "Explanatory Rites" (RCIA, 263). As such, too much cannot be claimed for it in terms of its importance for the celebration of baptism, but it is nevertheless an ancient usage which, intelligently observed, still retains its expressive power. When a child is baptized, the rubric suggests that it is desirable that the parents themselves provide the robe (RBC, 63). Ideally, perhaps, the mother might make it herself during her pregnancy as she thinks of the child she is carrying and of how the mercy of God already reaches out to her baby: "Before I formed you in the womb I knew you, and before you were born I consecrated you" (Jer 1:5).

The celebrant gives each child a white garment, and parents and godparents put it on the child:

(N., N.,) you have become a new creation,
and have clothed yourselves in Christ.
See in this white garment
the outward sign of your Christian dignity.
With your family and friends
to help you by word and example,
bring that dignity unstained
into the everlasting life of heaven (RBC, 63).

In the fourth and fifth centuries, the newly baptized used to wear their white baptismal gowns for a whole week. For this reason the Sunday after Easter in the Tridentine missal still bore the title "Dominica in albis [deponendis]": "the Sunday for laying aside the white garments." The entry chant for the Mass of that day was taken from 1 Peter 2:2—"Like newborn babes, alleluia, long for the pure spiritual milk, alleluia"; with Psalm 81, "Shout aloud to God our strength, shout for joy to the God of Jacob!" On this day they took their places for the first time among the ranks of the faithful, the believers. On each of the previous weekdays following their baptism on Easter Night, they had come to the church in their white garments to hear the bishop explain the meaning of the rites they had experienced that night, and to celebrate the Eucharist. This week of wearing white was, like the whole Easter season running from the paschal vigil to Pentecost, a period of joy and festivity, reminding them that through baptism they have become people of the future, people who, while still very much in this world, nevertheless belong to the new era of the world to come. "If then you have been raised with Christ, seek the things that are above, where Christ is, seated at the right hand of God. Set your minds on things that are above, not on things that are on earth. For you have died, and your life is hid with Christ in God.

When Christ who is our life appears, then you will also appear with him in glory" (Col 3:1-4).

11. *The Lighted Candle*

The proper name for the newly baptized is "neophytes," meaning "the newly enlightened." This name derives, clearly, from the Greek-speaking Churches, where those preparing for baptism are called *photizomenoi*, "those to be enlightened." These are ancient names, and if the rite of presenting a lighted candle is itself a comparative newcomer to the baptismal liturgy (being a medieval innovation), the idea behind it has been associated with baptism from the beginning.

According to St. John, Christ identified himself as "the light of the world" (John 8:12), promising that "he who follows me will not walk in darkness, but will have the light of life." This theme of the light shining in the darkness runs through all the pages of the New Testament and finds an echo in what is most probably an ancient baptismal hymn quoted in the letter to the Ephesians:

Awake, O sleeper, and arise from the dead,
and Christ shall give you light (5:14).

Each evening, the lighting of the lights served as an occasion for generations of Christian people to give thanks to God for Christ, "the true light that enlightens every man" (John 1:9), making known the God who "dwells in unapproachable light" (1 Tim 6:16). Another early Christian hymn, used for the lighting of the lights, celebrates this fact:

O radiant light, O sun divine
Of God the Father's deathless face,
O image of the light sublime
That fills the heavenly dwelling place.

Nowadays it is generally only at the beginning of the Easter Vigil that this ancient ritual survives, with the lighting of the paschal candle. Outside the Easter season, the paschal candle stands beside the font, ready, as a symbol of the risen Lord, to shine on all who pass from death to life, from darkness to light in the baptismal waters. It is this Easter candle which the celebrant now takes and holds out to the parents and godparents: "Receive the light of Christ."

One of the parents or godparents lights a small candle from the paschal candle on behalf of their child. Holding it carefully for the child, they hear the celebrant saying:

Parents and godparents, this light is entrusted to you to be kept burning brightly. These children of yours have been enlightened by Christ. They are to walk always as children of the light. May they keep the flame of faith alive in their hearts. When the Lord comes, may they go out to meet him with all the saints in the heavenly kingdom (RBC, 64).

The excellent custom has arisen in recent years of a special baptismal candle being prepared for each child with his or her name and appropriate baptismal symbols decorating it. This is then preserved to remind the child of baptism and to be lit perhaps on the anniversary of baptism or at confirmation, first Communion, or other significant moments in the Christian life, as a reminder to walk as a child of light, "for the fruit of light is to be found in all that is good and right and true" (Eph 5:9). Finally, it should burn beside the baptized as he or she lies dying, and stand, with the paschal candle, beside the coffin, as one makes that final journey through the impenetrable darkness of death into the light that is God. This burning candle, of course, is no more than a token of the light of Christ shining within the baptized. It is that light which will save this person, if he or she can remain true to it. "The kingdom of heaven shall be compared to ten maidens who took their lamps and went to meet the bridegroom . . ." (Matt 25:1ff.).

12. *The Ephphetha Rite*

In Mark 7:33-36, Jesus is recounted as having healed a man who was both deaf and suffering from a speech impediment. He did so by touching the man's mouth and ears, "and looking up to heaven, he sighed, and said to him, 'Ephphetha,' that is, 'Be opened.' And his ears were opened, his tongue was released, and he spoke plainly." Such an incident was remembered, not for its curiosity value, but because it summed up so perfectly what the presence of Jesus was about. He was on earth to enable people to hear the word of God and to respond to it. He was re-opening communications between God and the world, as the little aside about his looking up to heaven and sighing indicates.

This rite has been used for centuries in the preparation of candidates for baptism, preparing them to hear the gospel and to respond in words of faith and prayer. In the rite of adult initiation, it takes place on Holy Saturday morning, some hours before the baptismal vigil starts and in connection with their public recitation of the creed. Here, in infant baptism, it concludes the baptismal rites, and by so doing serves to point to the future, to the day when the children will be old enough to speak for themselves and to make their own the faith of Christ in which they have been baptized:

> The Lord Jesus made the deaf hear and the dumb speak. May he soon touch your ears to receive his word, and your mouth to proclaim his faith, to the praise and glory of God the Father (RBC, 65).

13. *Conclusion of the Rite*

The baptismal part of the liturgy of Christian initiation for children comes to an end with a procession to the altar for the recitation of the Lord's Prayer and the blessing and dismissal of the families and the whole congregation. In actual fact, this final scene is a reminder that only the first act is drawing to a close. The whole drama of initiation is not unfolded until the children have been confirmed with the gift of the Holy Spirit and taken their place at the table of the Lord. As the words of the celebrant indicate, the children are already children of God, but their initiation is not yet complete. They have yet to receive the seal of the Spirit and to partake of the body and blood of the Lord. According to the long established custom of the Western Churches, these further stages of initiation are now to be postponed until the children are of an age to be able to cooperate in their "christening," their assimilation to Christ.

In the meantime, and in anticipation of that day, we pray in their name to their Father and ours, to the God who has fathered us all by adopting us in Christ through the one Spirit whom he has given to us all.

There is one God, one Father of all:
he is over all, and through all:
he lives in all of us (RBC, 228).

PART THREE

CONFIRMATION

I

CONFIRMATION AND BAPTISM

Today as in the past, those who receive the call to faith as adults and submit to the sacraments of Christian initiation are confirmed immediately after the baptismal rites we have described, and are then admitted at once to the celebration of the Eucharist. The three sacraments together form a single climax to the long process of conversion. In the case of children, however, at least in the Western Church, confirmation and first Communion are generally separated from baptism by a time span of several years. Because of this, it is often found difficult to explain what the meaning of confirmation is, or to decide at what age it should be conferred, or indeed to know why it should be celebrated at all. We have already seen that the Holy Spirit is given in baptism, so what does confirmation do that baptism does not? In this chapter we shall be attempting to come to grips with these questions by looking at the history of confirmation in relation to baptism. This will prepare the way for a close look at the rite of confirmation in the next chapter.

1. *Baptism and the Spirit*

The Christian era is the era of the Holy Spirit. Just as the Old Testament was the era when human relationships with God were regulated by the Law, the New Testament is the time when human relationships with God are under the gracious influence of the Spirit. This was the Spirit whose outpouring the prophets had anticipated, whose coming Jesus had promised. As he prepared to pass from this world to the Father, he promised his disciples that "the Holy Spirit, whom the Father will send in my name, will teach you all things and bring to your remembrance all that I have said to you" (John 14:26). According to Luke, Jesus told his disciples after his resurrection not to leave Jerusalem but to await their baptism with the Holy Spirit, promising them: "You shall receive power when the Holy Spirit has come upon you; and you shall be my witnesses in Jerusalem and in all Judea and Samaria and to the end of the earth" (Acts 1:4-8).

According to John, it was on the day of the resurrection itself that Jesus poured out his Spirit upon his apostles. "Jesus came and stood among them and said to them, 'Peace be with you.'. . . Then the disciples were glad when they saw the Lord. Jesus said to them again, 'Peace be with you! As the Father has sent me, even so I send you.' And when he had said this, he

107

breathed on them, and said to them, 'Receive the Holy Spirit. If you forgive the sins of any, they are forgiven; if you retain the sins of any, they are retained'" (John 20:19-23). Luke, remembering the giving of the old Law in the dramatic theophany of Sinai, represents the promulgation of the new era as taking place at the feast of Pentecost, the feast when the giving of the Law was celebrated among the Jews. There the Spirit erupts among the apostles in tongues of flame and roars of thunder, flooding weak men with new courage and rendering their words of witness intelligible to all. Peter explained this with reference to the prophecy of Joel:

And in the last days it shall be, God declares,
that I shall pour out my Spirit upon all flesh,
and your sons and your daughters shall prophesy,
and your young men shall see visions,
and your old men shall dream dreams;
yea, and on my menservants and my maidservants
    in those days
I will pour out my Spirit; and they shall prophesy . . .
And it shall be that whoever calls on the name of
    the Lord shall be saved (Joel 2:28-32; Acts 2:16-21).

This new age had been made possible only by the death and resurrection of Jesus, to which the apostles were witnesses. "Being therefore exalted at the right hand of God, and having received from the Father the promise of the Holy Spirit, he [Jesus] has poured out this which you see and hear" (Acts 2:33). A share in this Spirit is the lot of all who put their faith in Jesus, Peter tells the Jews: "Repent, and be baptized every one of you in the name of Jesus Christ for the forgiveness of your sins; and you shall receive the gift of the Holy Spirit" (Acts 2:38).

These texts testify that there was an indissoluble connection between faith in Jesus, the forgiveness of sins and the gift of the Holy Spirit. These three things constitute membership of the new era into which people enter through the celebration of baptism. The Church, the Body of Christ, is constituted by faith, reconciliation and the common bond of the Spirit, so that a person shares all three upon entering the Church by baptism.

The living experience of the Spirit in the Christian life is something which goes beyond simple definition however. Even in the Scriptures, the Spirit of God is something felt and experienced rather than something which can be adequately described. In the Old Testament, the Spirit is the active power of God manifest among people in his creative and redemptive work. It seizes upon individuals, making each a chosen instrument of God's purposes, to serve as a judge or a king, a priest or a prophet. In the Gospels of Matthew and Mark, the Holy Spirit is understood in similar terms: as the unpredictable intervention of God to do battle on behalf of his people through Jesus against the evil spirits which enslave us.

For John and Paul, the presence among us of the Spirit is constitutive of the new era opened by the exaltation of Jesus. For Paul, it is the Spirit which forms the Church into an organic unity, the one body of Christ, "for by one Spirit we were all baptized into one body" (1 Cor 12:13). For John, the presence of the Spirit in the Church enables Jesus to continue his work of salvation (John 14:26; 16:8-14) and of glorifying the Father (John 4:23-24). To be baptized in the name of Jesus is to be baptized in his Spirit (1 Cor 6:11; 12:13) and to begin to live by the Spirit (Rom 8:1ff.). It is to be reborn as children of God by water and the Spirit (John 3:5ff.; 1 John 3:24). This may manifest itself in charismatic gifts (1 Cor 12:4ff.), but the purpose of them all is the building up of the Church (1 Cor 14:1ff.). Thus, while not forcing us but inviting our cooperation (1 Cor 14:32, 39; Gal 5:22-23), the Spirit moves us to faith (1 Cor 2: 7; 1 John 4:2), to love (Rom 5:5; 1 John 4:12-13), to prayer (Rom 8:15, 26), and to a moral life which contradicts the mendacity and corruption of an unbelieving world (Gal 5:22-23; John 16:8-11).

Luke, on the other hand, both in his gospel and especially in the Acts of the Apostles, emphasizes the missionary and prophetic drive of the Spirit. It is the Church itself which, like Jesus, is "clothed with power from on high" (Luke 24:49). This power is essentially a power of prophecy, enabling the community of believers to tell of "the mighty works of God" (Acts 2:11). This Spirit is poured out on all believers without distinction, men and women, Jews and pagans alike. But it seems to be given, not so much for the transformation of the individuals as to enable them to act as members of the prophetic community of believers. Thus the Spirit guides the Church in critical decisions (Acts 10:47; 15:28), gives prophetic foresight (Acts 11:28; see Luke 1:41, 67), enabling Church leaders to read the hearts of their adversaries (Acts 5:3; 11:9) and to discern the will of the Lord (Acts 10:19ff.; 11:12; 16:6). In Acts, as in John and Paul, the gift of the Spirit is associated closely with baptism. There are several instances where the presence of the Spirit is dramatically manifested in connection with baptism (Acts 9:17; 10:44-46; 11:15-17; 19:5-6), but equally significant is the repeated conviction that it was the Lord's initiative that lay behind the growth of the Church (Acts 2:47; 5:14; 11:24) and its consolidation (Acts 6:7; 8:31; 12:24; 16:5; 19:20; 28:30).

Thus the working of the Spirit is essential to the growth of the Church and the initiation of the individual, yet both of these are attributed to the rite of baptism. Outside the Acts of the Apostles, there is no reference to any rite of initiation except that of water and a form of words. In three famous texts in Acts, the link between baptism with water and the gift of the Spirit, so clearly evidenced everywhere else, seems to break down. In Acts 8:4-18, Peter and John go up from Jerusalem to Samaria to lay hands on the converts whom Philip the deacon had already baptized, "that they might receive the Holy Spirit; for it had not yet fallen on any of them, but they had only been baptized in the name of the Lord Jesus." The opinion seems to be gaining ground among modern exegetes, however, that this incident is cited by

Luke to emphasize the organic growth of the Church from the source-community in Jerusalem, where the Spirit had first been given. It is thus a story about the nature of the Church rather than about a second sacramental rite being necessary for the gift of the Spirit. In Acts 10:44, however, the Spirit comes down upon Cornelius and his pagan household even before baptism is given, thereby indicating that the mission of the Church is not only to the Jews but to all peoples. Once again, it is a story about the Church rather than about Christian initiation as such. In a third text, Acts 19:1-7, Paul is reported to have baptized some disciples of John the Baptist and then, "when Paul laid hands upon them, the Holy Spirit came on them; and they spoke with tongues and prophesied." This time the story is obviously recounted in order to say something about Christian initiation, but here it is precisely the difference between the baptism administered by the disciples of the Baptist and that administered in the name of Jesus which is at stake. The disciples of John the Baptist had to admit, "We have never even heard there is a Holy Spirit" (19:2), so that the point of the episode seems to be the same point made several times over in the gospels: that John baptized with water, but the baptism of Jesus would confer the Holy Spirit.

It is quite possible that Luke did know of a form of Christian initiation which used the double rite of washing in water and an imposition of hands, but there is no other New Testament evidence for it (except an obscure text in Heb 6:2). Nevertheless, later tradition will appeal to these Lucan texts to explain a practice which existed in the third century but whose origins are untraceable. Our earliest descriptions of the rites of initiation—the *Didache* and St. Justin—are ignorant of any such rite.

The same must be said of the subsequent use of New Testament texts to illustrate the meaning of the rites of "anointing" or "sealing" which followed baptism. In these cases appeal would be made to 2 Cor 1:22 and 1 John 2:20, 27. In 2 Corinthians Paul writes: "But it is God who establishes us with you in Christ, and has commissioned us; he has put his seal upon us and given us his Spirit in our hearts as a guarantee" (see also Eph 1:13; 4:30). This is a very important text, for it shows that in baptism God has marked us as his own by giving us his Spirit, and that the possession of his Spirit is a pledge of our future inheritance of a glory that is not yet given us. In the meantime, we are commissioned to do the work of God. In 1 John 2:20, 27 we are told: "You have been anointed by the Holy One . . . The anointing which you received from him abides in you, and you have no need that anyone should teach you; as his anointing teaches you everything, and is true, and is no lie, just as it has taught you, abide in him." Just as Jesus is the Anointed of God (Acts 4:27; 10:38; Luke 4:18), being anointed with the Spirit, so we too have been anointed with that same Spirit of truth, who will guide us into all truth and enable us to understand the revelation of Jesus (John 16:13-14). But in both cases a figure of speech is being used to express the gift of the Spirit: he is the "seal" with which God has marked us as his own and which is our guarantee of glory; he is the power with which God has "anointed" us to enable us to remain faithful to Christ and to his work.

We can summarize the evidence of the New Testament about initiation by saying that everything was given in a single rite of baptism with water, accompanied by a word of faith: forgiveness of sins, incorporation into Christ, the gift of the Spirit, the pledge of immortality. In the second century, this initiation came to be known by a whole series of names which, taken together, give us some insight into the richness of meaning which the simple rite of initiation was seen to contain. It was known as the water-bath, regeneration, illumination, the washing, the seal, grace, and perfection. The water-bath and the washing clearly refer to the rite itself; grace refers to the gracious initiative of God who loves us before we love him and saves us for himself; illumination refers to the new vision which faith and baptism set before us; regeneration refers to the wholly new life which is given us in the Spirit; the names "seal" and "perfection" refer to the unrepeatable, because irreversible, mercy of God who has established us permanently in his love, thereby giving us all good things.

Around the year 200, Tertullian speaks of a ritual of initiation which is considerably developed, as we have seen. The initiatory rites not only include a washing in water, but follow this up with an anointing, signing with the cross, and the imposition of hands. A few years later, in Rome, the *Apostolic Tradition* of Hippolytus lays down that the newly baptized, upon emerging from the baptismal waters, are to be anointed by a priest and then, after dressing, led to the bishop. The bishop is to pray over them with outstretched hand, asking God: "Make them worthy to be filled with the Holy Spirit . . . that they may serve thee according to thy will." He then pours consecrated oil upon the head and signs the forehead, saying: "I anoint thee with holy oil in God the Father Almighty and Christ Jesus and the Holy Ghost" (xxii, 1–3; Whitaker, p. 6).

At this stage, it should be remembered, the rites of initiation, while developing in the direction of greater complexity, were still administered in the course of a single ceremony: the paschal vigil. In the rite described by Hippolytus, the bishops, priests, deacons and sponsors are all involved, and the action takes them from the assembly out to the baptistry and back into the assembly again; yet it is still a single rite and the rite in its entirety was considered as effecting the initiation of a Christian. Different parts of the rite gave expression to different aspects of becoming a Christian, but there was no question as yet of asking at which stage of the rite a person became a Christian or received the Spirit. The whole process, as the culmination of the catechumenate, signified and brought about the transformation of a person into a Spirit-filled member of Christ in the Church.

It is only by trying to understand the practice of the Church in this way, and not allowing the categories of our later theology to impose themselves on earlier evidence, that we can hope to make any sense of the immense variety of initiation rituals which have existed in the Church. The Roman tradition has had two anointings after baptism, one by a priest, the other by the bishop, plus an episcopal laying on of hands. The non-Roman Churches of the West seem originally to have known a laying on of hands by the bishop after baptism, then to have added an anointing either by the priest or the bishop, and then to have ended up by substituting the anointing for the laying on of hands. In the East, the imposition of hands seems hardly to have been known at all; there the gift of the Spirit was associated with a post-baptismal anointing with consecrated oil. Even more confusing, the oldest liturgy of Syria seems to have had an anointing with chrism *before* baptism and to have led the newly baptized directly to the table of the Eucharist with no intervening rite!

As long as the various ceremonies which made up the initiation rite were thus united in a single liturgy, celebrated by the whole community and presided over by the local bishop, it was sufficient to acknowledge the rich transformation of the initiates without being too specific about what precisely happened when. The entire sacramental liturgy brought forgiveness of sins and the gift of the Holy Spirit, with all that that implies. In commenting on the rites of their own Church, the bishops could expound the meaning of Christian initiation by pointing to the different symbolic words and rituals which embody that meaning. In fact, it would be true to say that all the different rites were expressing the same mystery—the mystery of our sharing in the Lord's passover from this world to the Father—but that each of them gave new insight and complementary understanding of that single mystery. Just as there are four gospels all telling the same message, but each in its own way, so the liturgies of the different Churches could likewise afford to differ in the arrangement of their rites and yet still embody the same mystery of salvation.

It was when the different liturgies found it impossible to retain the organic unity of their initiation rites that theological and practical questions began to be asked about the specific value of the separated parts. We have already seen something of how this happened on a wide scale, but even before the spread of infant baptism in the sixth century there were instances where the baptism with water could not be followed immediately by an episcopal hand-laying or anointing. When this happened, was the status of the baptized person that of an "incomplete Christian"? Was it necessary to get that person to the bishop as soon as possible? Was salvation in jeopardy if the initiation ritual was not complete? If the initiate could be saved in virtue of being sacramentally baptized with water, what was the necessity of the anointing or laying on of hands by the bishop?

The first and most obvious instance of this sort of thing happening was when a catechumen fell dangerously ill and had to be baptized in an emergency. In such a case a priest, deacon or even a lay person could baptize the individual with water. But if this person recovered, was it necessary to go to the bishop to have the initiation ritual completed in the usual way? No one doubted that a simple baptism immediately preceding death assured salvation, but there seems to have been quite a strong feeling that, if at all possible, the person should have the rites completed at the hands of the bishop. There was no real attempt to work out a systematic case for this: it was in the first instance a matter of instinct, but it soon came to be justified by the fear that such a Christian, baptized but uncompleted, as one might say, had not received the Holy Spirit. In the fourth century, Eusebius of Caesarea quotes in his *History of the Church* a letter of Pope Cornelius (251–253) concerning the unpromising beginnings of the heretic Novatus:

> While the exorcists were still trying to help him he fell desperately ill, and since he was thought to be on the point of death, there as he lay in bed he received baptism by affusion—if it can be called baptism in the case of such a man. And when he recovered he did not receive the other things of which one should partake according to the rule of the Church, in particular the sealing by a bishop. Without receiving these how could he receive the Holy Ghost? (c. 43:20; Williamson, pp. 282–283).

Here it seems as though the enforced separation of what is by now two stages in Christian initiation has led to a specific value being attached to each: persons may be saved by being baptized, but the gift of the Holy Spirit is seemingly withheld until they are "sealed" by the bishop. This growing conviction was strengthened by consideration of the status of those baptized in heresy. We saw that the Church came to accept that baptism conferred by heretics could be a valid baptism if it was properly administered, so that they should not be rebaptized if they returned to the bosom of the Church. But did such people have the Holy Spirit? Could heretics give the Holy Spirit in their initiation ritual? It was generally agreed that they could not, for the Spirit dwelt in the Church and what the heretics did not possess, being outside the unity of the Church, they could not give. As Cyprian recognized, this was not a logical position, but it nevertheless prevailed and left the question of what to do with reconciled heretics. The ruling of the Council of Arles (314) expressed what was the standard practice in Africa and adopted it for Gaul:

> . . . if anyone should come over to the Church from heresy, they examine him on the creed, and if they find he has been baptized in the Father, the Son, and the Holy Spirit, they simply lay hands on him that he might receive the Spirit . . . (c. 8).

Later, in the fifth and sixth centuries, anointing came to replace the laying on of hands as the rite both of initiation and reconciliation, but the effect was the same. A person who had simply been baptized still needed the episcopal rite to receive the Spirit. Once the anointing came to replace the laying on of hands, however, in the East and in Gaul, the gift of the Spirit came to be associated more with the oil consecrated by the bishop than with the administration of the rite by the bishop himself. In this way, both reconciliation of heretics and the full rites of initiation could be done by priests, provided they used chrism consecrated by the bishop. Once again, a practice was growing whose full implications were by no means worked out in any systematic way, but whose effect was further to identify the post-baptismal anointing with chrism or episcopal imposition of hands with the gift of the Holy Spirit.

2. *Two Sacraments of Initiation*

While the ground had been laid for a separation of the rites of initiation by the position adopted on clinical baptism and the baptism of heretics, it was really the far more common and, from the early sixth century, virtually universal practice of infant baptism which finally drove the wedge between the baptismal and post-baptismal rites and led to their being regarded as two distinct, if related, sacraments.

In Gaul and Spain this only happened later when the Roman liturgy and its discipline were adopted. In the East it never happened at all. To this day, infants baptized in the Eastern Churches are given the full rite of Christian initiation by the priest. This was possible because of the way the gift of the Spirit was associated with the anointing, and because the effectiveness of the anointing was attributed more to the *myron* (consecrated oil) than to the minister, who could be either a priest or a bishop. An early witness to this tradition is St. Cyril of Jerusalem who, in the fourth century, was able to compare the sacrament of the oil to the sacrament of the Eucharist:

> Be sure not to regard chrism merely as ointment. Just as the bread of the Eucharist after the invocation of the Holy Spirit is no longer just bread, but the body of Christ, so the holy chrism after the invocation is no longer ordinary ointment but Christ's grace, which through the presence of the Holy Spirit instils his divinity into us . . . The body is anointed with visible ointment, and the soul is sanctified by the holy, hidden Spirit (*Myst. Cat.* 3:3; Yarnold, pp. 80–81).

In those Churches where there was only one anointing after baptism, the simple identification of such an anointing with the gift of the Holy Spirit was logical enough, and the willingness of the bishops to allow priests to administer it in cases where the bishop could not be present ensured that the sacraments of initiation remained united and that doubts about the meaning and worth of "confirmation" never really arose. In Rome, however, the situation was not so simple. We have already seen how Hippolytus, as early as the beginning of the third century, indicated that the Roman liturgy of initiation called for a post-baptismal anointing by a priest as soon as the newly baptized emerged from the water, and then for the bishop to lay hands on them, invoking the Spirit, before anointing them a second time. In both instances, chrism consecrated by the bishop was used. Because there were these two anointings, it became impossible for the first anointing, administered by a priest, to be identified as the moment when the Spirit was given. That was reserved for the episcopal anointing which followed, and the priestly anointing came to be regarded as a way of illustrating the newly baptized's conformity to Christ, the Anointed of God.

The Roman position on this matter of the post-baptismal gift of the Spirit was set out clearly in a letter of Pope Innocent I written in 416 to Decentius, bishop of Gubbio in central Italy:

> As far as the sealing of infants is concerned, it is clear that this may be done by no one but the bishop. Presbyters, after all, are priests of the second rank, and do not have the supremacy of the episcopate. Such belongs to bishops alone so that they alone should seal, or give the Spirit, the Paraclete; as is proven not only by the custom of the Church, but also by that passage in the Acts of the Apostles which states that Peter and John were sent to confer the Holy Spirit upon those who had already been baptized. While priests may anoint the baptized with chrism, whether in the absence of the bishop or when baptizing in his presence, as long as the chrism is consecrated by the bishop, they must not sign them on the forehead with that chrism, because that is for bishops alone to do when they confer the Spirit, the Paraclete . . . (DS, n. 215).

In Rome and southern Italy, such a ruling would perhaps have caused no great problem, since virtually every town was a diocese, a community presided over by its own bishop. Even when it was necessary to baptize an infant in an emergency, if the child recovered the parents would not have had far to go to have the child "sealed" with the Spirit by the bishop. It was probably this tight-knit community sense and easy access to the bishop which accounts for the late survival of the custom of baptizing even children only at Easter and Pentecost in Rome and its environs. On the other hand, the situation was quite different in the rest of Western Europe, where bishops usually had vast areas to cover. However, the Roman practice was not followed in these areas initially. In England it was introduced early, when Augustine imported it along with the rest of the Roman liturgy, which was eventually imposed on even the surviving Celtic Christians in Britain in the course of the seventh century. In Gaul, it was only the ecclesiastical and liturgical reform of Charlemagne which finally succeeded in putting an end to the sacramental post-baptismal anointing conferred by the priest in favor of the Roman practice of episcopal anointing. Thus it was only from the ninth century that the problem of the separation of baptism by a priest and confirmation by a bishop became really widespread.

It should be said that such a separation of the two stages of Christian initiation was not intended by the legislators of the Carolingian reform. It was also decreed that the Roman practice of reserving the sacraments of Christian initiation to the feasts of Easter and Pentecost should be universally restored, which would have assured that baptism and confirmation, together with first Communion, were kept together. However, in practice it meant that baptisms continued to be conferred within a short time after the child's birth without the sacramental anointing to "complete" the initiation, while the injunction to bring children to the bishop for baptism and confirmation at Easter was generally ignored. This situation had to be accepted, for the influence of Augustine's doctrine that children dying unbaptized would be unable to enter the kingdom of heaven was far too strong in the minds of both pastors and people for it to be set aside in favor of a practice which, however venerable, had little obvious meaning for the people of the early Middle Ages. A sense of the importance of the Easter celebration of Christian initiation depended upon a sense of the intrinsic association of baptism with the paschal mystery and also upon a strong sense of the local Church as an organic unity presided over by the bishop; whereas for most people, then as now, the bishop was a remote figure, the Church meant the local clergy and the sanctifying powers they possessed to baptize and shrive and consecrate the Eucharist, while baptism was identified as the sacrament of deliverance from original sin.

Nevertheless, in the early Middle Ages it was still supposed that a baptized child should ideally be confirmed as soon as possible after baptism. The *Ordo Romanus XV*, which represents the Roman liturgy as used and adapted in Frankish territory in the late eighth century, takes it for granted that a child will be baptized and given Communion by a priest, and then adds:

> Infants having been baptized, if they can secure the presence of a bishop, must be confirmed with chrism. But if on the actual day they cannot find a bishop, as soon as they find one, they must do this without delay (cited in J. D. C. Fisher, *Christian Initiation: Baptism in the Medieval West*, p. 71).

Even for that to be possible, though, it would have meant that bishops were willing and able to spend a great deal of their time travelling round their extensive dioceses. Synodal legislation called for bishops to carry out annual visitations of their dioceses, which would have meant that every child could have been confirmed within a year of its baptism, but such ideals were rarely realized. Consequently, while infant confirmation was still the accepted thing, in practice the tendency was for the two parts of Christian initiation to drift further and further apart and even for the second part, confirmation, to be dropped altogether. Ecclesiastical legislation tried to counteract this neglect, urging bishops to visit their dioceses, and parents to present their children for confirmation. Age limits came to be set beyond which confirmation should not be deferred. In England, the Council of Worcester (1240) set the limit at the age of one, threatening the parents with excommunication "provided they had access to a bishop, or it was well known that he was passing through the vicinity." In the diocese of Winchester, the age limit was three years. In Durham, in 1249, parents were ordered to ensure that their child was confirmed by the age of seven. In a council held at Lambeth in 1281, the "damnable negligence" whereby people grew old and died without being confirmed was condemned in a measure which forbade Holy Communion to be given to anyone not confirmed, except in danger of death, unless the person had been prevented from being confirmed by some reasonable cause. This rule is still observed in the Church of England.

A council held in Cologne in 1280, however, issued a ruling which was gradually to spread through the rest of Europe and to become the common practice in the sixteenth century: ". . . Let them bring to [the bishop] children of seven years or more" (Fisher, *Christian Initiation*, p. 123). Although there were still places where the ancient consciousness of the unity of Christian initiation survived well into the high Middle Ages, by and large baptism and confirmation were now and henceforth regarded as distinct sacraments, each with its own minister, its own discipline, and its own distinct meaning.

The meaning of confirmation apart from baptism, however, was not something which was immediately obvious. The very neglect into which confirmation fell was itself testimony to widespread uncertainty as to its importance and significance. The Church, it seemed, had practiced this rite from time immemorial, but what had it, other than its antiquity, to recommend it? In the patristic era, as we saw, it was rather vaguely identified in liturgical texts, commentaries, and disciplinary canons as the conferral of the Holy Spirit. I say "vaguely identified" because, whatever may be thought about baptism administered by heretics and schismatics, it could never be denied that the Spirit was operative and communicated in Christian baptism. So what did confirmation add?

Up until the ninth century, the rite of confirmation was frequently called the rite of "perfection," "completion" or "sealing." Even when the term "confirmation" was used, it was in a non-technical sense as the equivalent of these other terms, and as referring simply to the completing of the rites of initiation. It had much the same meaning as we have when we refer to a business being "signed and sealed": completed, finished, ratified, with all formalities observed. From the ninth century, "confirmation" is the name referring specifically to this part of the initiation process, to the sacrament which was meant to follow baptism. Whereas for the Fathers, "baptism" could refer to the whole process of making a Christian, and not just to the water-rite, so terms like "perfection," "completion," "confirmation" could also refer to the sacramental effects of initiation as a whole: it made a person a new creature, establishing one irrevocably in the mercy of God through incorporation into Christ. But the sense of the unity and richness of this one mystery itself disintegrated as the complex of initiatory rites fell apart to produce two separate sacraments.

Faced with the heritage of two related but distinct sacraments, the theologians of the high Middle Ages attempted to work out a systematic theology of each of them. They had little knowledge of the history of the rites, and even with regard to the teaching of the Fathers they relied on texts which had not been subjected to the rigor of historical criticism. In particular, they had recourse to a text which was generally attributed to Pope Melchiades (fourth century) but was in fact a ninth century forgery drawing largely, for its teaching on baptism and confirmation, from a sermon by Faustus, a fifth century bishop of Riez in southern Gaul. Faustus squarely faced the question of what good confirmation did for one who had already been reborn in Christ. He answered in a series of images. A soldier is enlisted and tattooed, but he also needs to be armed. Confirmation arms the baptized Christian with the Holy Spirit:

> So the Holy Spirit, who descended upon the baptismal waters bearing salvation, gave at the font all that is needed for innocence: at confirmation he gives an increase for grace, for in this world those who survive through the different stages of life, must walk among dangers and invisible enemies. In baptism we are born again to life, after baptism we are confirmed for battle. In baptism we are washed, after baptism we are strengthened . . . (cited in Milner, *Theology of Confirmation*, pp. 45–46).

This understanding of confirmation as being the gift of the Spirit for the arming and strengthening of the Christian in the world—as opposed to the gift of the Spirit for rebirth and salvation in baptism—became normative for understanding the two sacraments in the Middle Ages and since. It also helped to make sense of the delay in conferring confirmation. This had come about, in fact, for a series of accidental reasons, as we have seen, but it appeared increasingly proper to defer confirmation until a child began to need such assistance; namely, when one reached the age of discretion and moral responsibility. Not least, it fitted in with a way of understanding Christianity which has regarded it less in terms of our involvement in God's plan for the salvation of the world than in terms of saving one's soul by grace-aided moral endeavor.

The practice and understanding of confirmation thus developed in the Middle Ages was taken up and handed on to modern times by the influential Catechism of the Council of Trent. It describes the administration of confirmation to children under the age of seven as "inexpedient" and goes on to say:

> Wherefore, if not to be postponed to the age of twelve, it is most proper to defer this sacrament at least to that of seven; for confirmation has not been instituted as necessary for salvation, but that by virtue thereof we might be found very well armed and prepared when called upon to fight for the faith of Christ; and for this kind of conflict assuredly no one will consider children, who still want the age of reason, to be qualified (II, iii, 17; tr. Donovan, 1829, p. 184).

Dealing specifically with the effects of baptism, the Catechism reiterates the teaching of the Councils of Lyons (1274), Florence (1439), and Trent (1547) that confirmation is truly a sacrament and imparts "new grace." This includes the forgiveness of sins, as in the case of all sacraments, but also:

> . . . to confirmation it is peculiarly given first to perfect the grace of baptism; for those who have been made Christians by baptism still have in some sort the tenderness and softness, as it were, of new-born infants (1 Pet 2:2), and afterwards become, by the sacrament of chrism, stronger against the assaults of the world, the flesh and the devil, and their mind is fully confirmed in faith to confess and glorify the name of our Lord Jesus Christ, whence, also, no doubt, originated the very name [of confirmation] (II, iii, 19; Donovan, p. 185).

In the twentieth century, this sort of attitude toward confirmation has taken the explanation of the sacrament in further and different directions. It has been preached as the sacrament of Catholic Action, enabling a person to witness to Christ in the world; or as the sacrament of Christian growth, enabling the growing child to withstand the tumultuous years of adolescence; or as the sacrament of Christian maturity, to be celebrated when people are mature enough to reaffirm for themselves the commitment made in their name at baptism.

The problem with all these explanations of confirmation is that, like the explanation given by Faustus of Riez and the schoolmen of the Middle Ages, they are really quite arbitrary. We have inherited a sacrament which can only be given once, but which has no very clear and specific meaning; so what do we make of it? Moralists and militants, youth leaders and pastors have each staked their claim to it, suggesting a time for conferring it and a meaning to attach to it which both derive from considerations extrinsic to the sacrament itself. As Aidan Kavanagh has sagely remarked: ". . . the issue raised concerns far more than the appropriate age at which a rite as intrinsically modest as confirmation is to be administered. The issue concerns *why* one should be confirmed at all, and *how* one gets to the point of even wanting confirmation. In other words, the issue embraces the whole of the Church's policy on who a Christian is and how he gets to be that way" (in J. Gallen [ed.], *Made, Not Born*, 1976, p. 2).

A number of conclusions seem to suggest themselves when one reviews the history of the sacrament of confirmation. The first is that the sacrament of confirmation developed out of an initiation ritual which was originally very simple. The Church developed a fuller and more elaborate celebration of the original sacrament of Christian initiation so that it eventually came to take place in stages, but the stages retained their intelligibility as long as they were seen to be in strict continuity with one another, marking a single process of conversion and formation. Once the stages began to be considered as units each having a separate and distinct significance, the temptation was to make a somewhat arbitrary allotment of meaning to each section. A second conclusion would be that confirmation can best be understood if it is placed in its original context as the completion of baptism and as leading immediately to participation in the Eucharist. Thirdly, since the elaboration of the initiatory rites occurred originally in response to the need to give sacramental expression to what God was doing in people's lives, it would seem necessary to relate the stages of initiation liturgy to the actual growth of a person into the life of Christ in the Church. To see where confirmation fits into such a pattern today we shall study the rite itself, but it might be useful, since the question of the relationship between sacraments and personal growth has been raised, to look at this matter a little more closely.

3. *The Sacraments and Personal Growth*

One thing which the history of the theology of confirmation makes very clear is that the answers to questions about the sacraments (as about most things) are very much determined by the form in which the questions themselves are posed. As Kavanagh pointed out, the real question we are faced with today is not so much about the age at which baptism or confirmation should be given, but what the process of initiation is all about. It is possible, and necessary, for us to ask that kind of question today because we are confronted with the even more basic question of what it means to be a Christian at all. To answer that sort of question we have to have recourse both to our own experience and to the tradition of faith which can help us to understand our experience. This means that on the one hand we cannot dispense with the accumulated understanding of the Christian life which the Church, believing and celebrating through the ages, in fidelity to the gospel of Christ and under the inspiration of his Spirit, has acquired. On the other hand, it also means that we cannot simply return to the past, as if there were some golden age of faith after which the Church learned nothing new about the gospel entrusted to her.

As far as Christian initiation is concerned, we are in quite a different position from the Fathers on two important points of belief. Ever since St. Cyprian coined the phrase, "outside the Church no salvation," the experience of the Church has been such that it had to modify his dictum more and more. In view of our belief in God's universal salvific will, we have to believe that the large majority of the human race are confronted with God's offer of salvation and freely respond to it outside the visible Church. This in turn, by making us recognize that people must be able to be saved without being baptized as Christians, has forced the Church to abandon St. Augustine's uncompromising doctrine that children who die unbaptized are, through no fault of their own, condemned to eternal exclusion from the kingdom of heaven. In both these matters we are much less dogmatic than the Fathers were, and this in turn forces us to reconsider the role of the Church and her sacraments.

To put the whole thing in slightly different terms, we can say that we now recognize more clearly than before that the ongoing struggle between the mystery of salvation and the mystery of iniquity (2 Thess 2:7) constitutes the secret history and the hidden agenda of the whole of humanity. The role of the Church is not so much to be the sole means of salvation, for if that were so most of the human race would be condemned from the outset, since they have not even had the chance to be seriously confronted with the gospel. The role of the Church is rather to be a community of people who acknowledge what God is doing in human history and consciously commit themselves to that by submitting their lives to Christ in faith, so that with him they may do the will of the Father, and give him the acknowledgement he deserves. In the words of the epistle to the Ephesians:

> . . . he has made known to us in all wisdom and insight the mystery of his will, according to his purpose which he set forth in Christ as a plan for the fulness of time, to unite all things in him, things in heaven and things on earth.
>
> In him, according to the purpose of him who accomplishes all things according to the counsel of his will, we who first hoped in Christ have been destined and appointed to live for the praise of his glory. In him you also, who have heard the word of truth, the gospel of your salvation, and have believed in him, were sealed with the promised Holy Spirit, which is the guarantee of our inheritance until we acquire possession of it, to the praise of his glory (1:9-14).

The place of the sacraments in the Christian life needs to be seen in this context of a community of believers. They are the celebrations of the Church, whereby she acknowledges this mystery of faith and commits herself to it. They are the celebrations of the community and of the personal involvement of all its members, where the saving power of God is acclaimed and the working of evil is rejected. There the believers are drawn more deeply and more explicitly into the pattern of the crucified Christ by the power of his Spirit, "to the praise of his glory."

In her work of preaching the gospel, the Church proclaims that God has entered into the agony of the world and redeemed it in Christ, raising him from the dead to manifest the goal and meaning which he has given to every human life. To come to faith in Christ is thus to discover what God is doing in the world and to give oneself over to it, heart and soul. Since the passover of Jesus from this world to the Father is for all of us the only way to the Father, and the truth of human existence, and the only life that counts for anything, the Christian explicitly identifies with Jesus in his passover. This, we have seen, is the Christian faith: to share in the faith of Christ who abandoned himself to his Father and was not disappointed.

This is the fundamental mystery which constituted the Church and to which every one of her sacraments points. In each sacrament she celebrates the involvement of the individual and of the community in that "mystery of faith." The sacraments of initiation celebrate the insertion of the individual into that pattern of salvation. The Eucharist is the regularly repeated celebration of our common involvement with Christ in the Spirit: our self-sacrificial communion in the redemptive sacrifice of Christ. For one who has fallen away, penance is the sacrament of return to the life and work of God in the world. For the sick, the sacrament of anointing identifies them precisely in their suffering with the saving passover of the Lord. The love that prompted Christ to give himself for the world and to prepare a bridal community for himself in the form of the Church is manifested in the mystery of human love celebrated in Christian marriage. The gracious initiative of God who loved us first and sent his Son to save us is celebrated in the sacrament of orders, when the Church sends or ordains men to bring the word of grace and the sacraments of salvation to the people of God.

The meaning of each sacrament, then, is derived from two things: its reference to the paschal mystery and the particular situation of the individual or community upon whom the sacramental celebration focuses. The anointing of the sick is defined by reference to the passion of Christ on the one hand and the suffering of the Christian on the other; marriage by its reference to the saving work of Christ on the one hand and the love of two particular people on the other. And so on, through all the sacraments. Note that the reference is always to this particular person, this particular couple, this particular community. No two baptisms, no two weddings, no two Masses are ever quite the same, for each represents and realizes the participation here and now of these very particular people in the one saving mystery of redemption. Thus it will be even more true that baptism at the age of three weeks will not be the same as baptism at the age of seven, or seventeen, or seventy.

Seen from this angle, it is not really very helpful to ask what the grace of orders might be as opposed to the grace of matrimony, or the grace of penance as opposed to the grace of the Eucharist. Ultimately the grace is always the same: it is the Spirit of God drawing us into the passover of Christ. Yet obviously the situation of two people getting married is different from that of a man being commissioned for office in the Church; and that of the repentant sinner is not precisely the same as that of a member of the Sunday Eucharistic assembly. Similarly with baptism and confirmation: the "grace" is ultimately the same: that of initiation into the mystery of Christ, dead and risen and working in the world through his Spirit. But the situation of the person being baptized is different from that of a person who has already been baptized and whose initiation is now being completed. They are two stages in the same process, and what they mean for the individual concerned will depend more upon the actual situation vis-a-vis the mystery of Christ than upon any intrinsic difference in the grace of the two sacraments. It can happen, then, that if someone has just completed a full and rich catechumenate, the two stages will coalesce, and the person will be baptized and confirmed in a single liturgy. On the other hand, for someone baptized in infancy the deferment of confirmation will make that second stage all the more significant for the child, not *as opposed to* baptism, but in completion of it.

Nevertheless, there is also a very real sense in which one baptism is much like another, one marriage much like another. The situation may be new for the person or persons who are coming to it for the first time, but as part of the universal pattern of human experience this sort of situation has recurred many times before. This enables such situations to be ritualized, and the role of ritual is always to point to the deeper meaning of what is being experienced in a situation. The ritual of the Christian sacraments points to the meaning which Christ has given to such human situations. By proclaiming the word of the gospel and celebrating her ancient liturgies, the Church, the community of believers, *realizes* the profound significance of this occasion. The word "realize" is used here in both its senses. The liturgy makes us "realize" what is at stake when someone joins the Church or two people get married. We become aware of what is happening in their lives. On the other hand, the sacraments also realize that meaning in the same sense in which we speak of people realizing an ambition: they bring it to reality, to fulfilment. Thus the sacramental celebrations of the Church as "celebrations of awareness" are at the same time communicating the very realities they signify. They not only show that a person is becoming involved with Christ, they bring that involvement about. Thus the texts and ceremonies of the liturgy, taken globally as a single, significant unit, manifest and convey the whole mystery of salvation as being effective for this person or these people here and now. This is why we can look at the liturgy of baptism and confirmation in its entirety and discover in all the details some realization of what it means to become a Christian.

It would be wrong to emphasize one meaning of the word "realization" at the expense of the other when we are talking of the sacraments. If we emphasize realization as awareness, we are in danger of regarding the sacraments as mere illustrations of the sort of thing God is doing in the world. On the other hand, if we emphasize the sacraments as effective realizations of grace there is a danger that they might appear altogether discontinuous from the rest of life, as if grace could be found in the celebration of the sacraments and nowhere else. But we have already seen that the sacraments are celebrations of what is happening in life, not a substitute for or alternative to what is happening there. The Liturgy Constitution of Vatican II speaks of the liturgy as being "the summit towards which the activity of the Church is directed; at the same time it is the fountain from which all her power flows" (n. 10). What is true of the community as a whole is true equally of the individuals who make it up. The sacramental celebration is a source of their life in Christ, so that we live out of the union with Christ in the Spirit which the sacraments give us. Yet they are also summits, or climaxes to which we are being led. This means that the grace of the sacrament is already working in us even before we receive it. The sacraments not only lie at the root of what *will* happen in our lives; they in some way sum up and celebrate what has *already* happened.

Having already looked at baptism, we can see the truth of this ancient theological principle without too much difficulty. The catechumens who enter the baptismal waters on Easter Night will be the first to acknowledge that the Spirit has been drawing them through the years, so that their baptism is not only the beginning of all that will be, but also the culmination of all that has been. That is why, if a person died suddenly while still a catechumen and before baptism, that person was always given Christian burial. The candidate already belonged to Christ and to his Church. Similarly, it has long been taught that a person in mortal sin who was run over by a car on the way to confession could be assumed to have been forgiven in virtue of the desire for the sacrament. But the desire for the sacrament, more or less explicit, is already a sign of the working of the Spirit in a person's life. Under normal circumstances, that person will be drawn more and more into an obedient faith until the time comes when the need to ask the Church for the sacrament becomes clear. Similarly with the love of two people: their marriage is not only the beginning of their relationship in Christ, but the culmination of what the Spirit of God's love has accomplished in them.

The recognition that the sacraments are not exclusive moments of grace, but refer to what the Spirit has done and will yet do in people's lives, is important for our understanding of Christian initiation. Initiation is a process of growth. Vatican II calls it "setting out on a spiritual journey" (AG, 13). But a journey is an ongoing thing. Milestones mark the way, but they presuppose that a person is making progress; they tell how far one has come and still has to go. So with the sacraments of initiation, although they do not simply mark the progress made, but actually further it. Nevertheless, the journey is more important than the milestones, and the actual process of growth in faith is more important than the sacraments of initiation. In that sense, there is a continuing dialectic between sacraments and life, between the sacraments of initiation and the actual transformation of men, women, and children into mature Christians.

It was in the context of this sort of dialectic that the initiation liturgies of the different Churches developed. The rites of the catechumenate, baptism, and confirmation as we now have them reflect the Church's accumulated experience of what is involved in the process of making a Christian. If we return to our original question, asking what confirmation does that baptism does not, perhaps we are now in a position to answer it by saying that confirmation signifies initiation precisely as process of growth. Its meaning is thus not independent of baptism. Rather, it draws out that which is already communicated in the rite of baptism. It makes clear what baptism leads to. It provides new stimulus for the life that germinates there and an opportunity to "realize" what has already begun to develop. Perhaps we can gain a more concrete understanding of what this is if we now turn to the liturgy of confirmation itself.

II

THE LITURGY OF CONFIRMATION

1. *Preparation for Confirmation*

In the days when adult initiation was the norm, and when confirmation and baptism were administered in the course of a single liturgy, the catechumenate provided all the formation which was necessary. In the Middle Ages, the responsibility for ensuring that baptized children were properly prepared for confirmation was laid chiefly at the door of the godparents, as the following text from the Sarum Manual, in use in England up to the Reformation, picturesquely testifies:

> God faders and godmodyrs of thys chylde, whe charge you that ye charge the fader and te moder to kepe it from fyer and water and other perels to the age of vii yere. and that ye lerne or se yt by lerned the *Pater Noster. Au Maria.* and *Credo.* after the lawe of all holy churche and in all goodly haste to be confermed of my lorde of the dyocise or of hys depute . . . (Ed. A. J. Collins, Henry Bradshaw Soc., vol. XCI, 1960, p. 32).

A little later in the same Manual, we read that the godfathers and godmothers are responsible to God for the children and must admonish them, as soon as they are old enough, to be chaste, love justice, and preserve charity. They are also to ensure that the children know how to make the sign of the cross, as well as know the prayers already mentioned.

The Roman Pontifical, published in the late sixteenth century, laid down that no one was to be confirmed who was ignorant of the rudiments of the Christian faith; a directive which presumably gave rise to the common enough practice of the bishop asking the children questions about the faith before confirming them.

In the present revised Rite of Confirmation, responsibility for preparing the baptized for confirmation is given, like the task of preparing candidates for baptism, to the community as a whole, though it is acknowledged that this responsibility will, in practice, devolve upon the pastors. Still, it is perhaps worth remembering all the same that the process of initiation, of which confirmation and its preparation are a part, is something which is fundamental to the quality of Christian life in a community, and thus is of concern to all.

What is of particular interest in the provisions of the Rite of Confirmation for the preparation of candidates, is the preference apparently

125

expressed for a form of preparation based on the catechumenate. Adult catechumens, who are to be confirmed right after they are baptized, can look to their contact with the local community and to the program of their catechumenate to provide adequate formation for confirmation. The same will be true of children baptized at an age when they are old enough to profit from an adapted form of catechumenate (RC, 3.11), and also for those "who, baptized in infancy, are confirmed only as adults" (RC, 3). In the latter case, care is to be taken that such adults, already baptized, are not regarded as catechumens (RR, 5), but a program of formation, based on the steps of the catechumenate, is to be worked out for them (RC, 3).

The same is not said quite so explicitly for children who were baptized in infancy and who are reaching the stage when they should be confirmed. Parents are to "form and gradually develop a spirit of faith in the children and, with the help of catechetical institutions, prepare them for the fruitful reception of the sacraments of confirmation and the Eucharist" (ibid.). The Latin text makes it much clearer that what is involved is faith-formation, and that this is primarily the responsibility of parents, but that they will be helped in this by teachers who have charge of catechetical formation. But what should such "catechetical formation" programs consist of?

Since the document speaks of preparing for confirmation and Eucharist together, it might be worth remembering what the Directory of Children's Masses has to say about preparing children for first Communion:

> The preparation of children for their first Communion deserves special consideration. It should be aimed not only at teaching them the truths of the faith concerning the Eucharist, but also at explaining how from now on they are going to be able to share the Eucharist actively with the people of God and have a share in the Lord's table and in the community of their fellow Christians. Prepared by penance in proportion to their understanding, they are now going to be inserted fully into the body of Christ (n. 12).

This is set in the context of experiential learning (n. 9), of training in prayer (n. 10), and life within the Christian community (n. 11). There will be need for celebrations of various kinds which give children a sense of liturgical celebration and common prayer, while enhancing their appreciation of the Word of God (nn. 13–14). Nor is this divorced from the moral growth of the children (so that the sacrament of penance for children needs to be seen in the overall context of their Christian initiation); nor from learning to witness to the gospel and become involved in the fraternal charity of the Christian community (n. 11).

Now this is remarkably close to the kind of all-round formation envisaged by the catechumenate program. The Introduction to the Rite of Christian Initiation of Adults (which is intended to be adapted to the needs of children of catechetical age) defines the catechumenate as a four-point program of formation. It includes (a) a *doctrinal* formation leading "to a suitable knowledge of doctrines and precepts and also to an intimate understanding of the mystery of salvation which they desire to share"; (b) a progressive change of outlook and *morals*, together with the social consequences ensuing therefrom; (c) a *liturgical* formation; and (d) an *apostolic* formation, whereby they learn "how to work actively with others to spread the Gospel and build up the Church by the testimony of their lives and the profession of their faith" (*ibid.*, 19; see 41 and RC, 12).

With a formation of this sort behind them, even young children could come to confirmation with quite a vivid appreciation of the nature of this sacrament as the completion of Christian initiation begun in baptism, and as celebrating their being "bound more intimately to the Church" (LG, 11).

Fasting, too, has traditionally been associated with preparation for confirmation. It originated with the prebaptismal fast, and was still insisted upon, even for children, when confirmation became separated from baptism, although it was then understood as a pre-Communion fast. The Catechism of the Council of Trent ordained that adults are "to be admonished of the propriety of reviving that laudable practice of the ancient Church of receiving this sacrament fasting" (II, iii, 18; Donovan, p. 184). As we saw, the prebaptismal fast was a sacramental participation in the death of the Lord, for it was identified with the period during which he lay in the tomb. Perhaps today, particularly with children, it would be better to substitute some other form of spiritual preparation, such as a day's retreat.

2. A Celebration of the Church

Even before confirmation evolved as a second stage of Christian initiation, baptism was followed by the actual introduction of the newly baptized into the community of believers, assembled under the presidency of their bishop. So Justin remarks: "After thus washing him who has been persuaded and has given his assent, we bring him to those that are called the brethren, where they are assembled . . ." (*I Apol.* c. 65; Whitaker, p. 2).

This practice undoubtedly underlies what is pretty well the only consistent element in the variegated history of the sacrament: its association with the bishop. Whether this episcopal connection was retained by allowing only the bishop to confirm, as was the Roman practice, or by insisting that only chrism consecrated by the bishop could be used, the connection remained. One of our earliest references to this second stage of initiation makes this association quite clear:

> They who are baptized in the Church are brought to the prelates of the Church, and by our prayers and by the imposition of the hand obtain the Holy Spirit, and are perfected with the Lord's seal (Cyprian, Ep. 73, 9; Whitaker, p. 11).

The involvement of the bishop, then, is a constant and constitutive part of the sacramental sign of confirmation. But this is no arbitrary matter, as the Roman tradition was well aware. The bishop is involved because he presides over and in some way embodies in his own person the local Christian Church. As far back as the second century, St. Ignatius expressed this conviction powerfully and succinctly: "Wherever the bishop is, there let the people be, just as wherever Christ Jesus is, there is the Catholic Church" (ad Smyrn, 8:1). This image of the bishop presiding over his people in the name of Christ is taken up by Vatican II:

> Let [all] be persuaded that the Church reveals herself most clearly when a full complement of God's holy people, united in prayer and a common liturgical service (especially the Eucharist), exercise a thorough and active participation at the very altar where the bishop presides in the company of his priests and other assistants (SC, 41; see LG, 26).

The reason given for this is that "the bishop is to be considered as the high priest of his flock. In a certain sense, it is from him that the faithful who are under his care derive and maintain their life in Christ" (ibid.).

It is into this Church, presided over by the bishop whose membership of the college of bishops links the local community to the universal Church, that the sacraments of initiation give us entry. Confirmation, especially, is the celebration of our incorporation into this Spirit-filled community. "God has appointed apostles, prophets and teachers in the Church," says St. Irenaeus quoting 1 Cor 12:28, "as well as all the other workings of the Spirit, from which all who do not run to the Church cut themselves off, depriving themselves of life . . . For where the Church is, there is the Spirit of God; and where the Spirit of God is, there is the Church and all grace . . ." (Adv. haer. III, xxiv, 1).

Since the eighteenth century the Roman Church, too, has allowed priests to confirm, but only under extraordinary circumstances, as in missionary territories or when in danger of death. With the new rite, much more scope is given to priests to confirm, either as assisting the bishop or in celebrations at which a bishop is not present. It is the former case which is the more interesting, because it reveals more clearly the principle upon which this extension of the ministry of confirmation is made. Where there is a large number of confirmations, the bishop may associate priests with himself in the administration of the sacrament, but it is required that such priests either hold a diocesan post or have pastoral responsibility for those being confirmed. In other words, the priests concerned should themselves be people who have a particular job which enables them to be seen as in some way representatives of the bishop or at least as leaders in the local Church. It is because they, like the bishop, to some degree embody the local Church that they can be deputed to assist the bishop in celebrating the sacrament of incorporation into that Church.

However, the Church is first and foremost a community of people, and it is that community which, under the leadership of its bishop, makes the Church visible. Consequently, it is of great importance that confirmation should really be a community celebration:

Attention should be paid to the festive and solemn character of the liturgical service, and its significance for the local church, especially if all the candidates are assembled for a common celebration. The whole people of God, represented by the families and friends of the candidates and by members of the local community, will be invited to take part in the celebration and will express its faith in the fruits of the Holy Spirit (RC, 4).

At confirmation, as at baptism, all who are to be initiated should receive the sacrament at a common celebration (RC, 11), for they are being made members of one body by one sacrament and one Spirit. Ideally, this single celebration of initiation should lead to its fulfilment in a celebration of the Eucharist in which all will celebrate their unity in the body of Christ: "The newly confirmed should therefore participate in the Eucharist which completes their Christian initiation" (RC, 13).

Since we have been reflecting on confirmation as the sacramental celebration of a person's formal entry into the assembled and structured Church, it might be worth noting that confirmation is still today, as in the past, the sacrament for the reception of converts who have been baptized outside the unity of the Catholic Church. Pope Siricius wrote to Bishop Himerius of Tarragon in 385 about the Roman practice in receiving converts from schism and heresy: "We number them among the company of the Catholics simply by the invocation of the seven-fold Spirit and by the imposition of the bishop's hand: which is also the practice of the whole East and West . . ." (DS, n. 183). The present Rite for the Reception of Baptized Christians into Full Communion with the Catholic Church, which is an appendix to the Rite for the Christian Initiation of Adults, provides for a simple profession of faith, followed by confirmation and immediate admission to the Eucharist. Here confirmation is seen to be the sacrament of admission to that communion of faith and love which is celebrated in the Eucharist; so much so, that any priest who is entrusted with the reception of a convert automatically has the right and duty to confirm. This ecclesial dimension to confirmation is crucial to any understanding of the sacrament. It is a sacrament of the gift of the Spirit because it is a sacrament celebrating the incorporation of a person into the Church where the Spirit dwells: "There is one body and one Spirit, just as you were all called to the one hope that belongs to your call, one Lord, one faith, one baptism, one God and Father of us all" (Eph 4:4-6). This one Spirit penetrates to the heart of every believer and produces his own effects in each person's life, but the intended effect is the building up of the Church as an effective sign of the healing and unitive power of God's salvation. "Now there are varieties of gifts, but the same Spirit; and there are varieties of service, but the same Lord; and there are varieties of working, but it is the same God who inspires them all in every one. To each is given the manifestation of the Spirit for the common good . . . For by one Spirit we were all baptized into one body—Jews or Greeks, slaves or free—and all were made to drink of one Spirit" (1 Cor 12:4-7, 13).

3. *The Liturgy of the Word*

We have already discussed at some length the role of the word of God in the work of making a Christian. All that was said there applies equally well here, except of course that when the candidates are no longer infants, but at least children old enough to understand something of that word, it takes on an additional importance. For this reason, the rite calls for particular attention to be given to the proclamation of the word of God:

> It is from the hearing of the word of God that the many-sided power of the Holy Spirit flows upon the Church and upon each one of the baptized and confirmed, and it is by this word that God's will is manifest in the life of Christians" (RC, 13).

This statement expresses well the actuality of the word for the listening congregation: it is being fulfilled even as they listen, for the Spirit is working to help them understand and is arousing them to a response of faith.

The Scripture readings provided in the Lectionary would serve as an excellent starting point for a catechesis on the work of the Spirit in the Church and in the Christian life. What must be remembered is that they all speak of our situation *today*. The first five texts are taken from the Old Testament, but they are all prophetic readings referring to the messianic era in which we now live. As Jesus says in one of the gospel texts provided for confirmation, "I tell you that many prophets and kings desired to see what you see and did not see it, and to hear what you hear and did not hear it" (Luke 10:24).

The three readings from Isaiah are messianic texts, looking forward to the Anointed One who was to come to do the works of God. The gospel readings on the baptism of Jesus (Mark 1:9-11) and on the beginning of his public ministry (Luke 4:16-22) show how Jesus was that servant of God, anointed by the Spirit of God for the work of salvation. The readings from Acts show how Jesus in his turn has poured out his Spirit upon the Church which identifies itself with his mission, and itself shares his Spirit with all who die with him in baptism. The gospel readings from John point to the working of the Spirit in the Church, sustaining her in the truth from age to age and enabling her to understand Christ's revelation and to remain faithful to her witness to him. The role of the Spirit in unifying the Church is the special emphasis of 1 Cor 12:4-13 and Eph 4:1-6, whereas the other Pauline lessons speak more of the transformative power of the Spirit in the lives of individual members of the Church. He is the gift of God's love. He sets us free and enables us to pray, giving us spiritual wisdom and insight and enabling us to live lives which are characterized by joy, peace, love, and all the other "fruits of the Spirit." It is this same Spirit at work within us who makes it possible for us to live the gospel, making our faith productive (Matt 25:14-30; Luke 8:4-15) and pushing us to take the risks of the beatitudes (Matt 5:1-12). In short, the Spirit which was in Christ enables us to live by the same faith by which he lived and gave himself up to death and was raised to life.

Commitment to this kind of faith—"the obedience by which a person entrusts one's whole self freely to God"—should be the response to the hearing of the word. In confirmation as in baptism, the whole liturgy is a "sacrament of faith," but this faith now becomes explicit as the bishop, concluding his homily, invites those to be confirmed to make public profession of their baptismal faith.

If they were baptized as infants, this will be the first time they have made their personal profession of faith in public. And it is a personal profession. One by one, the candidates for confirmation are called up to the bishop. They are called by their baptismal names, summoned out of the crowd. No longer can they hide in the congregation and lose themselves in the anonymity of the crowd. Christ does not save crowds, he saves people, and he saves them precisely by confronting them with who they are and who he is. In the days of his life on earth, he met people in the streets and on country roads, in the synagogue and in the temple, by a well and even in a sycamore tree. Like Zacchaeus (Luke 9:1-10), we are called by name, but now Christ calls us through the ministry of his Church. So "each candidate is called by name and comes individually to the sanctuary" (RC, 21).

In every sacrament, the individual encounters Christ in the personal way, but that is not to say that each stands alone and unsupported. Those who were this person's godparents, or even one's own parents, may accompany the candidate, for they were the ones who then undertook, on behalf of the community, to lead the individual to Christ as he or she grew up. It used to be, because of the gulf between baptism and confirmation, that the baptized had to choose another sponsor for confirmation. This directive of the Code of Canon Law (can. 796) is now abrogated to emphasize the continuity of the process of initiation. Thus the candidate for confirmation will normally be accompanied either by the parents who presented the child at the font for baptism or by the godparent(s) to whom the Church entrusted the child emerging from the baptismal water. This should be no mere formality for, as the Rite of Adult Initiation points out, the sponsor's responsibility "remains important when the neophyte has received the sacraments and needs to be helped to remain faithful to the baptismal promises" (RCIA, 43; RC, 5). This in turn depends upon there being a real human relationship between the candidate and the sponsor, and upon the sponsor's ability to lend real help and support in living the Christian life. Apart from any legal disbarment, therefore, the rite insists that the sponsor be "sufficiently mature for this responsibility" and a fully initiated Catholic.

Formed in the Christian life by the word and example of parents and godparents, and through the experience of growing up in contact with the wider Christian community, the candidate for confirmation should now be at a stage to renew his or her baptismal promises (RC, 12). Perhaps "renewal of one's baptismal promises" is not really the best way of expressing what is happening in the case of a child baptized as an infant since, as we saw, the child did not make any promises at baptism, nor were the promises made in the candidate's name. On that occasion, it was the parents and godparents who publicly professed their own baptismal faith. Now the child is, for the first time, publicly professing his or her own faith. The candidate has gradually been learning what that faith involves and living by it, but this is the first time that this person stands before the gathered Church and proclaims the faith by which the Church lives to be the faith by which he or she too lives.

Once again, the formula of the profession of faith makes it clear that this is no statement of personal opinion, but a statement of commitment to a way of life: Christ's way of life as participated in by the community of his disciples who share his Spirit and follow their Lord under the sign of his cross. We have already seen what this means in our commentary on the rites of baptism. The candidate for confirmation therefore makes public a commitment to the baptismal way of life, so that one may be fully incorporated into the community which witnesses in word and life-style, in self-sacrificing charity and in Eucharistic celebration to its sharing in the death of the Lord. This is not the way of the world: it means a break with the conventional wisdom of the age. So the first question the bishop asks those to be confirmed is: "Do you reject Satan and all his works and all his empty promises?"

Assured of this, the bishop then inquires whether they put their faith in the saving power of God as revealed in Jesus:

Do you believe in God the Father almighty,
    creator of heaven and earth?
I do.
Do you believe in Jesus Christ, his only Son, our Lord,
    who was born of the Virgin Mary,
    was crucified, died, and was buried,
    rose from the dead,
    and is now seated at the right hand of the Father?
I do (RC, 23).

Although the group of candidates all answer together, each speaks for himself or herself. They say, not "we believe," as the community does at Mass; but, "*I* believe." Each candidate who was baptized as an infant was baptized in the faith of the Church and one's own faith was engendered and nurtured by the faith of others; but now that each is no longer an infant it is one's own faith which counts for salvation. A person must stand on one's own two feet and speak one's own mind. For this reason, confirmation should never be a mere formality for one who is old enough to know one's own mind.

In baptism, the final question put to the catechumens concerns their belief in the Holy Spirit and his role of bringing to completion the salvation inaugurated and revealed in Jesus. Here in confirmation that last question is broken into two in order to spell out a little more our belief in the reality of the Spirit and in his effective presence in our lives:

Do you believe in the Holy Spirit,
the Lord, the giver of life,
who came upon the apostles at Pentecost
and today is given to you sacramentally in confirmation?
I do (RC, 23).

The very same Spirit of God who was poured out on the Church at Pentecost remains with the Church today as the source of its life (theologians sometimes speak of the Spirit as the soul of the Church) and the guide and impetus behind the activity of the Church. To live and work in the Church means to live and work by the Spirit: "And all were made to drink of one Spirit" (1 Cor 12:13). It is this Spirit who will speak through us to the Church and to the world around us, each in one's own way but all for the same end: the building up of the Church and the ushering in of the kingdom of God. "Now there are varieties of gifts, but the same Spirit; and there are varieties of service, but the same Lord; and there are varieties of working, but it is the same God who inspires them all in every one. To each is given the manifestation of the Spirit for the common good" (1 Cor 12:4-7).

Finally, the bishop asks the candidates whether they put their trust in the presence of the Spirit in the community of believers and in his ability to transform their lives and bring them to union with the Father, which is the goal of all salvation history:

Do you believe in the holy catholic Church,
the communion of saints, the forgiveness of sins,
the resurrection of the body, and life everlasting?
I do.

The bishop then "confirms" their faith, by acknowledging that it is indeed the faith of the Church:

This is our faith.
This is the faith of the Church.
We are proud to profess it in Christ Jesus our Lord.
The whole congregation responds: Amen (RC, 23).

The whole process of initiation may be conceived of as a dialogue of faith in which the community and the catechumen, or the baptized but as yet unconfirmed believer, listen together to the voice of the Spirit of God and find themselves coming to a deeper and deeper unanimity of faith. This acclamation of the bishop and the community is their recognition that the Spirit has brought the candidates and the community to oneness of faith. It is a moment of joy which could well be expressed in music and song, for the candidates and the community have in a certain sense discovered each other, as two people discover each other when they suddenly find that they share something immensely important in common. They have all been led by the same Spirit to understand the same word and to commit themselves to the same Lord while sharing the same hope.

4. *The Laying On of Hands*

Nothing remains now but to seal this bond of faith with the sacrament of the Spirit who has brought it about. The bishop stands, with all his priests, and calls upon the assembled people of God to pray for their baptized brothers and sisters who have just given testimony of their Christian faith:

Let us pray to our Father
that he will pour out the Holy Spirit
to strengthen his sons and daughters with his gifts
and anoint them to be more like Christ the Son of God (RC, 24).

Towards the end of his gospel, St. John states explicitly the purpose of his work: "These [things] are written that you may believe that Jesus is the Christ, the Son of God, and that believing you may have life in his name" (20:31). For us "Christ" has become a proper name which we can use without adverting to the fact that it is a title. We should properly speak of "Jesus the Christ," for "christos" is simply the Greek translation of the Hebrew word "messiah," meaning "anointed." To believe that Jesus is "the Christ" is to believe that he is the one sent by God to carry out his plan for the salvation of the human race. To say that he is "the Son of God" is to say the same thing. To call Jesus the Son of God does also affirm his divinity, but in the New Testament it means equally that he has come from God, that God is coming to meet his people through him. He is the son sent by the great king to reclaim his vineyard, but who is rejected and killed by the rebellious servants (Matt 21:33-45).

When the bishop and the congregation pray that these baptized Christians may be anointed to be more like the Christ, the Son of God, they are praying that these people may be employed by God, as it were, as his emissaries to the world of today, as Jesus was to the world of his time. For this they must be anointed by the Spirit of God. Jesus himself began his work as "the one sent by God" after his baptism by John. As he came up out of the water, the Spirit descended upon him and began to "drive" him (Mark 1:10, 12; etc.). So, too, with the Church. The Church only began to take over the mission of Jesus and to proclaim the works of God when the disciples were anointed with the Spirit at the feast of Pentecost. In response to the bishop's invitation, therefore, the assembled believers pray that these newcomers to the Church may themselves be caught up by the Spirit into the missionary dynamism of the Church.

After a period of silent prayer, the bishop and his priests stretch out their hands over those to be confirmed. This ancient gesture is used in different ways in different sacramental liturgies—to exorcise catechumens before baptism, to invoke the Holy Spirit upon the gifts during the Eucharistic prayer, to give a solemn blessing to the congregation at the end of Mass, to ordain a priest, to bless a newly wedded couple, to absolve the penitent sinner. Each of these uses has a long history, stretching back as far as the Old Testament, but its precise meaning in each case is determined by the context in which it is used. In confirmation it has always been associated with an "epiklesis," that is to say, with calling down the Holy Spirit upon those newly baptized. The earliest texts seem to indicate that the bishop stretched out only his right hand over the whole group of those just baptized. Later on, under the influence of those texts in Acts which speak of a laying on of hands (in the plural), both hands came to be used, and the gesture itself came to be identified with the giving of the Spirit. However, there is no direct continuity between the apostolic period and the later practice of the Church of imposing hands on the newly baptized, so we would be right to see this solemn gesture as an immediate preparation for the anointing which follows and with which it is intimately linked. By the imposition of hands the gift of the Spirit is invoked, and by the anointing that gift is sealed. For a long time theologians argued about whether it was the laying on of hands or the anointing which conferred the gift of the Spirit. This is a somewhat futile argument, for the liturgy is an act of communication. Verbal communication is not made by one word, but by a sentence. Each word has meaning, but the sense is conveyed by the sentence as a whole. So with our liturgical celebrations. It is the rite in its entirety which "communicates" the Spirit of God, but each element in it is important. On the other hand, while stressing the importance of the laying on of hands and its contribution to the completeness of the rite and "to a clearer understanding of the sacrament," Pope Paul VI, in the Apostolic Constitution promulgating the revised rite of confirmation, directed that the anointing alone is absolutely essential and that in cases of "extreme necessity" the anointing alone would be sufficient.

It is really somewhat misleading to speak of an imposition or laying on of hands, for that suggests that the bishop lays hands on each candidate individually, whereas what we are in fact talking about is a gesture whereby the bishop stretches his hands out over all the candidates together. Nevertheless, in the context of confirmation, this is how the gesture has always been referred to. In the *Apostolic Tradition*, for example, we read:

> And the bishop shall lay his hand upon them invoking and saying: O Lord God, who didst count these worthy of deserving the forgiveness of sins by the laver of regeneration, make them worthy to be filled with thy Holy Spirit and send upon them thy grace, that they may serve thee according to thy will . . . (xxii, 1; Whitaker, p. 6).

However it is referred to, the meaning of the gesture is indicated, as we see here in Hippolytus, by the way the gesture is done and by the words which accompany it, as well as by the context in which it occurs. Our own ritual provides as follows:

> The bishop and the priests who will minister the sacrament with him lay hands upon all the candidates (by extending their hands over them). The bishop alone sings or says:

> All-powerful God, Father of our Lord Jesus Christ,
> by water and the Holy Spirit
> you freed your sons and daughters from sin
> and gave them new life.
> Send your Holy Spirit upon them
> to be their Helper and Guide.
> Give them the spirit of wisdom and understanding,
> the spirit of right judgment and courage,
> the spirit of knowledge and reverence.
> Fill them with the spirit of wonder and awe
> in your presence.
> We ask this through Christ our Lord. Amen (RC, 25).

This, unchanged at least from the early sixth century, is the traditional Roman confirmation prayer. In actual fact it is probably considerably older than that. The first part, even in English translation, is recognizably the same prayer as is found in the *Apostolic Tradition* in the early third century, while the rest of the prayer, invoking the gift of the seven-fold Spirit was certainly known at Rome in the fourth century, as we can tell from Pope Siricius' letter to the Spanish bishops (see p. 129 above).

In this prayer, the bishop is summing up the prayer of the whole congregation. He had asked them to pray to the Father to send his Holy Spirit upon these candidates, that they might be anointed with that same Spirit "to be more like Christ the Son of God" (RC, 24). From at least the fourth century, Hippolytus' prayer has been expanded to include a reference to the seven-fold Spirit of God mentioned in Isaiah 11:1-3. It is worth quoting this prophetic text:

> There shall come forth a shoot from the stump of Jesse,
> and a branch shall grow out of his roots.
> And the Spirit of the Lord shall rest upon him,
> the spirit of wisdom and understanding,
> the spirit of counsel and might,
> the spirit of knowledge and the fear of the Lord.
> And his delight shall be in the fear of the Lord.
> He shall not judge by what his eyes see,
> or decide by what his ears hear . . .

Jesse, of course, was the father of King David, and it was from the house of David that Jesus traced his own human lineage. He was, as Paul says, "descended from David according to the flesh and designated Son of God in power according to the Spirit of holiness by his resurrection from the dead" (Rom 1:3-4). It is of him, then, that Isaiah spoke. He was the one sent from God and anointed by this manifold Spirit of God. We pray that the Spirit which was in Jesus, which enabled him to do the works of God and glorify his Father, and which proved that he was indeed from God by breaking the stranglehold of death and raising him to life, may also be in those whom the Church confirms, that they may share the Spirit and mission and life of Jesus.

Notice that, although we have become accustomed to talking of the seven gifts of the Holy Spirit, the liturgy, following Isaiah, speaks of the *one* gift, the gift of the Spirit himself. This is very important, and it affects our whole understanding of how we live our Christian lives. We are not a people who are constantly trying to live up to the expectations of some law imposed on us from above. We are animated from within by the Holy Spirit who is poured out into our hearts. "Do you not know that your body is a temple of the Holy Spirit within you, which you have from God?" St. Paul asks (1 Cor 6:19). Our moral life is meant to be transformed into a credible sacrament of that Spirit, as a life characterized by insight and understanding of the things of God, a life lived under the guidance of his Spirit, resolute among people and reverential before God. The seven gifts are really one, not a check list of moral growth, therefore, but hopeful pointers to the different levels of life and areas of activity in which the Spirit will make his presence felt.

This prayer, taken together with the other prayers of the confirmation liturgy, such as those of the Mass formularies provided for confirmation, could serve as a useful starting point for a deepening understanding of the Spirit. Who is the Holy Spirit, anyway? If we try to answer that question by looking at the texts of the liturgy and at the scriptural readings, we will find ourselves following the same sort of process which the Church herself went through in history. We will start with an idea of the Spirit as a more or less impersonal force and move from there gradually to see that this force is not separable from God himself, but *is* God; and that he is not impersonal, but the very fruit of the personal love of the Father and the Son, and the source of the new person which is born in us when we come to share the divine life. But the fact that he is called "Spirit" means that we experience him as such. We speak of people being driven by a spirit of ambition, or anger or lust. Somehow, they are taken over by something in them, so that sometimes we can even talk of people being "beside themselves" with anger or impatience or desire. In fact, of course, much of what we do is done without a great deal of thought or commitment. We find ourselves doing things as if we had been handed over to an automatic pilot. This is part of being human, and it is everybody's experience. The point about the committed Christian, however, is that life has been surrendered to God in faith. In a sense, one deliberately chooses to "live beside oneself," to de-center one's existence that God's rule and kingdom may be at the heart of one's life. A person freely creates the space within for God to rule and guide one's life. This space, as it were, God fills with his Holy Spirit. This is why we speak of the Spirit as the "paraclete," which is a Greek word for someone who comes to another's help, an advocate. (That is why, in the prayer we have just been looking at, the translators, instead of saying "the Holy Spirit, the Paraclete," have preferred to paraphrase it as "Send your Holy Spirit upon them to be their Helper and Guide.")

It is this awareness of the Spirit as the driving force of God's presence in the world, the Church, and the individual, which we find in the liturgy. It is very rare indeed to find a liturgical prayer addressed to the Holy Spirit (although there are a few hymns which call upon him directly). Normally, as in this prayer, the Church prays to the Father to send his Spirit through Christ, "to complete his work on earth and bring us the fullness of grace." All grace is ultimately the gift and working of the Spirit, and the Spirit himself is grace, for he is a principle of life and strength to which we have no earthly claim, but which is God's absolutely free gift, the gift of the very love with which he loves the Son. The ultimate goal of the Spirit, therefore, is to transform us into the image of the Son, so that we can love the Father as Jesus loves him, and be loved by the Father who recognizes in us the Spirit and family likeness of his own beloved Son.

5. The Anointing with Chrism

The deacon brings the chrism to the bishop. If priests are to assist him in confirming, the bishop gives each of them a vessel of chrism, thereby indicating that they confer the sacrament in dependence on him who is the leader of the Church and the *minister originarius*, or source, of the sacrament of confirmation.

One by one the candidates come and kneel before the bishop. The person presenting the candidate introduces him or her to the bishop, and places the right hand on the protege's shoulder as a gesture of sponsorship and solidarity. The bishop dips his thumb in the chrism and traces a sign of the cross on the forehead of the person being confirmed, saying:

N., be sealed with the Gift of the Holy Spirit.

To which the newly confirmed replies: Amen (RC, 27).

While the candidates are being confirmed, the assembled people may sing a song commenting on and acclaiming the mystery which is being enacted. The following is taken from chapter six of the Adult Rite of Initiation:

How great the sign of God's love for us,
Jesus Christ our Lord:
promised before all time began,
revealed in these last days.
He lived and suffered and died for us,
but the Spirit raised him to life.
People everywhere have heard his message
and placed their faith in him.
What wonderful blessings he gives his people;
living in the Father's glory,

he fills all creation
and guides it to perfection (RCIA, 390:14).

Up until about the sixth century, plain oil was used, just as it was for the pre-baptismal anointing. The difference between the two in the time of Hippolytus, in the third century, was simply that the oil for the pre-baptismal anointing was exorcised, whereas this oil was blessed. This difference simply reflects the different uses to which the two kinds of oil were to be put. Hippolytus calls the blessed oil the "oil of thanksgiving," for its application after baptism is to express the positive gifts of God with which the life of the neophyte is enriched. We saw that in the New Testament "sealing" and "anointing" are used metaphorically of the communication of the Spirit of Christ to the faithful, for this gift completes their conformity to him and is the guarantee of the divine protection in this life and pledge of sharing his glory in the world to come. Given the common use of oil after a bath in the ancient world it is not difficult to imagine how that metaphor was soon translated into a ritual, a sign of the sacramental action of Christ compacting and sealing his union with the baptized with the gift of his Spirit.

From the sixth century onwards, the Western Churches adopted the Eastern practice of using perfumed oil for the sake of the additional symbolic overtones which this carries. Perfumed oil is naturally a sensuous sign of joy and well-being, but it also has romantic overtones, and it was to the love song of the Canticle of Canticles that many of the Eastern Fathers looked for their interpretation of this rite. There the attractiveness of the bridegroom is described in terms of his fragrance (1:3; 3:6; etc.); and similarly the bride (1:12; etc.). St Paul encouraged this association by speaking in 2 Cor 2:15 of the knowledge of Christ filling the world like a perfume

But thanks be to God, who in Christ always leads us in triumph, and through us spreads the fragrance of the knowledge of him everywhere. For we are the aroma of Christ to God among those who are being saved and among those who are perishing, to one a fragrance from death to death, to the other a fragrance of life to life.

As early as the fourth century, we find this prayer in a Syrian liturgy:

O Lord God . . . who has scattered the sweet odor of the gospel among all nations, do thou grant at this time that this chrism may be efficacious upon him that is baptized, so that the sweet odor of Christ may continue upon him firm and fixed; and now that he has died with him, may he arise and live with him (*Apostolic Constitutions*, 44:2; Whitaker, p. 34).

In this beautiful prayer we see how the anointing with chrism was understood both as signifying the unbreakable bond between the baptized and Christ (which we call the "character") and also the spiritual gift of the knowledge of Christ. While the former aspect of confirmation was emphasized in the West, with all its associated ideas of defense and strengthening, in the East the aroma of the chrism was seen as symbolic of a kind of emanation from God himself. The ability to smell the perfumed oil was symbolic of the Christian's sensitivity to the presence of God in the created world, in the Church and her celebrations, and in the hidden life of prayer and holiness. Thus confirmation is seen in Eastern theology as the sacrament of spiritual growth, of a developing interior life, of sensitivity to the things of the Spirit. This is not opposed to the more common Western idea of confirmation as the sacrament of entry into the witnessing community, for it is clear from the text of St. Paul, quoted above, that the attractiveness of Christ to the world is dependent upon the attractiveness of our own lives. This emphasis upon the Spirit of holiness and the inner authority which it engenders is an essential counterweight to the sometimes rather too extroverted and even militaristic conceptions of the Church's mission which have sometimes prevailed in the West, not least in the context of confirmation. We need to incorporate this understanding of confirmation into our own theology of this sacrament if we are not to continue to suffer from the tragic dichotomy between the active life and contemplative prayer, and between institutional structures and the spiritual life.

The bishop traces a cross on the forehead of the candidate. This may seem a somewhat meager way of applying the oil, especially when one thinks of St. Ambrose quoting Ps 133 about the oil running over Aaron's face and down his beard onto his collar! One may legitimately hope that the bishop will use strongly perfumed oil and that he will apply it generously, but the sign of the cross is significant, too. It is, after all, the seal or mark of Christ himself, and the gift of the Spirit is intended precisely to unite us to him and to make us like him. It is the risen and exalted Lord who gives us his Spirit, the one who has passed from death to life by way of the cross. It was the one who was still marked by the wounds of his crucifixion, according to John (20:19ff.), who breathed his Spirit upon his disciples. The gift of the Spirit to his friends was the first and immediate benefit of the redemptive death of Jesus: "For as yet the Spirit had not been given, because Jesus was not yet glorified" (John 7:39). Thus the Spirit, released for us by the death of Jesus, himself conforms us to our crucified Lord and is the pledge of our own passing from death to life by way of the cross. It is the Spirit who is the guarantee of the "new and everlasting covenant" between God and us which was established in the death and resurrection of the Lord. To be brought into that covenant with God in Christ, we must break our old alliances with the spirit of this world and be incorporated into the new covenant by water and the Spirit. It was not unusual for the whole rite of initiation to be called a "signing" or "sealing," for all the rites have the effect of making a person the inalienable property of God. But it is altogether natural that this aspect of becoming a Christian should especially be associated with the rite of anointing and with the gift of the Spirit, and that anointing itself should be done as a mark of the cross. Thus is a person saved from death by the blood of

Christ, marked forever by the cross of Christ, animated by the Spirit of Christ, fed by the flesh and blood of Christ, destined to be raised up with Christ to everlasting life in the kingdom of his Father.

In this way, then, a person's Christian initiation is completed and confirmed, "signed and sealed" by the hand of the bishop in the presence of the community of the baptized. The link between the two stages of initiation is to be found in the personal development of the candidate on the one hand, and in the person of Christ on the other. Whatever their difference of emphasis (and such difference should not be exaggerated), both baptism and confirmation refer to and initiate us into the single mystery of Christ. Thus Cyril of Jerusalem could tell those whom he had just recently initiated:

> Just as Christ was truly crucified, buried, and raised again, and you are considered worthy to be crucified, buried and raised with him in likeness by baptism, so too in the matter of anointing, Christ was anointed with the spiritual oil of gladness because he is the author of spiritual joy; and you have been anointed with chrism because you have become fellows and sharers of Christ (*Myst. Cat.* 3:2; Yarnold, p. 80).

6. *"Be Sealed with the Gift of the Holy Spirit"*

It is never a gesture alone, still less some material thing, which constitutes a Christian sacrament, but always a gesture—washing, anointing, breaking bread, touching—accompanied by a form of words which express and define the meaning of what is happening. This sacramental formula is a word of faith, an expression of the Church's faith in the meaning of what she is doing. Speaking of baptism in a well-known passage St. Augustine says:

> Take away the word and what is water but water? The word is joined to the element and the result is a sacrament, itself becoming, in a sense, a visible word as well . . . Whence this power of water so exalted as to bathe the body and cleanse the soul, if it is not through the action of the word; not because it is spoken, but because it is believed? (*On the Gospel of John*, 80, 3; Palmer, p. 127).

Thus the character of the Christian sacraments as sacraments of faith is maintained by the profession or prayer of faith which accompanies the sacramental gesture. But since no single formula can ever say all that can ever be said about the meaning of what is being done, it is not surprising to find that in most sacraments the formula of faith which constitutes an essential part of the sacramental sign has taken many varied forms. (The form of words used in the sacraments are therefore quite different from magical formulae in which the exact reproduction of a precise form of words is essential to the effectiveness of the ritual.)

In the third century rite of Hippolytus, the bishop simply says: "I anoint you with holy oil in God the Father almighty and Christ Jesus and the Holy Spirit." This was clearly felt to be inadequate, for in the sixth century the bishops of Rome were confirming people with the words: "The sign of Christ unto life eternal." In Spain this Roman formula was further expanded: "The sign of eternal life which God the Father almighty has given through Jesus Christ his Son to them that believe unto salvation." In some confirmation liturgies of the early Middle Ages there is no actual form of words to accompany the anointing, and the meaning of the rite is indicated in an adapted form of the prayer for the gift of the Spirit which precedes the anointing. On the other hand, the Churches of Ireland and the British Isles seem to have had a confirmation formula much closer to that of Hippolytus. For example, the Irish Stowe Missal has: "I anoint thee with the oil and the chrism of salvation and sanctification in the name of the Father and of the Son and of the Holy Ghost, now and throughout all ages of ages" (see Whitaker, pp. 188, 121, 220). Thus even in the Latin liturgies of Europe there were many different forms of words in use to accompany the anointing at confirmation. The form which we were used to, "I sign you with the sign of the cross and confirm you with the chrism of salvation, in the name of the Father . . . etc.," first appears in the twelfth century Roman Pontifical but was never in universal use until the post-Tridentine reforms established liturgical uniformity throughout the Latin Churches in the sixteenth century.

Since our old confirmation formula had little to recommend it, neither in terms of its content nor its age, and was really no help in trying to understand the meaning of the sacrament of confirmation, Pope Paul VI took the opportunity of the recent liturgical reform to change the formula at the anointing and to bring in a formula long in use in the East. There, too, many different formulae have been in use from the early and laconic "N. is signed in the name of the Father . . . etc." through to lengthy prayers and multiple formulae accompanying multiple anointings of different parts of the body. The one chosen for adoption by the Roman liturgy however is both brief and expressive. It is the formula used by the Church of Constantinople (and hence by the Russian and Greek Orthodox) since the fifth century, and is first found quoted by the Council of Constantinople in 381, although it is generally considered that the canon concerned (c. 7) is probably a fifth century interpolation, so that our formula cannot be dated with any certainty before that time.

In changing the formula of confirmation, Pope Paul was acting in accordance with the wish of the Fathers of Vatican II that confirmation be revised to make its place within the process of Christian initiation more clear (SC, 71). The use of the words "N., be sealed with the gift of the Holy Spirit" is a considerable improvement over the old formula for they indicate more clearly what it is that confirmation is about. Although the formula does not directly reproduce any New Testament text, its references to "sealing" and to the "gift" of the Spirit do echo a number of New Testament passages: "Repent and be baptized . . . and you shall receive the gift of the Holy Spirit" (Acts 2:38); "God's love has been poured out into our hearts through the Holy Spirit which has been given to us" (Rom 5:5); God "has put his seal upon us and given us his Spirit in our hearts as a guarantee" (2 Cor 1:22); "In him [Christ] you also, who have heard the word of truth, the gospel of your salvation, and have believed in him, were sealed with the promised Holy Spirit, which is the guarantee of our inheritance until we acquire possession of it, to the praise of his glory" (Eph 1:13-14). In these texts, as in the writings of the Fathers, it is impossible to separate the different graces of Christian initiation, for ultimately they are all one: salvation. This salvation consists of reconciliation with the Father through our identification with Christ his Son, both reconciliation and identification being the work of the Spirit of God. Thus the gift of God is the gift of the Spirit who saves and reconciles us in Christ. The gift of the Spirit is all good things now and in the future:

> You were anointed by [the Holy Spirit] and received him by God's grace. He is yours and remains within you. You enjoy the first fruits of him in this life, for you receive now in symbol the possession of the blessings to come. Then you will receive the grace in all its fulness, and it will free you from death, corruption, pain and change; your body too will last for ever and will be free from decay and your soul will not be liable to any further movement towards evil (Theodore of Mopsuestia, *Bapt. Hom.* III:27; Yarnold, p. 209).

Thus the gift of the Spirit is poured out into our hearts through the whole process of initiation, right from the very first stirrings of faith or a child's first arrival at the church through to this final sealing or anointing. It is a gift which affects us at every level of our being, which means reconciliation all-round, which heals our past and guarantees our future. The gift of the Spirit means that a person's life is no longer aimless and undirected. On the contrary, such people have found their place in the plan of God, in life, in the Church. Time and time again, the Fathers come back to Paul's words in 2 Cor 1:21-22:

> But it is God who establishes us with you in Christ,
> and has commissioned us;
> he has put his seal upon us
> and given us his Spirit in our hearts
> as a guarantee.

7. *The Kiss of Peace*

Having sealed the candidates with chrism and marked them with the cross of Christ, the bishop embraces each of them as a brother or sister: "Peace be with you"; to which the newly confirmed replies, "And also with you." This is an extremely ancient greeting, still found in the Middle East to this day where people greet each other with "Salaam!" or "Shalom!" It was the greeting with which the risen Christ addressed his stunned disciples: "Peace be with you" (John 20:19, 21). For one who has just completed the initiation into the messianic community, it has all sorts of prophetic overtones, for the prophets associated the blessings of peace with the end time, the era of God's rule and kingdom (Isa 9:7; Ezek 34:25; 37:26).

First and foremost, however, this is not a heavily symbolic ritual but a simple gesture of affection, congratulations and welcome. A new Christian is made; the bishop embraces him or her; the Church rejoices. Our earliest text of the Roman baptismal liturgy, Hippolytus' *Apostolic Tradition* (215), already mentions this greeting, and orders the kiss of peace to be exchanged throughout the community as soon as the prayers are over. (It was usual for the liturgy of the word to be concluded by all the believers exchanging the kiss of peace.) The even earlier description of baptism by St. Justin also mentions the kiss of peace being given when the newly baptized is brought "to where the brethren are assembled," but again this mutual greeting of peace was standard practice at the conclusion of liturgical prayer. But John Chrysostom, preaching at Antioch in the last quarter of the fourth century, remarks on the special joy and enthusiasm with which the greeting of peace was exchanged with the newly baptized:

> As soon as they come forth from those sacred waters, all who are present embrace them, greet them, kiss them, rejoice with them, and congratulate them, because those who were heretofore slaves and captives have suddenly become free men and sons and have been invited to the royal table (Stavronikita, 2:27; Whitaker, p. 41).

One has to remember that the newly baptized would be sharing the kiss of peace with their fellow Christians for the first time, since the kiss, like common prayer and attendance at the Eucharist, had hitherto been denied them. This must have been an intensely emotional moment, one which underlined so very strongly that initiation was initiation into the Christian community and that to be a Christian really meant something. One would have wished that the kiss of peace might have been extended to embrace others besides the bishop, instead of having to be deferred until just before Communion. Interestingly enough, a first tentative step in this direction is taken by the Rite of the Reception of Baptized Christians. We read:

> After the general intercessions the sponsor and, if only a few persons are present, all the congregation may greet the newly received person in a friendly manner. In this case the sign of peace before communion may be omitted (RR, 20).

While not seeming to condone the sort of abandon with which John Chrysostom was apparently familiar, this rubric does open the way to a restoration of an ancient and very meaningful custom. Perhaps it will creep back into the other forms of the liturgy of confirmation, too, as the faithful appreciate more and more the ecclesial and communitarian dimension of this sacrament.

8. *The General Intercessions*

With the restoration of the general intercessions or "bidding prayers" at Mass, their presence here in the confirmation liturgy may be taken for granted, especially if, as is usual, confirmation is followed immediately by the celebration of the Eucharist. Yet they, too, are a significant part of the ritual of Christian initiation. Throughout the early centuries of the Church, while adult initiation was the norm, non-Christians, schismatics and catechumens were never permitted to pray with the community of believers. The *Apostolic Tradition* states quite clearly:

> Each time the teacher finishes his instruction let the catechumens pray by themselves apart from the faithful.
>
> But after the prayer is finished the catechumens shall not give the kiss of peace, for their kiss is not yet pure (xvii, 1, 3; Whitaker, p. 3).

At the Sunday liturgy, the catechumens were always dismissed with a prayer after the homily, and then the community of the baptized offered their intercessions, the "prayer of the faithful."

The first privilege of the newly baptized, then, is to join the Church at prayer. Tertullian tells those preparing for baptism:

> Therefore, you blessed ones, for whom the grace of God is waiting, when you come up from that most sacred washing of the new birth, and when for the first time you spread out your hands in your mother's house, ask of your Father, ask of your Lord that special grants of grace and apportionments of spiritual gifts be yours. *Ask*, he says, *and ye shall receive.* So now, you have sought, and have found; you have knocked, and it has been opened to you (*On Baptism*, 20; Evans, p. 43).

To understand this, one would need to understand the high value placed upon the prayer of the assembled people. For the Fathers, it was nothing less than the prayer of Christ himself. Even the prayer of the individual is thought of having value only insofar as it is prayer offered within the Church. Here, for example, is a passage from St. Cyprian on the Lord's Prayer:

> Above all, the teacher of peace and master of unity [Christ] did not want us to pray individually and privately. We do not say "My Father who art in heaven," nor "give me this day my daily bread." Our prayer is common and public prayer. It is not for an individual, but for the whole people that we pray, because we are all one people in a single [body]. The God of peace and master of concord who has taught unity has willed that the individual should pray for all, just as he bore all men in himself . . .
>
> "They persevered in prayer," being of one mind in their praying, showing by their perseverence and their oneness of heart that God who "installs in his house those who are all of one heart" does not admit into his divine and everlasting habitation anyone except those whose prayer he finds to be of one accord . . . (*de Oratione Dominica*, 8).

Whereas in the baptismal liturgy the prayers (in the form of litanies) are offered *before* baptism and on behalf of those to be baptized, here the intercessions follow the administration of confirmation and provide an opportunity for the newly initiated Christians to join in the common prayer of the people of God. For the first time, they raise their hands in prayer in the house of their holy mother, the Church. For the first time they exercise their newly acquired baptismal priesthood, for through baptism they have been incorporated into Christ of whom the epistle to the Hebrews says that "he is able for all time to save those who draw near to God through him, since he always lives to make intercession for them" (7:25). Through the sacraments of initiation, they have been incorporated into the praying and celebrating Church, the sacramental body of Christ through which Christ is able to continue on earth his work of sanctifying humanity and glorifying his Father. As members of the community of faith they have the right and the duty to celebrate the sacraments of faith, to participate fully in the liturgical life of the Church, which is "the whole public worship of the Mystical Body of Jesus Christ, Head and members" (Pius XII, *Mediator Dei*, 20).

We have already seen in many different contexts that the rites of initiation commit people irrevocably to Christ, assigning them forever to the service of the Lord. Even should they subsequently fall away, there can be no question of repeating their Christian initiation. St. Augustine explained this by analogy with the "character," or stamp, which a coin bears: no matter where it goes, it still bears the imperial likeness. In the thirteenth century, St. Thomas Aquinas enormously enriched this concept by relating it to the way the baptized share in the priestly work of Christ:

> . . . each of the faithful is destined to receive or to give to others what pertains to the worship of God; and to assure this is the proper function of the sacramental character. Now the whole rite of the Christian religion is derived from the priesthood of Christ. It is clear then that the sacramental character is specially the character of Christ, to whose priesthood the faithful are likened or configured by reason of the sacramental characters, which are nothing else but certain participations of the priesthood of Christ, which are derived from Christ himself (*Summa Theol.* III, 1.63; tr. Palmer, p. 140).

It is this understanding of the rights and duties of all the baptized which lies behind the Sunday Mass obligation, and also accounts for the efforts of Vatican II, and of the popes from Pius X to Paul VI, to encourage the full, conscious and active participation of all the faithful in the liturgical celebrations of the Church.

Such active participation finds its highest form, of course, in the celebration of the Eucharist and the reception of Holy Communion. Nevertheless, the "bidding prayers" express very clearly the fact that the Church serves the world, and that the baptized have to exercise their priesthood not only on their own behalf but for the benefit of all the world. Speaking precisely of the prayers offered by the newly baptized with their fellow Christians, St. Justin reflects this sense of responsibility for the larger world community:

> After we have thus washed him who is persuaded and declares his assent, we lead him to those who are called brethren, where they are assembled, and make common prayer fervently for ourselves, for him that has been enlightened, and for all men everywhere, that, embracing the truth, we may be found in our lives good and obedient citizens, and also attain to everlasting salvation (*I Apol.* c. 65; Whitaker, p. 2).

St. Justin was writing in the middle of the second century, but exactly the same pattern and purpose of prayer is found in the general intercessions found in our own confirmation liturgy. The bishop calls the community to prayer in words reminiscent of the text of St. Cyprian cited above: "My dear friends, let us be one in prayer to God our Father as we are one in the faith, hope, and love his Spirit gives." The intentions for prayer, called out by the deacon or other minister, begin with the newly confirmed, move then to their parents and godparents "who led them by faith," then on to the universal Church, praying for its growth in unity of faith and love; then to "people of every race and nation" (RC, 30). Thus the prayer begins with those who have been the focus of the community's celebration and from there spreads out like ripples, overflowing the boundaries of the local community to embrace our brothers and sisters in the faith throughout the world, and finally including the whole of humanity. The actual texts provided do not have to be used, but they provide a pattern which must be followed if the faithful are to prove themselves sharers in Christ's universal concern and, in Justin's phrase, "good and obedient citizens."

9. Conclusion

The bishop sums up the prayer of the faithful in a concluding collect, and with that the ritual of confirmation comes to a close. In the normal order of things, suggested both by the introduction to the rite (RC, 13) and by the whole movement of the process of initiation (see Part IV below), the celebration of the Eucharist in which the new Christians partake of the Body and Blood of the Lord for the first time should follow immediately. If, however, because of special circumstances, this cannot be done, the liturgy is concluded with the common recitation of the Our Father. The Lord's Prayer concludes the baptismal liturgy when it is separated from confirmation and Eucharist, in anticipation of the newly baptized reaching their goal when they recite that prayer at the celebration of the Mass. At confirmation it has the same anticipatory character, but now takes on additional significance insofar as the newly confirmed have just celebrated their anointing with the Spirit who is the source of all prayer. "When we cry, 'Abba! Father!' it is the Spirit himself bearing witness to our spirit that we are children of God, and if children, then heirs, heirs of God and fellow heirs with Christ, provided we suffer with him in order that we may also be glorified with him" (Rom 8:15-17).

These last words of St. Paul take us back to where we began, when the newborn child was welcomed into the community of the Church with the sign of the cross. Time and time again throughout the process of initiation we have come up against the cross of Christ. The sacraments are not magic, not automatic, impersonal processes, but the media of an encounter with God in faith. God's offer of salvation, his gift of the Spirit, is always and everywhere available whenever these liturgies of the Church are celebrated, provided we have the kind of faith which Christ himself had and are prepared to "suffer with him in order that we may also be glorified with him." The sacraments of Christian initiation show us that there is no other way to the Father's kingdom except that of becoming disciples of the Crucified, no other wisdom but the wisdom of the cross.

Praise be the Father of our Lord Jesus Christ,
a God so merciful and kind!
He has given us a new birth, a living hope,
by raising Jesus his Son from death.
Salvation is our undying inheritance,
preserved for us in heaven,
salvation at the end of time (RCIA, 390:13).

PART FOUR

EUCHARIST

EUCHARIST

1. *The Promised Land*

Every living being, Theodore of Mopsuestia reminded his people, owes its life not only to the fact that its mother gave it birth, but also to the mother's ability to feed her offspring. In this way, he links the new birth of initiation to the celebration of the Eucharist to which the newly baptized are immediately admitted. But the source of life is the same in both cases: the saving death of the Lord:

> Just as through the death of Christ we receive the birth of baptism, the same is true of the food: we receive it sacramentally through his death . . . Bringing an offering and participating in the mysteries means commemorating the death of the Lord who gains resurrection for us and the enjoyment of immortality; for it is right that we, who through the death of the Lord, the Christ, have received spiritual birth, should receive through that same death the food of immortality. *We are fed at the same source which gave us birth . . . (Bapt. Hom.* IV, 6).

From the beginning, the sacraments of initiation led immediately to common prayer with the community of the baptized and to the celebration of the Eucharist. In Acts, the account of the first baptisms is followed at once by a summary description of the community life of the first Christians: "And day by day, attending the temple together and breaking bread in their homes, they partook of food with glad and generous hearts, praising God and having favor with all the people" (2:46-47). Justin's description of baptism (c. 150) is followed at once by his description of the post-baptismal Eucharist. This pattern was followed in the West for over a thousand years and is still the normal procedure in some Eastern Churches to this very day, even in the case of the baptism of infants.

This participation in the Eucharist from which they had hitherto been barred, was, for the newly baptized, participation in the fullest sense. This meant that they could join with the rest of the faithful, not only in attending the celebration and joining in the responses, but also in making their offering and participating in the sacrificial meal. Thus the *Apostolic Tradition* of Hippolytus ordains that those to be baptized are to bring nothing with them to the baptismal vigil except their offering for the Eucharist to follow: "For it is right for everyone to bring his oblation then" (xx, 9; Whitaker, p. 4). In the early centuries, the bringing of gifts by all who had something to give was an essential part of the Eucharistic celebration. (What was not used for the

Eucharist was afterwards distributed by the bishop and his deacons to the poor.) Those who were barred from Communion were also barred from offering.

On the other hand, Hippolytus also mentions another custom which must have been a peculiarity of the Eucharist which culminated the baptismal vigil of Easter. After the prayers have been concluded and the kiss of peace shared, the gifts are brought to the bishop by the deacons and set upon the altar for him to consecrate. Besides the usual bread and wine, however, two extra cups are placed on the altar, one filled with water and the other with milk and honey. The water is symbolic of the baptism of the "inner person," that it "may receive the same as the body" (xxiii, 3). The cup of milk and honey is explained as being "in fulfilment of the promise which was made to the Fathers, wherein God said, 'I will give you a land flowing with milk and honey'; which Christ indeed gave, his flesh, whereby they who believe are nourished like little children . . ." (*ibid.*, 2; Dix, p. 40). Some scholars believe that this may be a surviving relic of the time when the Eucharist was still celebrated, as it was in apostolic times, in the course of a meal. However, given the baptismal context, it is easy enough to take the explanation given in the text of Hippolytus at its face value and to recognize that the newly baptized were being treated as the heirs of the promise made to the Israelites of old: "The Lord said to Moses: 'Depart, go up hence, you and the people whom you have brought up out of the land of Egypt, to the land of which I swore to Abraham, Isaac, and Jacob, saying, 'To your descendants I will give it . . . Go up to a land flowing with milk and honey'" (Ex 33:1, 3). However, the people's infidelity to the covenant made their hold on that land—"a land flowing with milk and honey, the most glorious of all lands" (Ezek 20:6)—very tenuous. Not surprisingly, then, the new people of God, who were heirs of the new covenant forged in Christ, saw themselves as being the ones who would inherit this land. But just as the covenant was a spiritual covenant, so the land was no geographical area any more; it was the land of life, of immortality. Nearly three hundred years after Hippolytus, this custom of presenting the newly baptized not only with the body and blood of the Lord but also with the cup of milk sweetened with honey, still survived at Rome. John the Deacon answered a question from his friend Senarius on this matter as follows:

> You ask why milk and honey are placed in a most sacred cup and offered with the sacrifice at the Paschal Sabbath. The reason is that it is written in the Old Testament and in a figure promised to the New People: *I shall lead you into a land of promise, a land flowing with milk and honey* (Lev 20:24). The land of promise, then, is the land of resurrection to everlasting bliss, it is nothing else than the land of our body, which in the resurrection of the dead shall attain to the glory of incorruption and peace. This kind of sacrament, then, is offered to the newly baptized so that they may realize that no others but they, who partake of the body and blood of the Lord, shall receive the land of promise; and as they start

upon their journey thither, they are nourished like little children with milk and honey . . . (12; Whitaker, pp. 157–158).

For the newly baptized to share in the Eucharist, then, is the most obvious and natural thing. They have passed through the waters and entered the Promised Land. They are fed now with the food with which God sustains his own people, for in a sense they have arrived and the fulness of life and joy is theirs. In another sense, though, they are still pilgrims and this is only a foretaste of glory, an anticipation of the great feast to be held in the kingdom of God (Luke 14:15-24).

Even infants and small children were admitted to Holy Communion after baptism, especially if their baptism occurred in the course of the paschal vigil. The cup of milk and honey does not appear to have found much favor outside Rome and even there it was allowed to lapse in the sixth century, but the practice of giving baptized infants Communion continued in Rome and was universally accepted. Shortly after the time of John, the Gelasian Sacramentary makes no mention of the cup of milk, but the Ordo Romanus XI in the seventh century states unequivocally:

> After [the completion of baptism and confirmation] they go in to Mass and all the infants receive Communion. Care is to be taken lest after they have been baptized they receive any food or suckling before they communicate.

> Afterwards let them come to Mass every day for the whole week of the Pascha and let their parents make oblations for them (103–104; Whitaker, p. 204).

The tenderness of the children's age was no more thought to be a reason for postponing Holy Communion than it was for postponing baptism. In fact, it was generally considered that the two were inseparable. In the fifth century, Pope Innocent I wrote: ". . . it is stupid to think that children can be given the reward of eternal life without the grace of baptism. Unless they have eaten the flesh of the Son of Man and drunk his blood they shall not have life in them [John 6:53f.]" (DS 219).

When infant Communion finally died out in the twelfth century (at least as a universal practice; it continued longer in some places), this was due less to any fear of irreverence than to the fact that the laity rarely received Holy Communion anyway. The problem of spilling the sacrament was overcome easily enough, either by giving Communion by intinction (as is the custom in the East) or under the form of wine only, the priest administering it to the infant on the end of his finger. Certainly the growing realism with which people regarded the presence of Christ in the sacrament contributed to making people shy away from Communion anyway and to making the giving of the sacrament to children too young to understand increasingly inappropriate. In 1215 the situation had become so bad that the Fourth Lateran Council had to order every baptized person who had attained the age of discretion to go to confession and Communion once a year, under pain of excommunication and refusal of ecclesiastical burial! However, no mention was made of infants in this context and in the sixteenth century the Council of Trent was able to declare that the sacrament of the Lord's body and blood could in no way be regarded as necessary for the salvation of children below the age of reason (DS, n. 1730).

The problem with this was that it led to the situation in which, even when adults were baptized, it was no longer considered right to admit them to Communion either, with the result that the celebration of the Eucharist no longer capped the celebration of initiation, and the sacraments of initiation were no longer seen as leading to participation in the Eucharist. In the nineteenth and twentieth centuries, even the traditional order of administering the sacraments—baptism, confirmation, first Communion—was abandoned when the emphasis on early first Communion meant that children went to Communion before they were confirmed, not only in the exceptional case, but as a general rule. This was just the last and ultimate symptom of the slow disappearance of any integrated understanding of the sacraments of initiation as celebrating a process of Christian formation. Before anything else, therefore, Vatican II had to try to ensure that a sense of the continuity of the sacraments of initiation should become part of our Christian heritage again. The General Introduction to the initiation liturgies begins with a very clear statement of this principle. It is worth quoting in full:

> Through baptism men and women are incorporated into Christ. They are formed into God's people, and they obtain forgiveness of all their sins. They are raised from their natural human condition to the dignity of adopted children. They become a new creation through water and the Holy Spirit. Hence they are called, and are indeed, the children of God.
>
> Signed with the gift of the Spirit in confirmation, Christians more perfectly become the image of their Lord and are filled with the Holy Spirit. They bear witness to him before all the world and eagerly work for the building up of the body of Christ.
>
> Finally they come to the table of the Eucharist, to eat the flesh and drink the blood of the Son of Man so that they may have eternal life and show forth the unity of God's people. By offering themselves with Christ, they share in his universal sacrifice: the entire community of the redeemed is offered to God by their high priest. They pray for a greater outpouring of the Holy Spirit so that the whole human race may be brought into the unity of God's family.
>
> Thus the three sacraments of Christian initiation closely combine to bring the faithful to the full stature of Christ and to enable them to carry out the mission of the entire people of God in the Church and in the world (GICI, 2).

Because of this essential unity of the sacraments of initiation, it is now the policy of the Church that whenever adults, or children who have reached the age of discretion, come to the church for baptism, they will be baptized, confirmed and make their first Holy Communion in the course of a single liturgy (RC, 11). No explicit provision in this sense is made for children baptized in infancy, yet the whole thrust of the rites demands that at least the order of the sacraments of initiation should, as far as possible, be respected. In their case, the process of initiation may need to be spread out over a period of years, yet it should still be intelligible as a single process, the culmination and completion of which is their admission to the celebration of the Eucharist, the sacrament and pledge of their arrival in the land of promise, the land of milk and honey.

2. *The Mystery of Faith*

It has sometimes been suggested that had someone spoken of the "blessed sacrament" to St. Paul, he would have presumed that it was baptism which was in question. Certainly St. Paul had a high estimation of baptism and he also had a great respect for the celebration of the Eucharist (see 1 Cor 11:17ff.), but the value of them both lay precisely in the fact that they were means whereby we can participate in the mystery which they both communicate: God's hidden purpose for his people now revealed and realized in Christ, and still in process of being realized until the end of time sees its completion. This mystery is the Good News preached by the Church and celebrated in all her sacraments. Thus baptism and Eucharist are both celebrations of the same "mystery of faith." The Church, which is the visible manifestation of this mystery of salvation in a gathered community, initiates people into the mystery in the sacraments of baptism and confirmation and maintains herself as a community living by this mystery in the regular celebration of the Eucharist. The individual who is led to faith by the Spirit of God is drawn into the mystery of salvation through the sacraments of initiation and sustained in the new life by regular participation in the Eucharist. Thus the Mass is the celebration of the baptized, while baptism is the necessary initiation which leads to the celebration of the Eucharist. The grace of baptism and confirmation leads directly and inevitably to reception of the gift of the Eucharist, which is the celebration of our unity with Christ and one another in faith and love. The sacraments of initiation mark the process of entering into communion; the sacrament of the Eucharist is the sacrament of the gift of Communion.

This is not the place to attempt a consideration of all that the Mass means, but it might be helpful, since we are speaking of the Eucharist as the completion of Christian initiation, to point out some of the ways in which the Mass takes up the themes we have found in baptism and confirmation.

In Christian initiation we become members of the Church and are incorporated into the unity of the one body of Christ. Our unity with Christ, therefore, is expressed and realized by our entering into human community which is the local Church and which in turn is part of the universal Church of God throughout the world. There is no "direct link" to Christ. We can only become one with him by becoming one with one another. Thus the Church is the communion of saints, and the Eucharist, the fraternal meal, is the sign and sacrament of that unity in Christ. It both celebrates the unity we have been given and urges us to deepen our unity and to overcome our divisions:

> The new birth has made [the newly baptized] grow into a single body; now they are to be firmly established in the one body by sharing the body of our Lord, and form a single unity in harmony, peace and good works. Thus we shall look upon God with a pure heart; we shall not incur punishment by communicating in the Holy Spirit when we are divided in our views, inclined to arguments, quarrels, envy and jealousy, and contemptuous of virtue . . . In this way, by communion in the blessed mysteries, we shall be united among ourselves and joined to Christ our Lord, whose body we believe ourselves to be, and through whom we become partakers of the divine nature (Theodore Mopsuestia, *Bapt. Hom.*, V, 13; Yarnold, pp. 246–247).

If we are one body in Christ, it is because we are one in faith; that faith whereby we entrust our lives to God. We have already seen how the sacraments of initiation are sacraments of faith, and how both the community and the individual express their faith commitment in the very celebration of the sacraments after hearing the word. So, too, at Mass. The weekly assembly of the people of God is confronted with the word of God as a word of judgment and of hope, denouncing evil and holding out the offer of salvation. The prayers, the creed, and above all the Eucharistic prayer itself, these are the Church's confession of faith in response to that word. We speak of the "eucharist," a Greek word which is perhaps best translated as "acknowledgement." The Eucharistic prayer is a grateful acknowledgement of what God has done and is doing in our lives. Remembrance leads to intercession: for the present and for the completion of God's plan in the future. We have already seen an instance of this sort of prayer in the blessing of baptismal water (see page 71 above).

But this act of faith is no mere lip service; it is a renewal of commitment, a renewal of the covenant. This covenant was made between God and his people in Christ, but each of us became party to it in our own baptism. In that sense, the offering of oneself with Christ to God in sacrifice is an affirmation of one's baptismal commitment and a rediscovery of one's baptismal identity. The mystery of faith we proclaim is that Christ has died, and is risen, and is coming; we proclaim his passover, and do so only that we might offer ourselves with him to share his passover as we continue, day by day, upon the spiritual journey begun in baptism. In sharing the sacrament of the Lord's body "given up for you" and the cup of his blood "poured out for you," we reaffirm that "we were buried . . . with him by baptism into death, so that as Christ was raised from the dead by the glory of the Father, we too might walk in newness of life" (Rom 6:4).

But this, we saw, is the work of the Spirit. The same Spirit of God who was at work in the sacraments of initiation is at work in the Mass. In the course of the Eucharistic prayer we pray not only that the Spirit may come down upon the gifts, "to make them holy, so that they may become for us the body and blood of our Lord Jesus Christ," but also "that we, who are nourished by his body and blood, may be filled with his Holy Spirit, and become one body, one Spirit in Christ." Thus St. Cyril of Jerusalem could say:

> The offerings are holy since they have received the presence of the Holy Spirit, and you are holy because you have been accounted worthy of the Holy Spirit (*Myst. Cat.* 5:19; Yarnold, p. 93).

In this way, the celebration of the Eucharist keeps alive the gift given us in baptism: the gift of our assimilation to the dead and risen Christ and the life of the Spirit in the Church. It is the formal acknowledgement of all that God has done for us, in the history of the world and in the story of our own lives. It is the supreme act of witness and praise, the fulfilment of that sacred charge which we accepted in baptism and confirmation, to be "a chosen race, a royal priesthood, a holy nation, God's own people, that you may declare the wonderful deeds of him who called you out of darkness into his marvelous light" (1 Pet 2:9).

It is no arbitrary matter, therefore, that the Church insists that we assemble each week, on the first day of the week, to renew our identity as the disciples of the risen Lord, and to declare the deeds and sing praises of our God. Nor is it an arbitrary matter that confirmation, which completes our baptismal process and dedicates us to the building up of the unity of the Church and to the work of witness, should normally take place in the context of a Eucharistic assembly and immediately issue in the great prayer of acknowledgement and in the sharing of the bread and the cup. Baptism, confirmation and Eucharist belong together, so that the meaning of each is gravely impoverished if it is detached from its relation to the rest. All three are but different aspects of a single mystery of divine benevolence, drawing us into an ever deeper union with the Father through the Son in the Holy Spirit. Tertullian, at the turn of the third century, expressed this richness beautifully when he summarized the whole process of becoming a Christian as he knew it in the liturgy of his own Church:

> The flesh is washed that the soul may be spotless; the flesh is anointed that the soul may be consecrated; the flesh is signed [with the cross] that the soul too may be protected; the flesh is overshadowed by the imposition of the hand that the soul also may be illumined by the Spirit; the flesh feeds on the body and blood of Christ so that the soul as well may be replete with God (*De Res. Carnis*, 8; Whitaker, p. 10).

3. *Christians, remember your dignity.*

Life is not all celebration, and Christian life is not all liturgy. The sacramental celebrations of the Christian people draw upon the experience of day to day living and point back to it. It is there, in the toil and the leisure, in the laughter and the tears, in the bearing of burdens and the cheerful, even courageous perseverance in the face of all life brings, that the realities symbolized in the sacraments enter almost imperceptibly into the very stuff of life. It is there that the way of Satan and his world have resolutely and persistently to be brushed aside. It is there that the wisdom of the cross has to be discovered by taking the sort of risks which the world—our world—considers folly: the risks involved in bearing with one another, in loving unconditionally, in unstinting generosity, in humble service, in real concern for justice and for truth, in genuine delight in all that is good and beautiful and true. Sacraments are not just sacred rituals; they are patterns upon which to build a life-style.

How is the Christian to survive in a de-christianized world? How is one to grow strong enough to offer that world the word of life? Week by week, we will gather with the assembly of the faithful on that day "when life first dawned for us, thanks to Christ and his death," and we will renew our baptismal commitment and give thanks for our baptismal gift as we partake of the bread that is broken and the cup that is shared. This will be the source of our inner strength, an inner strength which lends the authority of Christ to us as we live and work among other people. The Eucharist will be our "viaticum," the unfailing source of nourishment for our continuing spiritual journey. For the journey does not end when initiation is completed. It has only just begun. It will continue until we make our final surrender to God in death, thus fulfilling in our own bodies the mysteries we have experienced in the sacraments. It will continue as we move through the successive chapters of our lives in the world, and it will continue as an inner journey of growth in prayerful union with God in the Spirit. As we travel on, we will discover that the sacramental celebrations of the Church help us to make sense of the confused pattern of our lives, but that the experience of life, too, will gradually reveal for us the meaning of the sacraments we celebrate. For ultimately all is one, thanks to the incarnation of Christ which has revealed to us the presence of God among us in our world. Pope St. Leo the Great (d. 461) marvelled at this great mystery in one of his Christmas sermons:

> Let us give thanks, dear friends, to God our Father, through his Son, in the Holy Spirit; to him who, of his great mercy, loved us and took pity on us; who "even when we were dead through our trespasses, made us alive together with Christ" [Eph 2:5], that we might be a new being, a new creation, in him. Let us then "put off the old nature with its practices" [Col 3:9] and, being sharers in the divine nature, let us renounce the ways of the flesh. Christian, remember your dignity: you are a sharer in the divine nature, so do not relapse into the degenerate life-style of the past. Remember who your head is and to whose body you belong. Remember that you have been snatched from the power of darkness, and transferred to the light and kingdom of God. By baptism you have been made a temple of the Holy Spirit (In Nativ. Dni, Sermo II; SC 22, pp. 73–74).

Besides the weekly Eucharistic assembly, the Church had other ways of helping the newly baptized to remember their dignity. The first of these was to make the most of their baptism by following it up with a week of celebration. From the Easter Vigil until the following Saturday inclusive the newly baptized wore their new white baptismal tunics, so that they were immediately recognizable and could be greeted and congratulated by the whole community. Each day throughout this week, too, there was a special assembly every morning at which the bishop prayed and celebrated with them, and instructed them concerning the meaning of the rites they had experienced. Egeria, the Spanish pilgrim who visited Jerusalem shortly after 380, has left us this vivid eyewitness account:

> Then Easter comes, and during the eight days from Easter Day to the eighth day, after the dismissal has taken place in the church . . . it does not take long to say the prayer and bless the faithful; then the bishop stands leaning againt the inner screen in the cave of the Anastasis [site of Christ's tomb], and interprets all that takes place in baptism. The newly baptized come into the Anastasis, and any of the faithful who wish to hear the Mysteries; but, while the bishop is teaching, no catechumen comes in and the doors are kept shut in case any try to enter. The bishop relates what has been done, and interprets it, and, as he does so, the applause is so loud that it can be heard outside the church. Indeed the way he expounds the mysteries and interprets them cannot fail to move his hearers (47:1–2; Wilkinson, pp. 145–146).

This sort of instruction of the initiates, or "mystagogy" as it is called, is strongly recommended in the new rite for the initiation of adults (RCIA, 37–40). It is envisaged as a period in which, after the completion of their initiation, "the community and the neophytes move forward together, meditating on the gospel, sharing the Eucharist, and performing works of charity" (*ibid.*, 37). It is a period for deepening in an experiential way the sense of what the paschal mystery is about and how it affects our daily living. It is a period of settling into the Christian community for the neophytes, but it is also a period in which the local community itself enjoys something of a boost, for it is hoped that "the neophytes, helped by their sponsors, may enter into a closer relationship with the faithful and bring them renewed vision and a new impetus" (*ibid.*, 39). In other words, the Church has something to learn from the experience of those who have been initiated. Their own attentiveness to the Spirit and enthusiasm for the things of God might rub off on the local faithful. This is obviously more likely to happen with adult converts, but there is good reason for thinking that a comparable attempt to fete those who have just been confirmed and made their first Communion would help both the children and the parish, especially if, as is suggested in the adult rite, the sacraments are celebrated at Easter or during the Easter season and the festivity is prolonged until Pentecost.

There was also for many centuries the custom in the Roman Church of celebrating the *pascha annotinum,* or anniversary of baptism. It was a sort of "class reunion" for the baptized, their sponsors, and the bishop, at which they celebrated the Eucharist together on what might be called their Christian birthday. The sense of the occasion is well caught in the opening collect of the Gelasian Sacramentary:

O God, by your providence, the memory of the things that happened remains, while all that we could hope for in the future has been promised. Let the solemn occasion which we recall be permanently effective in our lives, so that we may remain faithful in practice to what we commemorate now.

If ever the celebration of Christian initiation begins to play the role in Christian community life that it used to play in the past, when it was the great community festival of the year, perhaps such annual reunions of the baptized will also revive. In the meantime, a growing awareness of our baptismal identity may make it more common for Christians to know at least the date of their baptism and to give thanks to God for his mercy on each successive anniversary.

On the other hand, there is already an occasion on which all the baptized may remember the grace of their initiation and give thanks for it. Even though it is rare nowadays to have adults or even children initiated at Easter, the liturgy of Easter is still a baptismal liturgy, as all the readings and prayers of the vigil make clear. Particularly now that a celebration of the renewal of baptismal promises is included in the rite, it is the annual commemoration and reaffirmation of our baptism. The fact that it takes place at the same time for everyone, irrespective of when they were actually baptized, can serve to underline the fact that we are all sharers in one Lord, "one faith, one baptism" (Eph 4:5), and that the baptism of one is the renewal of all. Indeed, the annual communal renewal of our common baptismal commitment is a most important occasion for becoming aware that baptism, far from being a private matter, is in fact constitutive of the very Church itself.

Unfortunately, the term "laity" is no longer a proud title, yet the word derives from that lovely and ancient scriptural name, *laos tou theou,* "people of God." To call oneself a layperson is to claim membership of the people whom God has gathered to himself in Christ. Far from meaning unprofessional, it is rooted in a profession, the baptismal profession of faith. Every Sunday this is renewed and the Church itself is renewed. Each Easter is the great festival of the laity, the baptismal people, the Church of God. Thus, every year at Easter, every week on the Lord's day, every day as they sign themselves with the cross of Christ, Christian laypeople remember their dignity and their birthright and gird themselves to do the work of God to which they are committed.

. . . the laity, by their very vocation, seek the kingdom of God by engaging in temporal affairs and by ordering them to the plan of God. They live in the world, that is, in each and in all of the secular professions and occupations. They live in the ordinary circumstances of family and social life, from which the very web of their existence is woven.

They are called there by God so that by exercising their proper function and being led by the spirit of the gospel they can work for the sanctification of the world from within, in the manner of leaven. In this way they can make Christ known to others, especially by the testimony of a life resplendent in faith, hope, and charity. The layman is closely involved in temporal affairs of every sort. It is therefore his special task to illumine and organize these affairs in such a way that they may always start out, develop, and persist according to Christ's mind, to the praise of the Creator and the Redeemer (LG, 31).

The individual is baptized, not for his or her own salvation alone, but for the salvation of the world. If a person has been wrested in baptism from the kingdom of Satan and anointed with the Spirit of Christ, it is so that the structures of the world itself may be exorcised by the Christian's presence to become sacraments of the Spirit. Thus the face of the earth shall be renewed, that it may appear to the Father to bear the likeness of his Son. The city of the world shall give way to the holy city, "the new Jerusalem, coming down out of heaven from God, prepared as a bride adorned for her husband; and I heard a great voice from the throne saying, "Behold, the dwelling place of God is with men. He will dwell with them and they shall be his people, and God himself will be with them; he will wipe away every tear from their eyes, and death shall be no more, neither shall there be mourning nor crying nor pain any more, for the former things have passed away" (Rev 21:2-4).

Such is the hope which God, in his mercy, has given us and which we celebrate in baptism, confirmation, and the Eucharist. For this is the Christian made, that the world itself may be "Christened," transformed into the image of Christ.

Since, then, we have here such a fountain and our life here is such, since our table groans under the weight of countless blessings and spiritual gifts abound on every side, let us come forward with a sincere heart and with a clean conscience, that we may receive his grace and mercy to help us in our need, by the grace and kindness of the only begotten Son, our Lord and Savior Jesus Christ, through whom and with whom be to the Father and the life-giving Spirit glory, honor and power, now and forever, world without end. Amen (John Chrysostom, *Sermon to the Neophytes;* Hamman, p. 172).

INDEX